Microsoft Operations Manager 2005 Field Guide

Andy Dominey
Garry Meaburn

Apress®

Microsoft Operations Manager 2005 Field Guide

Copyright © 2006 by Andy Dominey and Garry Meaburn

ISBN 978-1-59059-709-5

Trademarked names may appear in this book. Rather than use a trademark symbol with every occurrence of a trademarked name, we use the names only in an editorial fashion and to the benefit of the trademark owner, with no intention of infringement of the trademark.

Lead Editor: Jonathan Gennick
Technical Reviewer: Judith Myerson
Editorial Board: Steve Anglin, Ewan Buckingham, Gary Cornell, Jason Gilmore, Jonathan Gennick, Jonathan Hassell, James Huddleston, Chris Mills, Matthew Moodie, Dominic Shakeshaft, Jim Sumser, Keir Thomas, Matt Wade
Project Manager: Richard Dal Porto
Copy Edit Manager: Nicole Flores
Copy Editor: Damon Larson
Assistant Production Director: Kari Brooks-Copony
Senior Production Editor: Laura Cheu
Compositor: Linda Weidemann, Wolf Creek Press
Proofreader: Elizabeth Berry
Indexer: Toma Mulligan
Artist: Kinetic Publishing Services, LLC
Cover Designer: Kurt Krames
Manufacturing Director: Tom Debolski

Distributed to the book trade worldwide by Springer-Verlag New York, Inc., 233 Spring Street, 6th Floor, New York, NY 10013. Phone 1-800-SPRINGER, fax 201-348-4505, e-mail orders-ny@springer-sbm.com, or visit http://www.springeronline.com.

For information on translations, please contact Apress directly at 2560 Ninth Street, Suite 219, Berkeley, CA 94710. Phone 510-549-5930, fax 510-549-5939, e-mail info@apress.com, or visit http://www.apress.com.

The information in this book is distributed on an "as is" basis, without warranty. Although every precaution has been taken in the preparation of this work, neither the author(s) nor Apress shall have any liability to any person or entity with respect to any loss or damage caused or alleged to be caused directly or indirectly by the information contained in this work.

This is dedicated to my loving wife Suzanne;
without her love and patience, this book
would not have been possible.
—Garry Meaburn

This book is dedicated to all my family and friends.
You give me the strength to carry on when times are hard,
and without you, none of this would have been possible.
To Liz, thank you for supporting me and being there for me.
Finally to my father, Brian, who sadly is no longer with us.
—Andy Dominey

Contents at a Glance

Contents

About the Authors

Andy Dominey has been in the IT industry for 7 years. He started out as a field service and support engineer and worked his way up to systems administrator, responsible for MOM, Active Directory, Exchange, web hosting, storage, and clustering for an exchange hosting provider based in the United Kingdom. He is currently working as a MOM/infrastructure consultant for 1E, an automated deployment and Windows management specialist based in the United Kingdom. He has been responsible for the IT systems of many large-scale customers, including the British Army and a company supplying mobile phone services to major UK mobile operators. He has also been awarded the Most Valued Professional (MVP) award for MOM from Microsoft. Andy can be contacted at andyd@1e.com.

Garry Meaburn lives in the United Kingdom and works for a large multinational company. His current role is Active Directory team leader, in which he manages a global team supporting over 500 domain controllers. He is also responsible for a MOM 2005 implementation to monitor Active Directory, SMS, and Exchange in a large enterprise environment. Garry can be contacted at garry@msmanage.com.

About the Technical Reviewer

Judith M. Myerson is a systems architect and engineer. Her areas of interest include middleware technologies, enterprise-wide systems, database technologies, application development, web development, software engineering, network management, servers, security management, information assurance, standards, RFID technologies, and project management. Judith holds a Master of Science degree in engineering, and is a member of the IEEE organization. She has reviewed/edited a number of books, including *Hardening Linux, Creating Client Extranets with SharePoint 2003*, and *Microsoft SharePoint: Building Office 2003 Solutions*.

Acknowledgments

Thanks to all of the production team at Apress; without their help, this book would have been much less readable and much less useful. Jonathan, Judith, Jim, and Richard: a big thank you for all your hard work and patience in helping us produce this book.

Introduction

Systems management is one of today's hottest topics in IT, but it is also one of the most undervalued. What it lacks in glamour it makes up for in importance. Systems management is not new; the idea has been around since IT became integrated into business. As business becomes more dependent on technology, so do the requirements for a robust, dependable solution that can cover multiple platforms and also scale to large enterprise environments. And that's where Microsoft Operations Manager (MOM) 2005 comes in; MOM is a flexible solution that can be deployed in the most complex environments, but is accessible to most systems engineers. Using MOM 2005, you can monitor the key systems in your infrastructure, and you'll benefit from knowledge that has been developed by the product teams at Microsoft.

MOM is a product that aims to monitor a distributed computing environment. It seeks to do so by providing functionality such as the following:

- *State view*: Provides you with a real-time, consolidated look at the health of the computers within the managed environment by server role, highlighting the systems that require attention.

- *Diagram view*: Gives you access to a variety of topological views in which servers and relationships are defined by management packs.

- *Alerts view*: Provides a list of alerts requiring action and the current state and severity of each alert.

- *Performance view*: Allows you to select and display one or more performance metrics from multiple systems over a period of time.

This book is designed to be both a guide and a reference, containing practical instructions and recommendations to help you better carry out the tasks you'll be performing with MOM 2005, including best-practice tips on how to deploy MOM into your environment. You'll also find real-world examples on how to configure and manage your MOM environment, and tips and reference suggestions for obtaining more information about a topic.

Who Is This Book For?

This book is aimed at those people who have been using MOM and are familiar with either the current or previous version of the product. It is designed to help you get the most out of the product by utilizing tips and tricks that we have discovered along the way.

What Does This Book Cover?

This book covers all aspects of MOM, from installation to configuration and troubleshooting, as well as some information on extra tools and utilities for enhancing MOM, such as the MOM Resource Kit. This book covers MOM's ability to connect to different management appliances and help desk systems using the MOM connector framework. The MOM Reporting component is also covered in detail, and we have included a section on creating custom reports to help you further integrate MOM into your environment.

What Do You Need to Use This Book?

Since this is not a basic guide to MOM, previous knowledge of the product is necessary. In order to get the best from this book, you will need to have the following software installed in addition to having a functioning MOM infra-structure:

- MOM 2005 Software Development Kit (SDK)
- MOM 2005 Resource Kit
- Visual Studio .NET 2003 (for SQL 2000) or Visual Studio 2005 (for SQL 2005)

Conventions in This Book

The following typographical conventions are used in this book:

`Monospace font: Indicates Commands, code examples, performance counters, URLs and SQL statements.`

Note Indicates a suggestion or general note. For example, we'll tell you if you need to use a particular software version or whether an operation requires certain privileges.

Caution Indicates a warning or caution. For example, we might warn you that the account that a service runs under must not be changed.

Recommendation Indicates a recommendation from the authors. For example, we might recommend that you create a new security group to manage access to the application.

CHAPTER 1

■ ■ ■

Architecture

Before looking at deploying Microsoft Operations Manager (MOM) 2005, you should have a clear understanding of what your requirements are. You need to consider business objectives, operational requirements, and the network topology. These are the first crucial steps for a successful deployment. Otherwise, the risk is high that the solution you implement will fail to meet the needs of the business, be overly complex, or result in a project failure. The main reasons to deploy MOM are as follows:

- The need for a proactive approach to identifying and resolving issues before users are impacted. This is specifically important within a Windows Active Directory infrastructure supporting strategic business applications like Microsoft Exchange Server 2003.

- The need to specifically monitor services such as Active Directory or Exchange.

- The need to reduce operational costs.

MOM 2005 Supported Configurations

When planning your MOM installation, you should never exceed the maximum supported values. These are shown in Table 1-1.

Table 1-1. *Maximum Supported Configurations in MOM 2005*

MOM 2005 Feature	Maximum Supported
Operations Database Size	30 GB
Agent-managed computers per management group	4,000
Agent-managed computers per management server	2,000
Agentless-managed computers per management server	10

Continued

Table 1-1. *Continued*

MOM 2005 Feature	Maximum Supported
Agentless-managed computers per management group	60
Management servers per management group	10
Levels in a multitiered MOM configuration	3
Source management groups per destination management group in a multitiered MOM configuration	10
Alerts per day that can be forwarded to the destination management group in a multitiered MOM configuration	400,000
MOM consoles per management server	15
Reporting subsystems per MOM database	1
Management servers per agent for multihoming	4

Design Best Practices

Business, administrative, user, and security requirements directly affect how you implement your MOM solution, so you should create a requirements document that at a minimum can answer the following questions:

- Are there any special security requirements that must be adhered to?
- How many servers will be monitored?
- Will any servers be monitored that are separated by a firewall?
- What are your redundancy requirements?
- Will console scopes be required?
- Will reporting be required for historical and trend analysis reports?
- If historical data is required, how long does this need to be kept?
- Do you require MOM to integrate into a management framework (e.g., IBM Tivoli)?

Once the requirements document has been created, it must be approved by the project sponsor, and any changes to the scope of the project must be reflected in an updated copy of the requirements document authorized by the project sponsor.

The requirements document and a copy of the network utilization and topology reports will be the basis of the design document. You should take into account the following design best practices:

- Limit the number of management groups to reduce the complexity. A multihomed agent can belong to no more than four management groups. The use of console scopes should be first evaluated to see if this meets your requirements.

- Use multiple management groups if different administration teams have to manage the same server but have different requirements.

- Use a unique name for each management group and ensure that this is enforced; otherwise, if in the future you want to use multihomed agents or alert forwarding, this would not be possible without a large amount of reworking.

- Evaluate the current network usage and topology to ensure optimal placement of management servers.

- Break the design and deployment down into phases.

- Deploy only the management packs that are required initially. It is better to start with the core, and then increase once the environment has stabilized.

- Have a clear and agreed requirements document before going into design phase.

- Evaluate the disk input/output (I/O), as MOM is disk I/O intensive; if a bottleneck occurs, it would most likely be in this subsystem.

- Analyze integration requirements, as MOM can be integrated into existing management frameworks using product connectors. You should carefully analyze the integration requirements, as you may need to do some custom development to ensure that all requirements are met.

- Evaluate the management group configurations that will be appropriate for your requirements.

The remaining sections in this chapter show you how to use common configurations when deploying new management groups in various scenarios.

Single Management Group with a Single Management Server

The simplest way to deploy MOM is to run it from a single server, using a single management group. All MOM 2005 agents that are deployed in this scenario report to a single management server. This server will host the Operations database and optionally the Reporting database. Figure 1-1 shows a single management server with the OnePoint database.

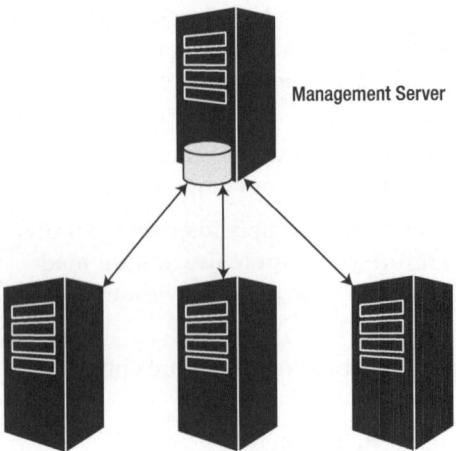

Management Server

Figure 1-1. *Single management group*

Note This configuration is only suited to a small-scale deployment of MOM—for
either a lab environment or a small company with a limited number of servers to manage.
Microsoft states that a single server (if of suitable hardware specification) will support 10
agentless-managed computers per management server and 2,000 agent-managed computers per management server.

Experience has shown that this configuration should only be used if you are monitoring less than 200 agents, do not require reliance on the infrastructure, and have a monitored environment that is not expected to grow in the foreseeable future. You can expand
the infrastructure at a later stage if you are required to add management servers and
separate databases to individual servers.

Single Management Group with Agent Failover

The simplest way to add a degree of resilience to the MOM infrastructure is
to add an extra management server to the management group. Figure 1-2
shows a single management group with multiple management servers.

The management group in Figure 1-2 allows for an increased number
of agents to be managed, and offers resilience, as the agents will fail over to
the other management server if their primary management server is offline.
The light blue arrows in Figure 1-2 show the agent failover path. The agents
can be load-balanced between the two management servers.

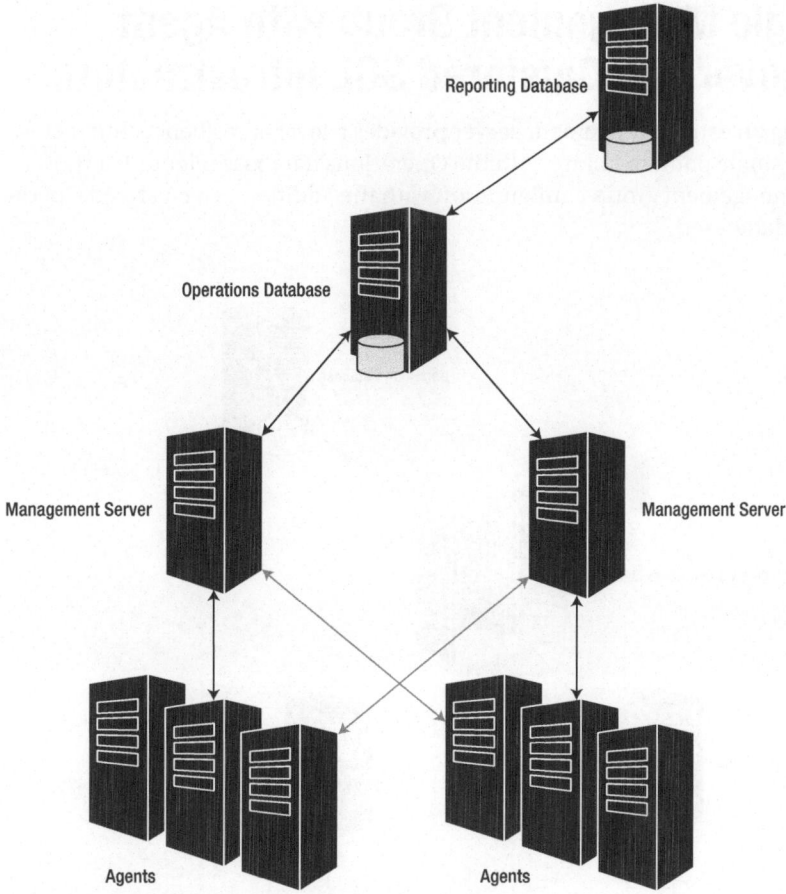

Figure 1-2. *Single management group with agent failover*

■**Note** This configuration is a good starting design for your MOM implementation. The design can easily manage a greater number of agents, and it also has a greater degree of resilience due to the use of two management servers. The maximum number of agents that a management group can support is 4,000. Although each management server has a limit of 2,000 supported agents, in the event that the primary management server becomes unavailable, the secondary server needs to be able to take on the load from the primary server without going over the limit. Additional management servers can be added to this configuration, up to a maximum of ten. The Operations database in this configuration does not have any resilience, so if high availability is required, then this configuration should not be used.

Single Management Group with Agent Failover and Clustered SQL Infrastructure

Adding an extra management server provides a level of resilience, but it creates a single point of failure with the Operations database. Figure 1-3 shows the management group configuration with the addition of a clustered Operations database.

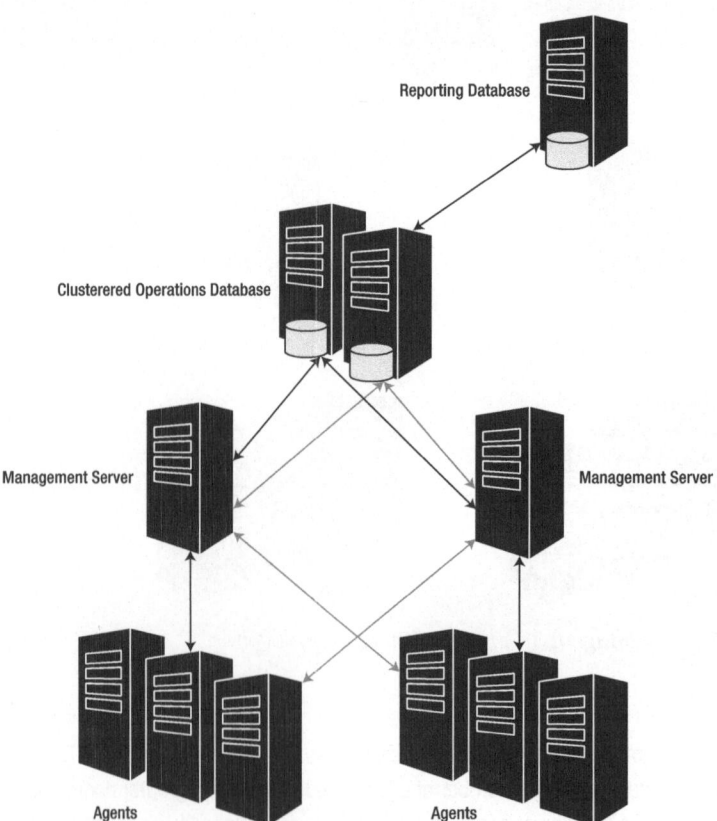

Figure 1-3. *Single management group with SQL cluster*

The management group in Figure 1-3 contains two management servers, and the agents can be load-balanced between them. The Operations database is clustered to offer resilience in the event of a failure of one of the Operations database servers. The light blue arrows in Figure 1-3 show the agent failover paths for the agent and the SQL server.

■Note This configuration offers full reliance on the management infrastructure. Only the MOM database components, the MOM agent, and the MOM Reporting database and components can be installed on a SQL server cluster. The management server and consoles cannot be installed on a SQL server cluster. This design increases the complexity of the MOM environment, but it offers resilience and no single points of failure. If you need a clustered SQL infrastructure, then you should choose this design.

Single Management Group with Agent Failover and Warm Standby SQL Server

Introducing a clustered Operations database increases the complexity and cost of the MOM infrastructure. However, it is still possible to eliminate the single point of failure by configuring a second SQL server as a warm standby server; this is shown in Figure 1-4.

The management group in Figure 1-4 contains two management servers, and the agents can be balanced between the them. A secondary database server is configured and has a Data Transformation Services (DTS) job running between the primary database and the warm standby. The process for configuring this configuration is available in the Establishing MOM 2005 Service Continuity.doc file, found in the MOM 2005 Service Continuity Solution, which is available for download from the Microsoft web site. The light blue arrows in Figure 1-4 show the failover paths for the agent and the SQL server.

■Note This configuration offers full reliance on the management infrastructure, but requires a manual step to point the management servers to the hot standby SQL server. This configuration reduces the complexity of the MOM environment, and still offers reliance and no single points of failure.

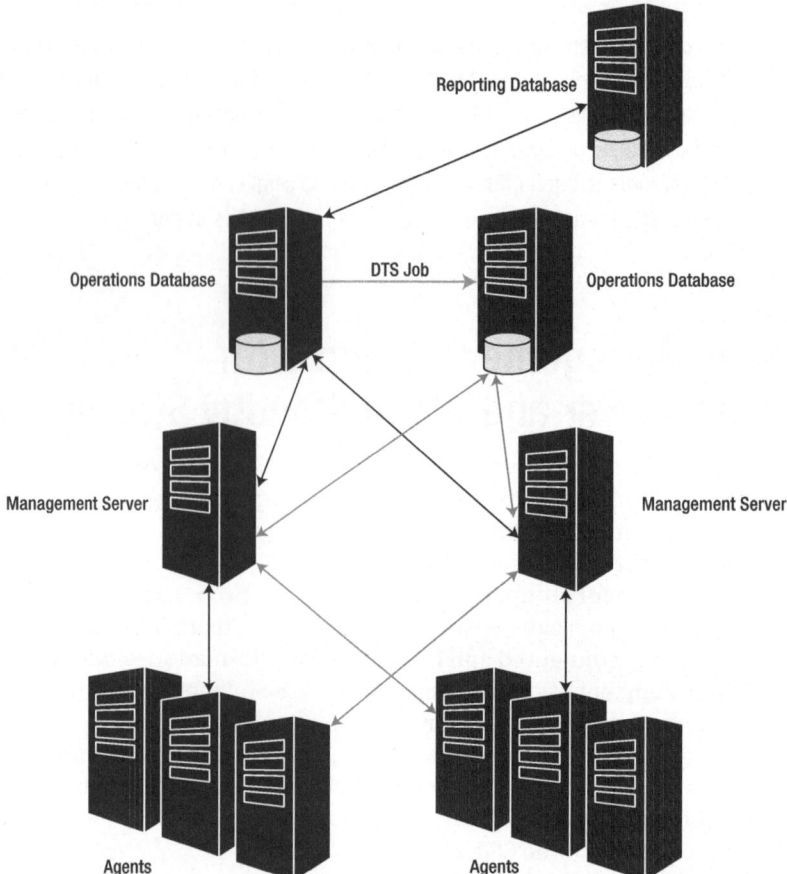

Figure 1-4. *Single management group with warm standby SQL server*

Multiple Management Groups with Multihomed Agents

It is possible in MOM for an agent to report to one or more management groups. In Figure 1-5, all MOM 2005 agents in computer group A report to two management groups.

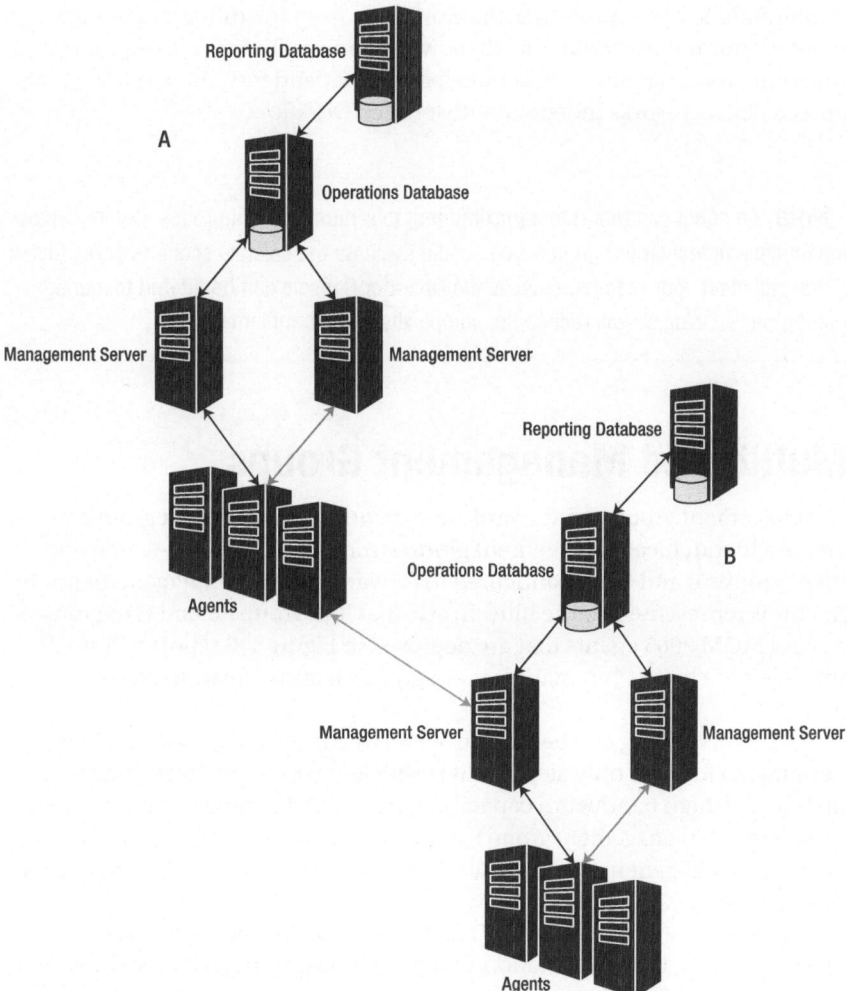

Figure 1-5. *Multihomed agents*

The agents in Figure 1-5 are multihomed. The term *multihomed agent* is used by MOM to refer to an agent that has been configured to be a member of two or more different management groups. Multihoming a MOM agent can be achieved when an enterprise has multiple administration groups managing different aspects of a common server. For example, one administration team might manage only the base operating system (OS) of a server, while a separate administration team manages the Active Directory component on that server. Multihoming an agent will not install multiple agents.

A multihomed agent processes the workflows from the different management groups independently, so there will be no conflict of rules—processing rules are processed and data is transferred independently. In addition, guaranteed delivery works independently of each workflow.

■Note An agent can report to a maximum of four management groups. Before deploying multiple management groups, you should evaluate the console scope features to see if that will meet your requirements, as the Operator Console can be filtered to management groups. Doing so will reduce the complexity of your implementation.

Multitiered Management Groups

A management group can forward alerts to other management groups to create a hierarchical management group structure. In Figure 1-6, management groups B and C are configured to forward alerts to management group A. This is represented by the blue arrows that link groups B and C to group A.

All MOM 2005 agents that are deployed in Figure 1-6 report to a single management group, but management groups B and C forward alerts to group A.

Alert forwarding can be used to achieve centralized monitoring. It is designed to forward only alerts, so it is very efficient, even for regions that do not have high bandwidth capacity. Alert forwarding enables management servers in one management group to send alerts to another management group, creating an efficient hierarchical alert management structure for large enterprise networks.

A source management group can forward to only one destination management group, but a destination group (such as group A) can receive the forwarded alert from as many as ten source management groups.

Duplicate alert suppression is primarily done at the source management group. Duplicate alerts received by the source management group are not forwarded to the destination management group. Only the repeat count for the alert is forwarded. Management packs need to be synchronized between the source and destination management groups. Alert suppression is also done at the destination, at which an alert from a source management group can suppress alerts coming from another source management group, depending upon the rule's alert suppression settings and logic. Rules also need to be synchronized between the source and destination management groups for the correct knowledge to be displayed for the alert.

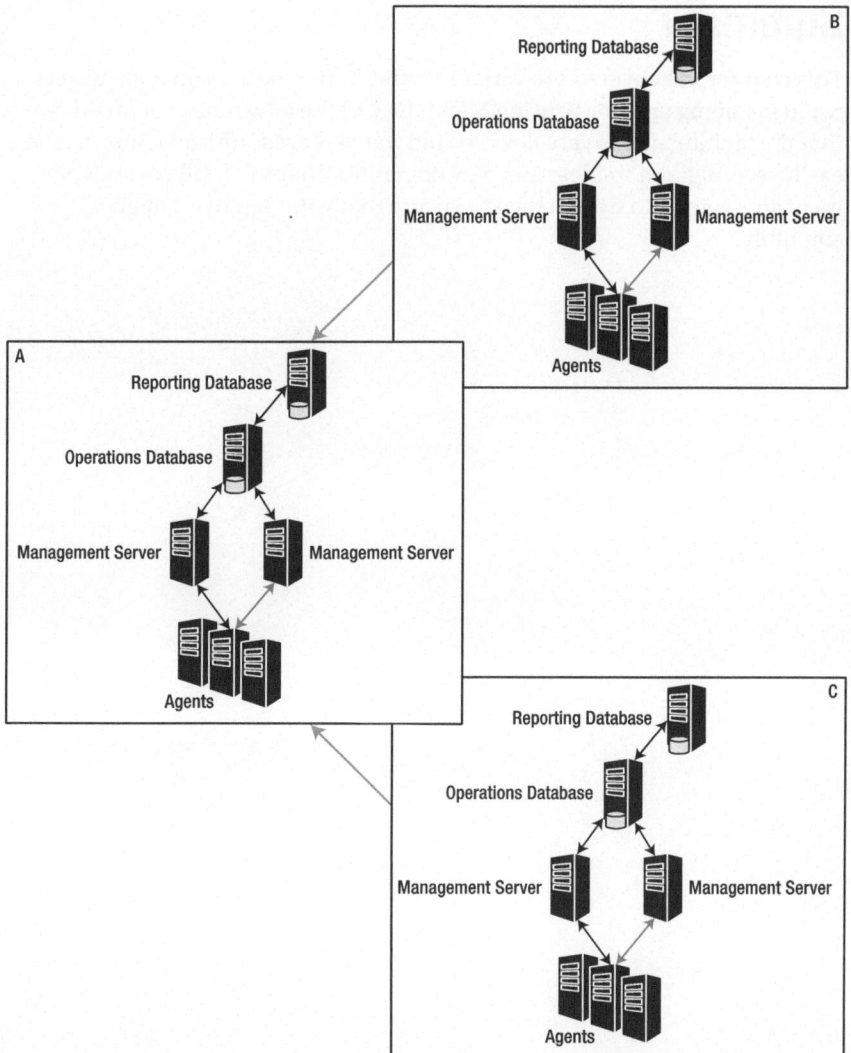

Figure 1-6. *Multitiered management groups*

Note This configuration can be very difficult to manage. However, if you require a centralized view of the whole environment, and you have network restrictions that force you to deploy multiple management groups, then this solution is your best option. The management group server configuration can be any of the sample configurations that are listed in this chapter.

Summary

This chapter has covered the various configuration options that are available when installing and configuring MOM. One of the advantages of MOM is that the architecture is very flexible, and the deployed infrastructure can be easily reconfigured to meet any new demands. Chapter 2 will cover deployment strategies and tips on how to ensure that your deployment goes smoothly.

■ ■ ■

Planning and Deploying

In this chapter, we will look at how to plan for a MOM infrastructure, including selecting hardware, planning for disk capacity, and RAID configuration. We will look at the MOM Sizer and the System Center Capacity Planner, which can assist you in your planning. We will also look at the deployment of MOM 2005. We will not show you detailed instructions on how to deploy MOM, but we will make recommendations and mention advanced configurations, such as multihoming agents, multitiering, clustering the MOM databases, and installing MOM onto 64-bit architectures. Finally, we will look at some points to consider as you decide how the MOM consoles will be used and how monitoring responsibilities will be distributed. We will also look at how to use MOM console scopes to make these decisions easier.

Initial Planning

Before attempting to deploy MOM, you should first decide whether MOM is the correct product for your environment. First, look at the devices you are monitoring. Are they mostly Windows servers? If the answer is yes, then MOM would be a great choice to monitor and maintain these devices. If the answer is no, and you have a large number of non-Windows devices to manage, MOM may not be the best tool to monitor your infrastructure (or it may be better used to augment another management appliance, such as IBM Tivoli or HP OpenView, using the Microsoft connector framework to link MOM to these appliances). The MOM-to-MOM product connector, which uses the MOM connector framework, is covered in Chapter 10.

Once you have decided to consider MOM, you should endeavor to gather a list of requirements from your business and align those requirements with the product. An example of these requirements might be as follows:

- Providing event log consolidation

- Providing proactive monitoring of key systems (i.e., Microsoft Exchange, Microsoft SQL Server, etc.)

- Providing capability for trend analysis

These requirements would all be met by MOM, since MOM collects data from the event logs of servers. It scripts proactive tests into the most common Microsoft applications, such as Exchange, Active Directory, and SQL Server, and it provides trend analysis using the Reporting database, which is covered in Chapter 7.

Once you have matched your requirements to MOM and you have made the decision to use MOM as your monitoring and management appliance, you can begin to plan for the MOM 2005 deployment. The first step is to decide the architecture of your MOM deployment (architecture is explained in more detail in Chapter 1). You may decide on a simple single server, or you may plan to deploy MOM in a complex configuration using multihoming, multitiering, or a combination of these. You may also choose to roll data from multiple MOM management groups into a single reporting data warehouse.

The first step to take once you have decided on the architecture of your MOM infrastructure is to calculate the hardware necessary to run MOM. The following section will show you how to do that using the MOM Sizer and System Center Capacity Planner tools.

Sizing the MOM Infrastructure

Sizing your planned MOM infrastructure is an important part of the planning process of your MOM implementation project. When planning the hardware requirements for your MOM infrastructure, you must take into account the following points:

Number of agents to be deployed: When estimating the number of agents that will be deployed, you should take into account any planned changes of your organization—for example, any planned expansions, merges, or reductions. The number should also cover the normal growth of your business. The MOM infrastructure can be easily expanded when required, but it is advisable to allow for (when possible) 12 months of growth for the initial design.

What will be monitored: If you are planning to use MOM to collect security audit data, you may want to consider a separate management group for that purpose. It is a best practice to separate audit data into another management group due to the volume of data that will be collected and stored.

Network constraints: Can you manage all your agents from a central management group? Are you going to have to deploy management servers on remote sites? Are you going to install multiple management groups? When you design the location of the management servers, it is always better to keep them as close as possible to the OnePoint database server.

Another important aspect you need to calculate is the expected volume of data that the management servers will receive. Microsoft has released the average capacity that is required to store one performance counter, alert, and event in the database, and the estimated number of such items that will be generated on average per agent. Table 2-1 shows the average size per item and the estimated volume of data (number of items) per agent-managed system.

Table 2-1. *Data Collection*

Type	Size in Bytes	Collected per Managed Server per Day
One performance counter	200	2500
One event	2500	200
One alert	6000	4

The values in Table 2-1 can be used to estimate the impact on the network and the capacity requirements for the OnePoint database. This is how you manually calculate the capacity requirements when you are monitoring 500 agents. The first step is to use the following equations to compute the total number of events, alerts, and performance agents and the daily capacity:

```
Events = (Events Collected per day * Size) * Number Agents
Alerts = (Alerts Collected per day * Size) * Number Agents
Performance = (Counters Collected per day * Size) * Number Agents
Daily Capacity = Events + Alerts + Performance
```

The second step is to substitute the values in the equations as follows:

```
Events = (200 * 2500) * 500 = 250000000
Alerts = (4 * 6000) * 500 = 12000000
Performance = (2500 * 200) * 500 = 250000000
Daily Capacity = 250000000 + 12000000 + 250000000 = 512000000 bytes
512000000 bytes is approximately 489MB per day
```

This data can then be used to estimate the growth for the OnePoint database and help in planning network usage. The figures used to estimate the capacity are averages based on the use of well-tuned management packs.

In addition to knowing about the formulas just given, you should know that Microsoft has released two tools that can be used to help estimate the capacity requirements for a MOM infrastructure: the MOM 2005 Sizer and System Center Capacity Planner 2006.

MOM 2005 Sizer

The MOM 2005 Sizer is a free spreadsheet that is available from `https://www.microsoft.com/downloads/details.aspx?FamilyId=93930640-FA0F-48B3-8EB0-86836A1808DF&displaylang=en`. This simple spreadsheet allows you to estimate the hardware requirements and potential network usage for the management servers, and it also estimates the Reporting server database sizes. The spreadsheet estimates the event, alert, and performance data using the same formulas used in the manual calculation. Figure 2-1 shows the spreadsheet being used to estimate the hardware requirements to monitor 500 agents.

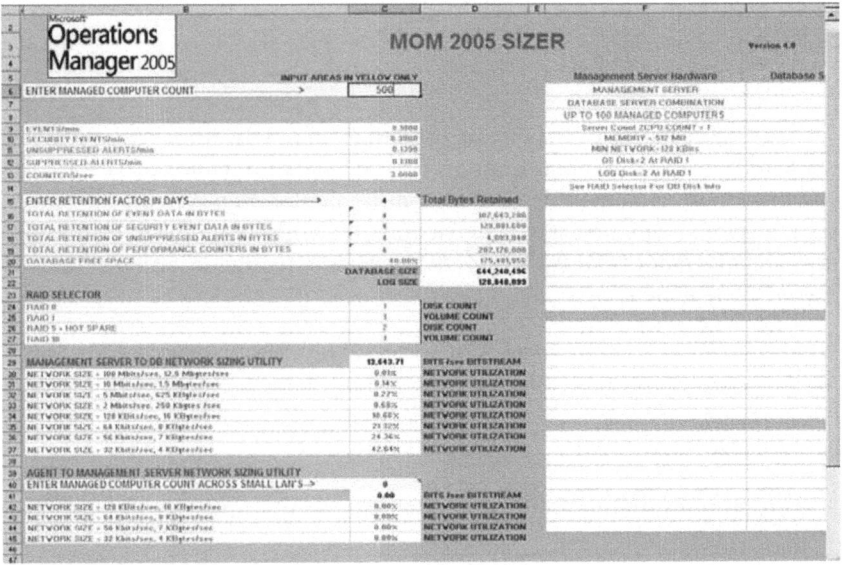

Figure 2-1. *MOM Sizer spreadsheet*

The MOM Sizer spreadsheet is OK for giving you an estimate on hardware requirements, but it does not cover different scenarios that could affect the hardware you need to purchase. As with all sizer tools, the spreadsheet should be used just to provide a guide rather than a definite answer.

System Center Capacity Planner 2006

System Center Capacity Planner 2006 allows you to create a model that simulates application and hardware infrastructure for Microsoft Exchange Server 2003 and MOM 2005. You can use System Center Capacity Planner to run numerous "what if" scenarios to evaluate the effects of adding extra servers to manage, changing network links, and increasing or decreasing the hardware specifications on the management server. It can also be used for evaluating the performance implications of combining roles. The current version of System Center Capacity Planner will only simulate a single MOM configuration group. System Center Capacity Planner is only available as part of a TechNet Plus or MSDN subscription.

In this section, Systems Center Capacity Planner will be used to model a proposed new implementation of MOM 2005 to monitor a typical branch office configuration of 23 servers split over a central site and 3 branch offices. Figure 2-2 shows the infrastructure that needs monitoring.

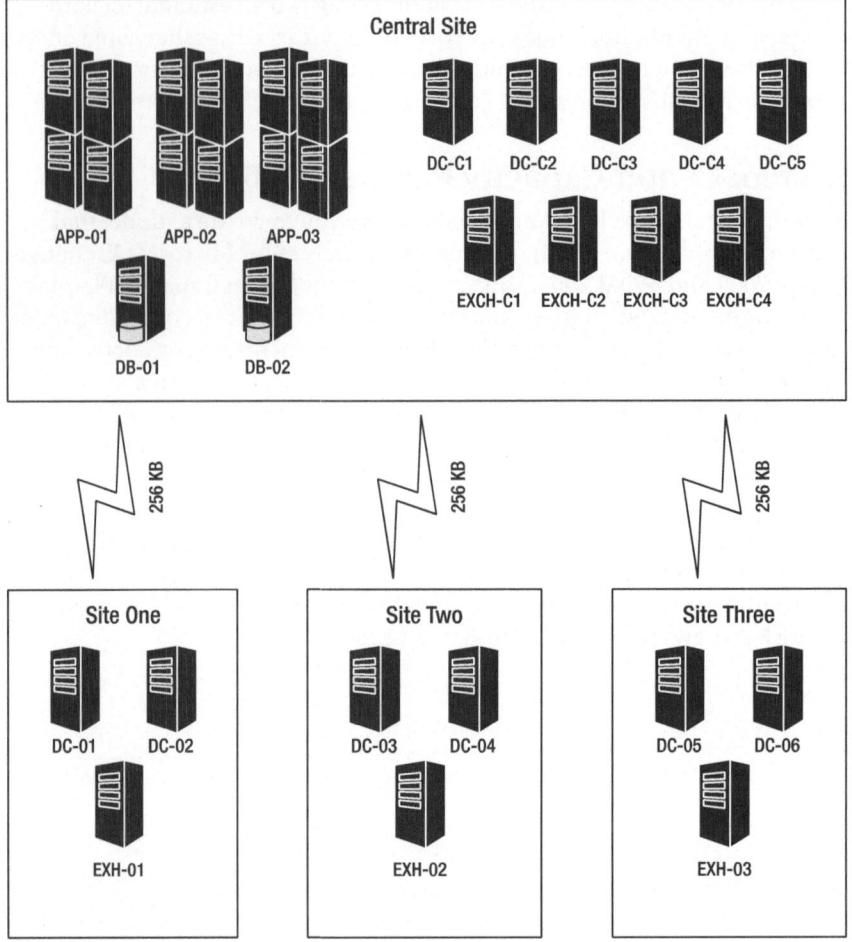

Figure 2-2. *Current environment that needs monitoring*

When you start Systems Center Capacity Planner, there is an option to model either an Exchange or MOM environment. In this example, you will choose the MOM option to create a new system architectural model, as shown in Figure 2-3. Select Microsoft Operation Manager 2005 as the application to model, and then Click "Create a model with the Model Wizard" to continue.

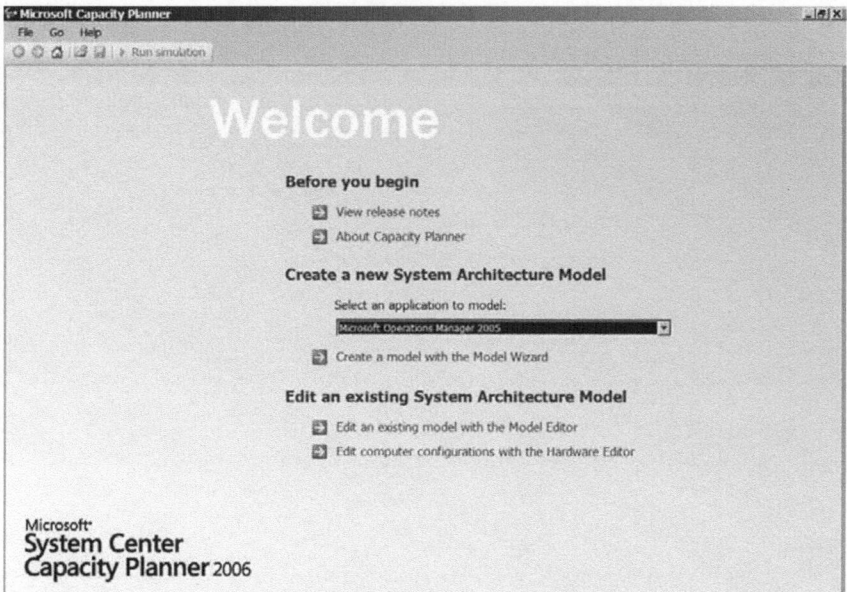

Figure 2-3. *Selecting an application to model*

Next, you will need to configure the site numbers and the network links. Initially, you can select only one network connection speed to use for all links. Once the model has been created, however, you can alter the connection speed and utilization on each separate network link. For the model that is required for the scenario in Figure 2-2, three remote sites have been added in this example, and the network link speed is set to 256 Kbps. This is shown in Figure 2-4.

On the next screen, you can configure the number of servers that you will be monitoring on each of the sites. Figure 2-5 shows the server type for each of the sites.

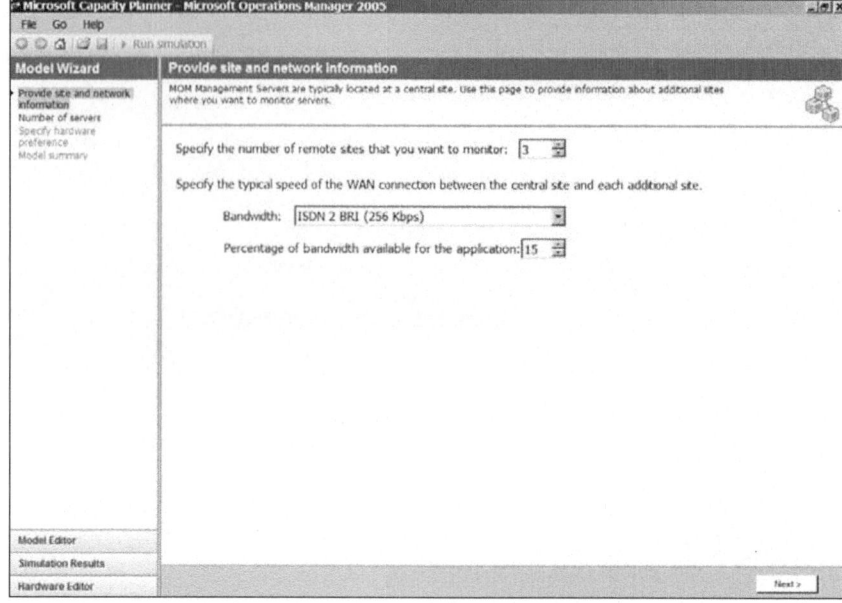

Figure 2-4. *Configuring networks and number of remote sites*

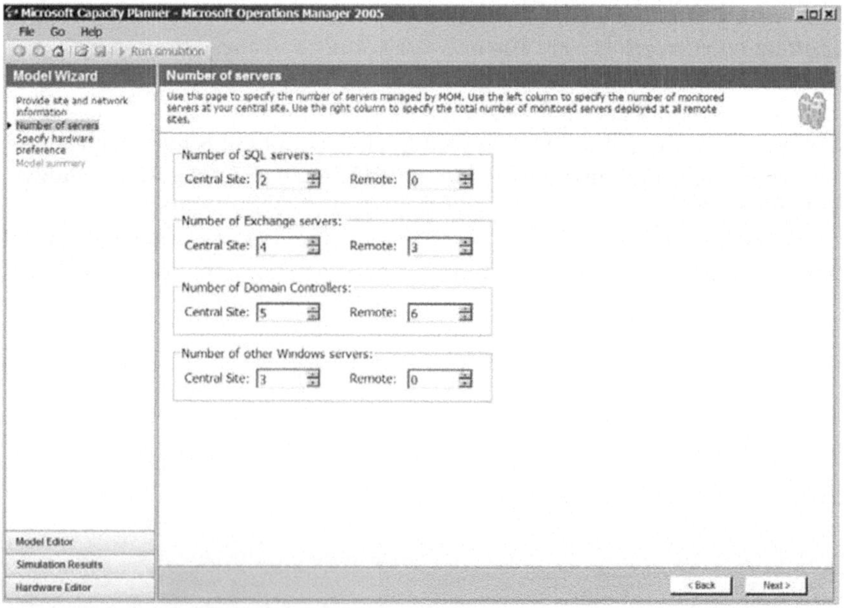

Figure 2-5. *Specifying the number of different server types*

On the screen that follows, you can configure different hardware configurations so that you can model utilization and performance on the MOM
infrastructure. There are also options you can use to evaluate if it is possible
to merge different MOM roles onto the same server—for example, a management server could also host the OnePoint database. As shown in Figure 2-6,
the roles will not be merged. Redundancy is also required for the management servers.

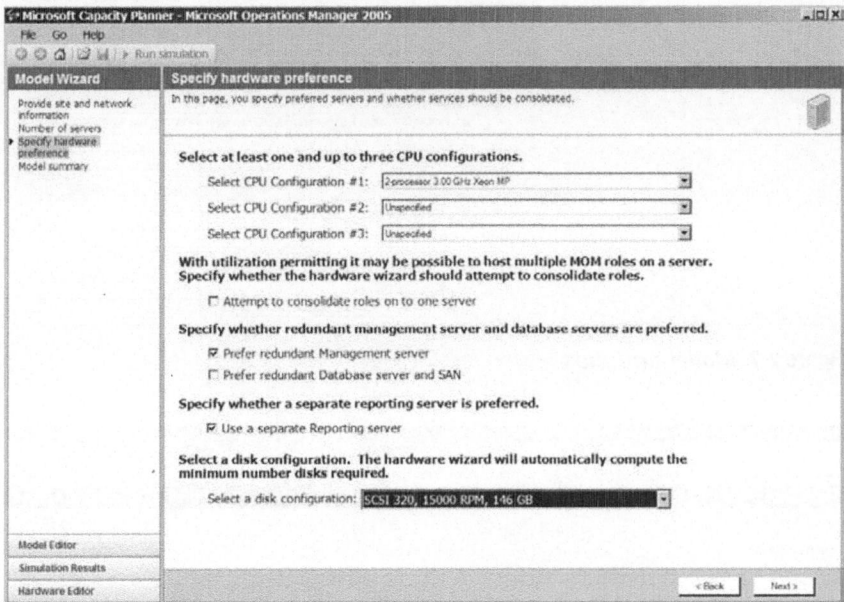

Figure 2-6. *Configuring the hardware specifications*

The summary screen in Figure 2-7 shows the number of servers required
for the MOM infrastructure and also the hardware specifications for each
server.

Figure 2-7 shows the main model that you've created. When you get to
the screen shown in Figure 2-8, you can run simulations and also configure
the individual network connections if required. You can also add and remove
sites as required by clicking a site and selecting Delete from the context
menu.

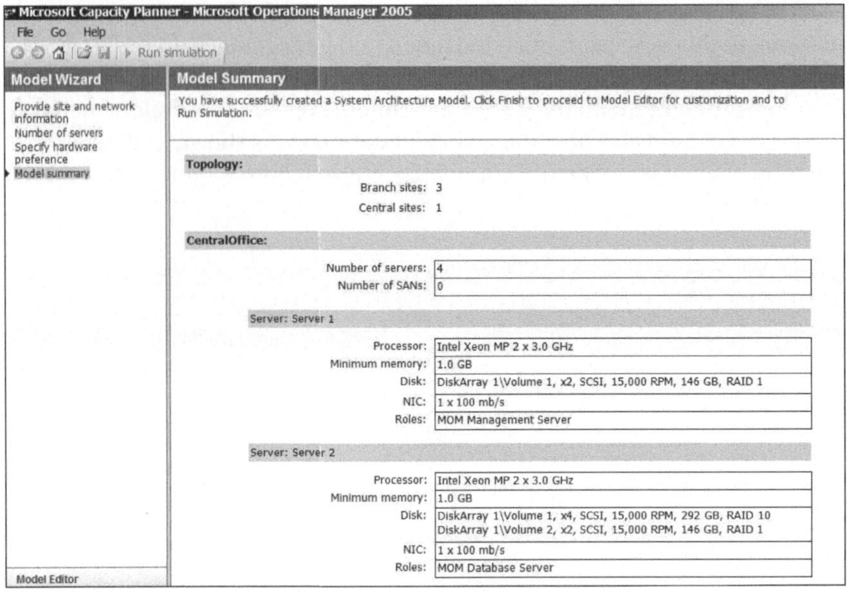

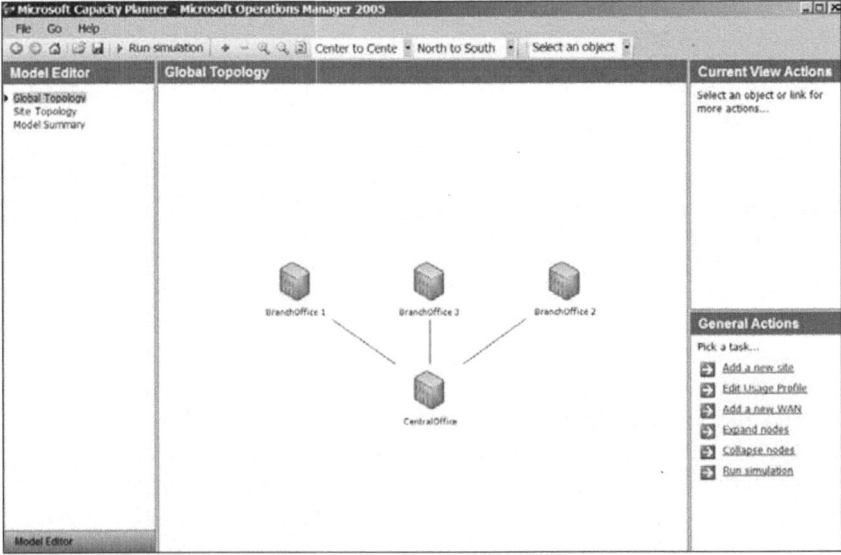

Figure 2-7. *Model summary*

Figure 2-8. *Topology diagram*

To configure the different network connections, double-click the network connection that links the sites that you want to change (shown in Figure 2-8). This will then bring up a screen like that shown in Figure 2-9.

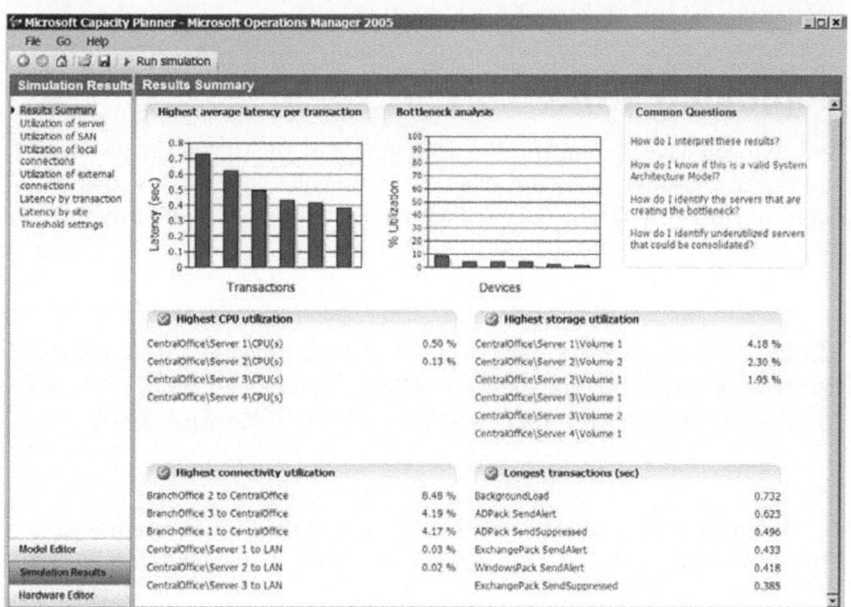

Figure 2-9. *Network connection speeds*

Once you have run the simulation, you will be presented with a summary screen, as shown in Figure 2-10.

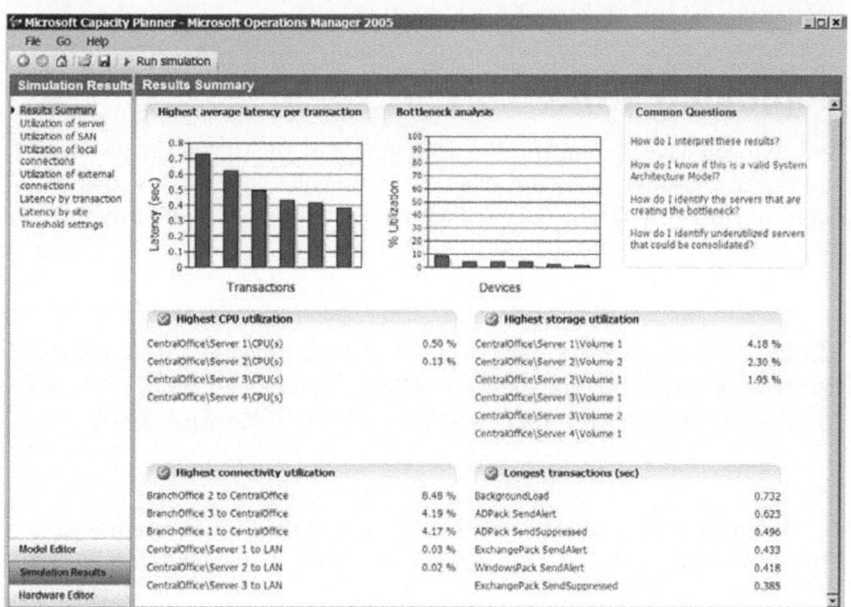

Figure 2-10. *Summary view*

From the summary screen, you can use the side menus to look at different reports on the utilization of the different components that make up the infrastructure (e.g., the utilization of network connections, the utilization of the management servers, and so forth). Report data can be exported to Excel if required. As with the MOM 2005 Sizer, the results should be used as a guide.

One thing to remember is that in addition to planning for a brand new infrastructure, you can use Systems Center Capacity Planner to model changes to your *existing* MOM infrastructure. If, for example, you need to add extra sites or servers to your current infrastructure, you can model the performance impact of adding these servers and sites and evaluate whether extra hardware is required.

When planning for a MOM deployment, it is also important to plan resources for the project. Such planning will not be covered here, as the resources required will vary depending on your company structure. Microsoft has produced a document that assists in planning a MOM deployment and selecting a team to ensure that the deployment is successful. The Microsoft Operations Manager 2005 Deployment Planning Guide can be downloaded from the following location (valid at the time this book goes to press): www.microsoft.com/downloads/details.aspx?familyid=F3D68268-DF08-431B-8D0D-2D184E81E161&displaylang=en.

Deploying MOM

Now that you have planned for the deployment of MOM, you can go ahead and install the software. By way of example, we will assume that you are deploying MOM 2005 with Service Pack 1 (SP1). MOM SP1 and its requirements are covered in more detail in Appendix A.

Note We will be referring to MOM 2005 both with and without SP1 in this section. You should assume that we are referring to MOM 2005 without SP1 unless SP1 is explicitly defined (i.e., MOM 2005 SP1, which refers to the MOM 2005 full product with SP1).

Before deploying MOM, it is necessary to run the MOM Prerequisite Checker to confirm that all requirements of MOM are installed. The Prerequisite Checker is run from the setup.exe file on the MOM 2005 CD. The Prerequisite Checker is shown in Figure 2-11.

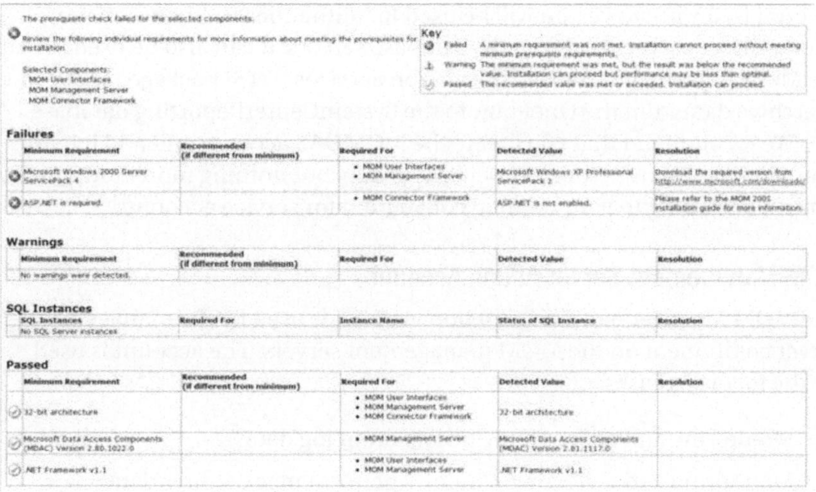

Figure 2-11. *MOM Prerequisite Checker results showing successes and failures*

If you are installing the base version of MOM 2005 (i.e., not SP1) onto SQL Server 2000 SP4 (SQL Server 2005 is not supported by the non-SP1 version of MOM), the installation Prerequisite Checker will fail, stating that MOM requires Microsoft SQL Server SP3a or above. This is due to the fact that the Prerequisite Checker looks for a particular registry key that is different in Microsoft SQL Server SP4. You can bypass the Prerequisite Checker to prevent this error from occurring. To do this, run a silent install of MOM with the following parameter: `PREREQ_COMPLETED=1`.

Note If you are using the `PREREQ_COMPLETED=1` parameter, ensure that all prerequisites are met before trying to install MOM, or else the installation may fail.

Installing MOM

Before installing MOM, ensure that you have set up the required user accounts in Active Directory. The following subsections describe the accounts that you'll need.

MOM Data Access Service Account

The MOM Data Access Service (MOMDAS) account is used by the Data Access Service (DAS) component on the MOM management servers. This account is low privilege and will be used for authentication between the management servers and the SQL database servers. It can also be used to run the MOM Reporting Data Transformation Services (DTS) package task used to archive data from the OnePoint to the SystemCenterReporting database.

We recommend that you create the MOMDAS account and add it to the Domain Users Active Directory security group, but nothing more. You should name it according to your naming convention for service accounts.

MOM Management Server Action Account

The MOM Management Server Action account is used by the management server component on the MOM management servers. The account is used for the following tasks:

- Monitoring and collecting Windows event log data
- Monitoring and collecting Windows performance counter data
- Monitoring and collecting Windows Management Instrumentation (WMI) data
- Monitoring and collecting application-specific log data, such as IIS (Internet Information Services) logs
- Running management pack responses, such as scripts or batch files
- Running managed code responses (*managed code* refers to code written upon the .NET Framework)

The MOM Management Server Action account requires higher privileges than the MOMDAS account since it will be required to run tasks on the MOM management servers. It will require additional local permissions on the MOM management servers because the MOM agents are installed manually during deployment. Due to the large number of tasks that the MOM Management Server Action account will perform on the MOM management servers, we recommend that this account be granted local administrator rights on the two MOM management servers.

We recommend that you configure this account as a member of the Domain Users Active Directory security group. Since this account may be used to deploy agents, you may wish to add it to the local administrators group on each machine that you'll be deploying an agent to. This account will require administrative rights on any management servers that you install.

If you decide not to elevate the permissions of this account, some MOM tasks may not run and you will need to specify a high-privilege account when installing agents. You should name it according to your naming convention for service accounts.

MOM Exchange Mailbox Access Account

The MOM Exchange Mailbox Access account is used by the Microsoft Exchange Server 2003 Management Pack. Use the Microsoft Exchange Server Management Pack Configuration Wizard to configure the necessary settings on the Exchange servers to enable the management pack to carry out monitoring correctly. This wizard will also create a user account and an Exchange mailbox in each Exchange database store (or one for each Exchange server depending on the options selected in the Exchange Management Pack Configuration Wizard). These mailboxes will be used by MOM to carry out Exchange database and mail flow monitoring. The Exchange Mailbox Access account will be granted permissions to these mailboxes in order that a single account can be used to carry out monitoring of a number of separate Exchange databases. Using a single enabled domain account to connect to multiple mailboxes helps to maintain the highest level of security possible while providing rich monitoring of Exchange, such as database and mail flow monitoring. You should configure this account with low privileges.

We recommend creating this account and adding it to the Domain Users Active Directory security group. The Exchange Server Management Pack Configuration Wizard will add the required permissions to this account and create additional monitoring accounts and mailboxes as required according to the options you specify in the wizard. The Exchange Server Management Pack Configuration Wizard should be run from a machine that has Exchange Server System Manager installed and executed with an account with Exchange administrator rights. You should name the MOM Exchange Mailbox Access account according to your naming convention for service accounts.

After you have created the user accounts and finished running the Prerequisite Checker, click the Install Microsoft Operations Manager 2005 option from the MOM 2005 Setup Resources dialog (shown in Figure 2-12). Once you have clicked the option, the MOM 2005 Setup Wizard will start. Simply follow the wizard, specifying the options as required for your environment. You will need to specify database locations and sizes, and MOM user accounts, as well as input exactly what you want to monitor.

After MOM is installed, you should do the following:

- Consider installing MOM Reporting (covered in Chapter 7). This is an optional component of MOM. You don't have to install it, but we recommend that you do since in addition to providing a rich graphical, reporting interface, it also keeps the MOM operational (OnePoint) database streamlined by archiving old data to the Reporting database.

- Install the management packs and agents as required.

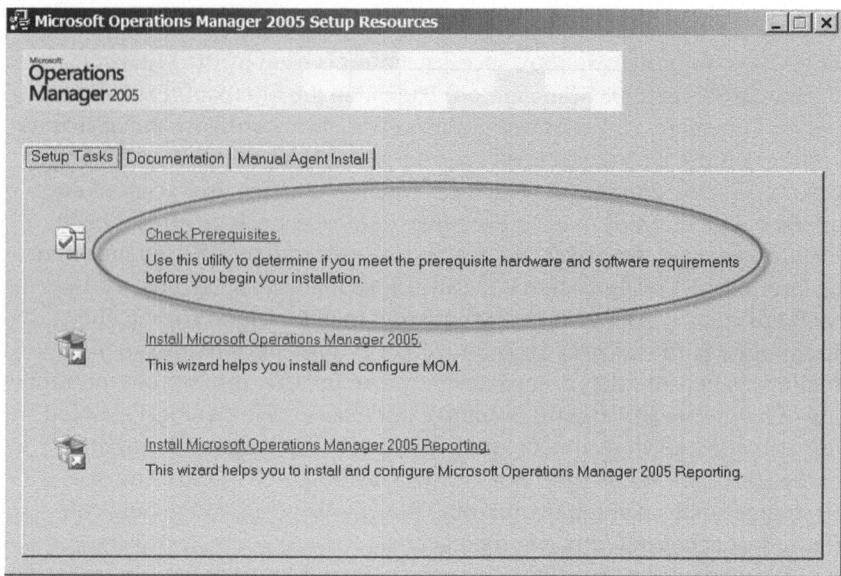

Figure 2-12. *The Setup Tasks tab on the MOM 2005 Setup Resources dialog*

There are various recommendations on installing management packs and agents. We personally choose to import the required management packs, tune the alerts (from our own experience), and then roll the agents out. The Microsoft best practice for deploying management packs, though, is to deploy the agents and then install the management packs one at a time, carrying out alert tuning on one management pack at a time. (Management packs are covered in more detail in Chapter 3.)

Advanced Configurations

Depending on your infrastructure, you may want to install MOM in an advanced configuration. Agent multihoming, MOM multitiering, passing reporting data to a single data warehouse, and installing onto a cluster are all examples of advanced configurations.

Multihoming

In some environments, it is necessary for MOM agents to report to two separate MOM management groups simultaneously. An example of when you might need to do this is when you have a requirement to collect security information from your agents. A good way to collect such information would be to have a separate management group for security events and multihome the agent. Configuring the agent to multihome is fairly simple. Once you have the two management groups established, you can either run an agent installation from both management groups one at a time, or run a manual installation of the agent for each of the management groups. The agent will only be installed once, but will be configured (via registry settings) with the information of all of the management groups it is reporting to. Figure 2-13 shows such a configuration.

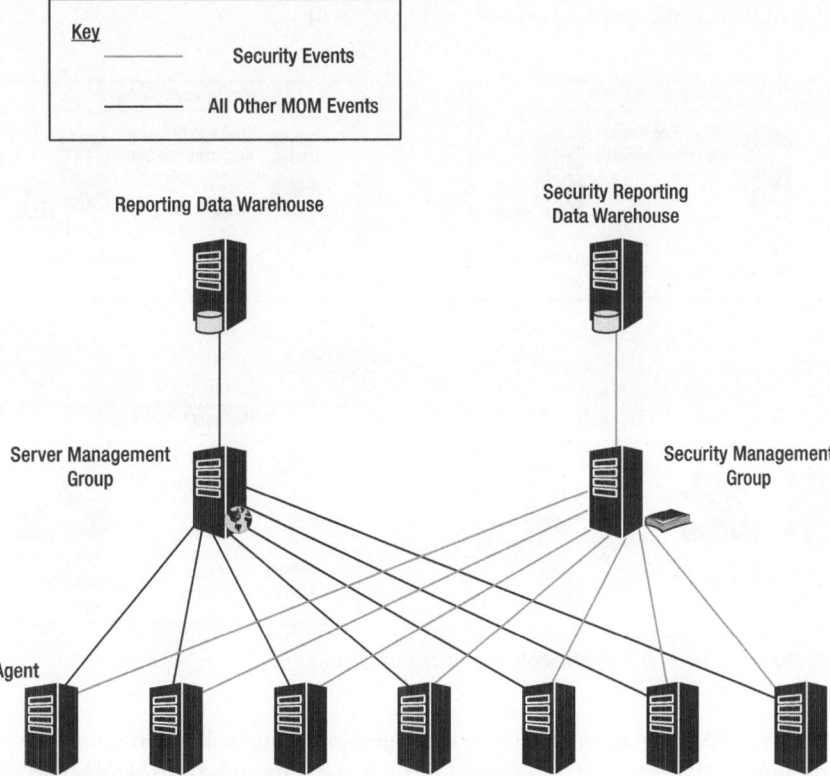

Figure 2-13. *MOM multihoming*

Multitiering

Multitiered configurations can be used in various situations. One such example would be a large enterprise with servers at different geographical locations. You could deploy a separate MOM management group at each location and create a top-level management group in which alerts from all other management groups would be rolled up. This would allow the monitoring of all locations from a single MOM Operator Console. Configuring multitiering using the MOM-to-MOM product connector is covered in more detail in Chapter 10.

Multiple Management Group Rollup to a Single Reporting Data Warehouse

In some environments, it may be necessary to hold all archived MOM data in a single reporting data warehouse. In such a case, you should configure the MOM infrastructure for multiple management group rollup. The architecture of this configuration is shown in Figure 2-14.

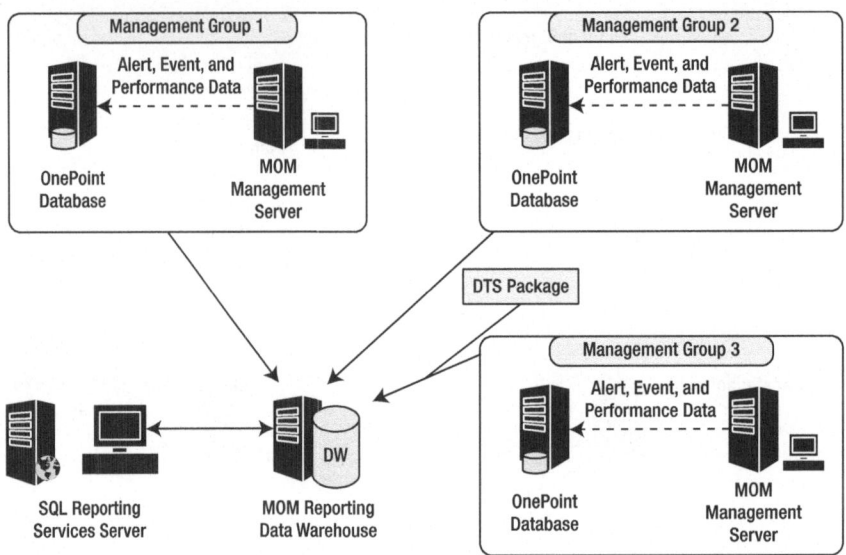

Figure 2-14. *Multiple management group rollup*

In order to configure multiple management group rollup, you need to manually create the DTS packages for the management groups. The MOM Reporting database schema has been written to support this configuration, and it is both valid and supported. More information can be found in the Multiple Management Group Rollup Solution Accelerator from Microsoft, available from www.microsoft.com/downloads.

Cluster Installation and Redundancy

Management servers cannot be clustered. To provide for management server redundancy, MOM supports the installation of up to four management servers per management group. You can split agents across these management servers by configuring the computer discovery rules in the Administrator Console appropriately. If a management server fails, all agents that report to it will automatically fail over to their secondary management server. Failover behavior is configured in the MOM Administrator Console on the Failover tab of the Management Server Properties dialog.

MOM databases, on the other hand, *can* be clustered. The MOM One-Point and SystemCenterReporting databases can be installed on a clustered instance of SQL Server. The MOM database can be installed in the same way as when installing onto a stand-alone server. The only difference is the fact that the setup program should be run on both nodes independently. First run setup on the active cluster node (the node currently running the SQL Server virtual server), and then run it on the passive node. When installing on the passive node, you should click the check box indicating that you are installing on the passive node in the MOM setup dialog. This simply tells the MOM setup program not to try to install the database again, but rather to install only the necessary files and registry keys to enable MOM to function correctly in the event of a cluster resource group failover.

One important point to note relates to the installation of the OnePoint and SystemCenterReporting databases onto 64-bit architectures. First, the System-CenterReporting database does not support 64-bit architectures, and therefore can only be installed on 32-bit editions of SQL Server. When installing the One-Point database onto 64-bit editions of SQL Server, the standard setup wizard cannot be used. In this case, you should use the `momcreatedb.exe` tool from the `Support Tools\ia64` directory on the MOM 2005 CD. This tool lets you create the database without using the setup wizard.

Assigning Monitoring Roles Using Console Scopes

Once MOM 2005 has been installed and configured, and you are starting to monitor agents, you will need to decide who monitors what. This will be easy in organizations in which a single person or team is responsible for all alerts; but in businesses in which there are multiple teams responsible for different aspects of the IT estate, you will need to separate monitoring responsibilities among the teams.

Separation of monitoring responsibility can be accomplished in MOM using console scopes. Console scopes are configured in the MOM Administrator Console, and are used to limit a user to viewing data and alerts from only selected computer groups in MOM. For example, an Exchange administrator can be limited to view only data relating to the Exchange servers in the organization. The console scope screen is shown in Figure 2-15.

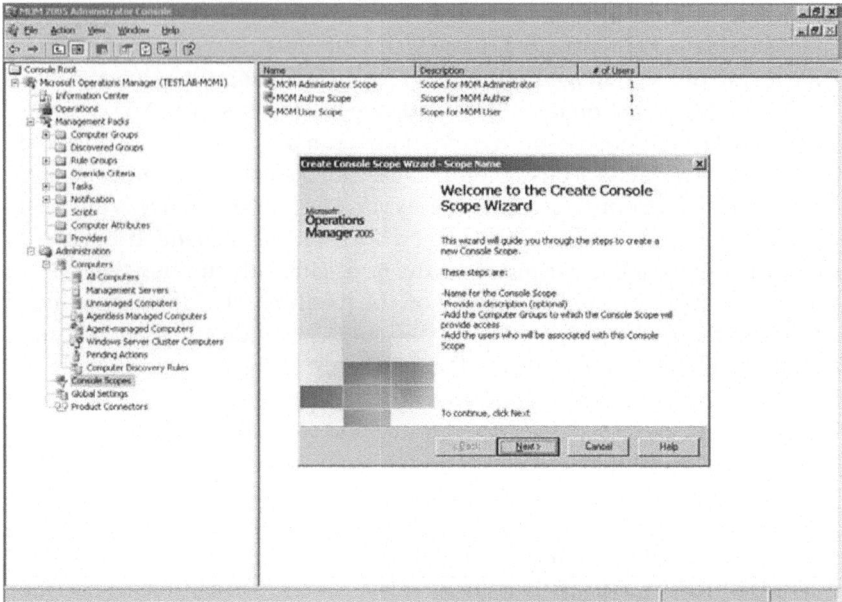

Figure 2-15. *The console scope screen, including the Create Console Scope Wizard*

Creating a console scope is straightforward: you simply need to give it a name, select the computer groups it is allowed to view, and finally apply it to a user account, a group of accounts, or a user group.

Once you have created a console scope, launch a MOM Operator Console running under the user credentials of one of the users the new console scope applies to, and verify that the users are only able to view data from the selected computer groups. Figure 2-16 shows the results of launching the Operator Console of a user that is limited to viewing Exchange Server data in a console scope.

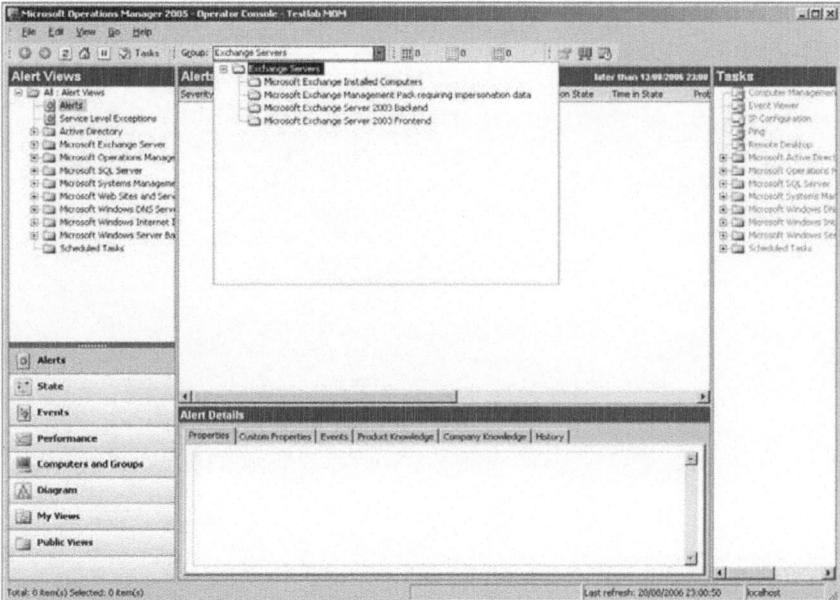

Figure 2-16. *Operator Console view limited by a console scope*

Summary

In this chapter, we looked at the planning and deployment of MOM, including deploying MOM into advanced configurations. We also looked at how to assign monitoring responsibilities using MOM console scopes. In the next chapter, we will look at installing and configuring management packs.

CHAPTER 3

■ ■ ■

Management Pack Installation and Configuration

Management packs are one of the core components of your MOM infrastructure. Without them, no monitoring would take place, as MOM would not know what to look for. One of the most common mistakes made is the installation of more management packs than are actually required. The more management packs that are installed, the more alerts there are to tune and the more data there is to be collected from the agents.

The aim of this chapter is to show you the minimum management pack installation for monitoring your systems, and how you should manage changes and/or introduce new management packs into your MOM environment. It will cover the following areas:

- Management pack definition
- Management pack installation best practices
- Management pack requirements to monitor various Microsoft products
- The rules assigned to an agent

What is a Management Pack?

A management pack is collection of configuration settings that allow you to monitor a system. Management packs are available from Microsoft and third-party vendors. You can also create your own packs for your specific requirements.

A management pack can consist of all or a selection of the following configuration settings, depending on the complexity of the management pack:

- Rules
- Schemas

- Attributes to be collected for computer groups
- Computer group rules
- Relationships
- Provider instances
- Rule groups
- Views
- Reports in a separate XML file
- Knowledge bases
- Tasks
- Notification groups
- Scripts
- Topology diagram definitions

Computer Groups

Computer groups are groups of computers that are based on attributes or manually selected. An example is the Microsoft Windows 2003 Servers computer group, which is created when you install Microsoft Windows Server Base Operating Systems Management Pack for MOM 2005. This will contain all the computers that have Windows 2003 installed, and allows you to use computer groups for the following:

- Rule targeting
- Rollup views
- Console scopes
- Computer group views
- Rule override targeting

Computer groups can be nested—containing other computer groups—and a computer group or computer can be a member of multiple computer groups. The membership of the computer groups can either be dynamic or static. Group membership can be defined by wildcard or regular expression on a domain and computer name, based on attributes (e.g., a registry key or value) or the inclusion of another computer group. The group membership is calculated continuously as discovery data is updated for the agent. Static membership is defined by the MOM administrator using a list of computers that you want to include or exclude from the group.

■**Note** One important difference between MOM 2000 and MOM 2005 is that in MOM 2000, the management console showed which computers had been discovered and were populated in the computer group. In MOM 2005, the discovered servers do not show up in the Administrator Console—they are instead displayed in the Operator Console.

Management Pack Installation Best Practices

When a management pack is imported, in most instances the pack will include computer groups that have attribute-based membership criteria and enabled rules. Once the management pack is installed, it becomes active. The following subsections outline some best practices for installing new management packs. Follow these practices to help avoid any adverse impact when installing new packs.

Creating a Sandbox Environment

Using either spare hardware or a virtual server environment, you can create a sandbox environment that is isolated from the production environment. This will be used to test the initial install of a management pack and the creation of new rules. When possible, this should contain the main components of your production environment (e.g., an Exchange server and a domain controller).

To start initial tuning of the management pack, you should do the following:

1. Carry out any post-installation configuration requirements.
2. Check that the installation of the new management pack has not impacted any of the existing management pack installations (e.g., after installing the first release of the Availability management pack, it accidentally deletes a number of the Exchange computer groups).

After you complete the steps, you should export the management packs into a staging environment (which is our topic for the next section). You should document any changes to the management pack.

Creating a Preproduction Staging Environment

Creating a preproduction staging environment will allow you to mirror the main components of your production environment and also contain all the live management packs. This staging environment can be made up of virtual machines and multihomed machines from your production environment. The deployment to the multihomed agents should only take place once you have tuned the management pack.

If the main management pack is in place, do the following:

1. Create a management server performance baseline before the new management pack is installed. See Chapter 4 for details on how to do this.

2. Import the new management pack.

3. Start a new management server performance baseline.

4. Compare the before and after baselines to ensure that the new management pack does not overload the management server.

5. Do the same for the agent performance baseline to ensure that the agent's performance is not impacted.

6. Analyze the alerts received from the new management pack. You should check the following:

   • That only valid alerts are being received—not alerts generated by misconfigurations (e.g., incorrect access rights).

   • That thresholds have been tuned to match your environment and alerts are being generated accordingly.

   • That the volume of alerts is at an acceptable level. If a management pack is "noisy," then operations teams may ignore the alerts that are being generated, and event storms may happen.

Tip The Alert Tuning Solution Accelerator (which you can download from `http://go.microsoft.com/fwlink/?LinkId=33861&clcid=0x409`) has a number of reports that can be used to analyze the alerts generated by the management pack.

After you carry out most of the tuning, you should deploy the management pack to the multihomed agents. This will allow you to check the management pack against your production environment in a controlled manner. When possible, you should test at least two multihomed agents: one on a well-connected site and one on a site with poor network links. This method of testing will highlight alerts that are triggered by slow networks. You should use rule overrides whenever possible in these scenarios to configure the alert thresholds for well-connected and poorly connected agents. You should be ready to export the management pack into your production system.

You should document any changes to the management pack, and you should update this documentation every time you make changes.

Note Override targets are not exported when you export a management pack. To get around this issue, either document the overrides that have been configured and recreate them in the production system, or use the `Overrides.exe` file, which is available in the MOM 2005 SDK. Using this tool, you can export the management pack, and then export the override targets using the `Overrides /dump filename` command. You can then import the management pack and the override targets into the production system by using the `Overrides /create filename` command.

Best Practices for Customizing Management Pack Rules

A typical MOM installation can have over 1,000 management pack rules. Typically, you will need to change the default configuration on a number of these management pack rules to meet your needs. The issue is that when you import a new version of a particular management pack, you may lose your configurations. Even if you select the merge rule, only the enabled/disabled flag and the company knowledge entries are retained.

Each rule has a unique rule GUID (globally unique identifier), so renaming the changed rule will not overcome this issue during the import. The rule will be overwritten, as it is identified by GUID rather than name.

The following process should be followed to ensure that the impact of importing updated management packs is reduced:

1. Create a new rule group based on the management pack name from which the rules are going to be copied (e.g., *Company Name* - Microsoft Operations Manager). If necessary, create any child rule groups based on the names of the original child rule group (e.g., *Company Name* - Operations Manager 2005). This allows you to easily see where the rules have come from, and also allow the rule targeting at the child rule group level as required.

2. Copy the rule that you are going to modify into this new structure, and then disable the original rule.

3. Change the name of the newly copied-over rule back to the original name, as "Copy of" will have been appended to the rule's name.

4. Populate the Knowledge Base entry in this rule, as it will be empty, and isn't copied over by default. To populate this field, you have two options: either share knowledge between two rules or simply copy and paste the Knowledge Base entry from the original rule into the company knowledge section of the new rule.

5. Once all rules have been copied over, associate the parent and child rule groups with the correct computer groups. You must match this association with the association of the original rule groups to ensure that the rules are applied to the correct agents.

Figure 3-1 shows an example of the configuration rules that you will have modified in the MOM rule group.

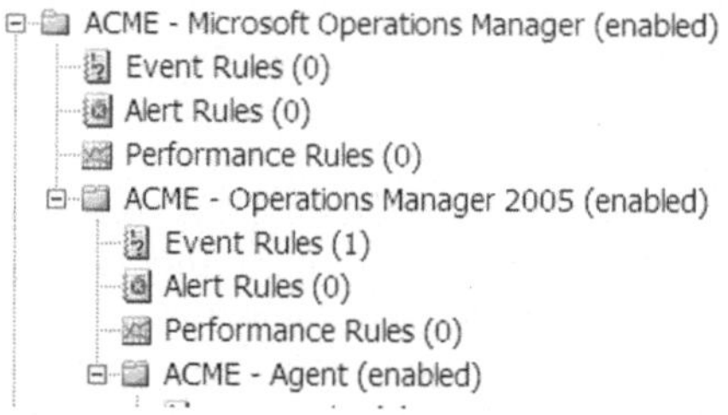

Figure 3-1. *Modified rule group*

This process may seem time-consuming, but in reality, the number of rules that you will customize will be relatively few. If you customize the rules in their original locations, you can avoid the difficulties of trying to manage the import of an updated management pack into your environment.

Management Pack Requirements

The aim of this section is to provide information on the management packs that should be installed to monitor the following:

- Active Directory
- Exchange
- Internet Information Services (IIS)
- Windows clusters
- Simple Network Management Protocol (SNMP)
- SQL 2000 and 2005

The Management Pack and Utilities catalog, which provides further information, is located at www.microsoft.com/management/mma/catalog.aspx. We will give more details later in this section.

Active Directory

Active Directory is the backbone of most companies' Windows infrastructures. It is therefore critical that proactive management is carried out to avoid business outages. The main components that need to be monitored are as follows:

- OS (Windows 2000 and Windows 2003)
- Distributed file system (DFS)
- File replication service (FRS)
- Domain name system (DNS)
- Group policy (GPO)
- Server hardware
- Directory services

Install the following management packs to monitor the Active Directory server environment:

- Active Directory (AD) Management Pack for MOM 2005
- Group Policy Management Pack for MOM
- Microsoft Windows Distributed File System Service Management Pack for Microsoft Operations Manager 2005
- Microsoft Windows Server Base Operating Systems Management Pack for Microsoft Operations Manager 2005
- Domain Name Service (DNS) Management Pack for MOM 2005
- Microsoft Windows File Replication Service Management Pack for Microsoft Operations Manager 2005

Depending on the hardware used to host the Active Directory environment, one or more of the following management packs should be installed:

- HP Server Management Packs for MOM 2005
- Dell Management Pack for MOM 2005
- IBM Director 5.10 (for integration of IBM Director with MOM 2005)

■Note The File Replication Service management pack relies heavily on having Ultrasound installed in your environment. A MOM agent should be installed on the server that hosts the Ultrasound installation. You should ensure that your process for managing FRS alerts also includes resolving the alerts in Ultrasound, as the management pack does not send alert status changes back to the Ultrasound server.

Exchange Servers

Since businesses have become dependent on e-mail, many processes and procedures are integrated with the environment of sending and receiving e-mail. Therefore, it is critical that the messaging environment is monitored closely. The messaging environment is also one of those areas on which managers like to have reports and statistics for service level agreement (SLA) reporting. In this section, we will focus on Exchange 2000/2003, as Exchange 5.5 support ended on December 31, 2005.

Install the following management packs to monitor an Exchange Server environment:

• Microsoft Exchange Server Management Pack for MOM 2005

• Microsoft Exchange Server Best Practices Analyzer Management Pack for Microsoft Operations Manager 2005

• Microsoft Operations Manager 2005 SLA Scorecard for Exchange

• Microsoft Availability Reporting Management Pack for Microsoft Operations Manager 2005

• Microsoft Windows Server Base Operating Systems Management Pack for Microsoft Operations Manager 2005

Depending on the hardware that is used to host the Exchange environment, one or more of the following management packs should be installed:

• HP Server Management Packs for MOM 2005

• Dell Management Pack for MOM 2005

• IBM Director 5.10 (for integration of IBM Director with MOM 2005)

Note If you install Microsoft Operations Manager 2005 SLA Scorecard for Exchange, there is a misconfigured rule. The Service Control Manager event for the Service Stopped/Started rule should have the This Rule Generates Alert check box unchecked—otherwise it will generate an alert for every event ID 7036. The rule should be just a collection rule, not an alert-generating rule. If it is not unchecked, your Operator Console will be flooded with critical alerts.

You can also utilize some of the features of the Active Directory management pack to ensure that the Active Directory environment that has to service the Exchange environment is responding as expected. This can be achieved when you add the Exchange servers into the Active Directory Client Side Monitoring computer group. This allows the Exchange server to test whether Active Directory is available by the following:

- Pinging (using both Internet Control Message Protocol [ICMP] and Lightweight Directory Access Protocol [LDAP])

- Searching Active Directory

- Confirming that a sufficient number of global catalog servers are available

- Detecting primary domain controller PDC availability and responsiveness

If you are concerned about installing extra components on the Exchange servers, you can add a server that is on the same physical site as the Exchange server, and this server will carry out the checks.

IIS

Web sites are utilized heavily by businesses now. A web site may be the first encounter a potential new customer has with a company. It is important, then, that any issues that could potentially cause downtime or poor performance—such as broken links, unavailable sites, and security breaches—are alerted on.

Install the following management packs to monitor the IIS server environment:

- Internet Information Server (IIS) Management Pack for MOM 2005

- Microsoft Web Sites and Services Management Pack for MOM 2005

- Microsoft Windows Server Base Operating Systems Management Pack for Microsoft Operations Manager 2005

Depending on the hardware that is used to host the web servers, one or more of the following management packs should be installed:

- HP Server Management Packs for MOM 2005
- Dell Management Pack for MOM 2005
- IBM Director 5.10 (for integration of IBM Director with MOM 2005)

If you wish to monitor the Live Communication Server (LCS) web component, then also install the Office Communicator Web Access Management Pack for MOM 2005.

You should pay particular attention to the Web Sites and Services management pack, as you will be able to closely monitor the availability and functionality of the web site or web service. Out of the box, this management pack does not contain any preconfigured rules that allow you to monitor a web application or web service. You must take time to configure the management pack to meet your requirements. The following link has more information on the management pack: www.microsoft.com/technet/prodtechnol/mom/mom2005/maintain/momwssmpguide_3.mspx.

Note If you don't have the current IIS management pack installed, ensure that you disable the following rules:

Security: Error 401: "Access Denied" Error - Alert

Security: Error 401: "Access Denied" - Event Consolidation

It has been known for the IIS management pack to randomly add IP address and domain name restrictions to all web sites on the local computer. These rules must be disabled for IIS 5 and 6.

Windows Clusters

Clustering allows the delivery of higher levels of service and availability so that you can ensure that the clustered environment meets the business needs. For this reason, you need to carefully monitor these clusters. Install the following management packs to monitor the cluster environment:

- Server Clusters Management Pack for MOM 2005
- Microsoft Windows Server Base Operating Systems Management Pack for Microsoft Operations Manager 2005

Depending on the hardware that is used to host the clusters, one or more of the following management packs should be installed:

- HP Server Management Packs for MOM 2005
- Dell Management Pack for MOM 2005
- IBM Director 5.10 (for integration of IBM Director with MOM 2005)

These management packs will monitor the core components of the cluster installation. Additional management packs should be installed based on the applications that will be hosted on the cluster (e.g., Exchange or SQL).

Once you have installed the management pack and discovered the cluster, you need to go to the Windows Server clusters in the Administrator Console Right-click them and select Start Managing. It is also recommended that you disable event log replication to avoid generating duplicate alerts. If you decide to leave event log replication enabled, then you need to allow the agent proxying for the cluster nodes; otherwise, you may receive security alerts in MOM. You can disable event log replication via a built-in task in the MOM Operator Console, or by entering **EnableEventLogReplication=0** at the command prompt on a cluster node.

The use of clusters in your environment may have an impact on some of the management packs, such as the Microsoft Operations Manager 2005 SLA Scorecard for Exchange, which currently does not support clusters.

SNMP

MOM 2005 can monitor SNMP traps. This allows you to configure MOM to monitor non-Windows systems (e.g., UPS, routers, etc.). You are required to make the configurations rather than just upload a management pack. The following example will show how to monitor the HP StorageWorks Reference Information Storage System (RISS) via SNMP. In this example, the RISS has only three traps that we are interested in. These are described in Table 3-1.

Table 3-1. *SNMP Traps*

Trap ID	Description
1.3.6.1.4.1.14701.6.6.1	A notification will be sent if any SmartCell goes into the dead state.
1.3.6.1.4.1.14701.6.6.2	A notification will be sent if any host is down.
1.3.6.1.4.1.14701.6.6.3	A notification will be sent if any service listed in PCC has the state CRITICAL.

The RISS system does not come with any management information base (MIB), so the translations have to be done inside MOM. To set up MOM to receive SNMP traps, you need to set up the management server and the SNMP rule group.

Setting Up the Management Server to Collect SNMP Traps

It takes five steps to set up the management server to collect SNMP traps. The following sections show you how you perform them.

Step One

To ensure that the SNMP service and WMI SNMP provider are installed on the management server, do the following:

1. Open Add/Remove Programs.
2. Click the Add/Remove Windows Components button.
3. Select Management and Monitoring Tools from the Windows Components dialog.
4. Click the Details button, and install SNMP and the WMI SNMP Provider.

Note On Windows 2000, you can find the WMI SNMP Provider on the Windows 2000 CD, in a file called WBEMSNMP.EXE.

Step Two

To configure the SNMP service to accept traps, do the following:

1. Go to Computer Management ➤ Services and Applications, and double-click the SNMP service in the Services window.
2. In the SNMP Service Properties window, click the Security tab.
3. Ensure that the Accept SNMP packets from any host check box is checked, as shown in Figure 3-2.

Note SNMP is insecure, so when possible you should rename the community name to something other than the default PUBLIC.

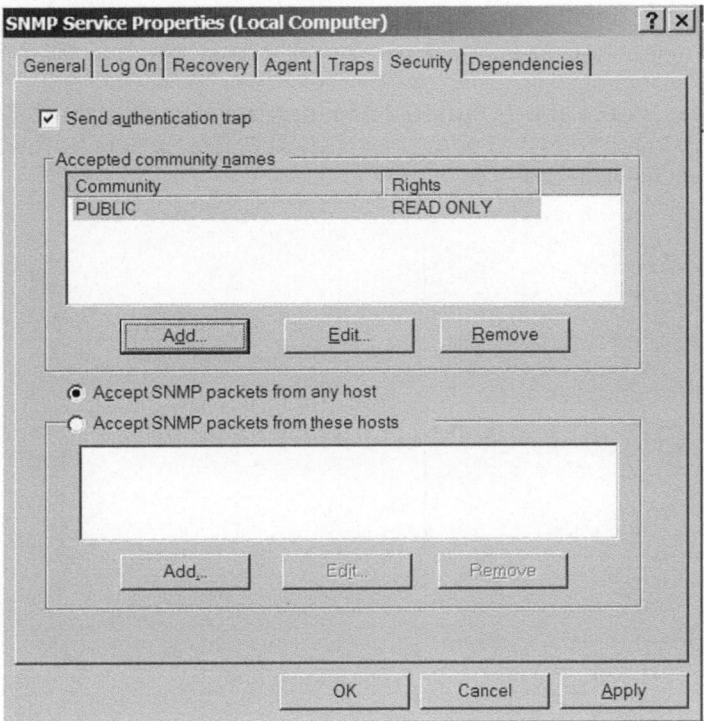

Figure 3-2. *The SNMP Service Properties window*

4. On the General tab, you should configure the service to start up automatically. Once you've done that, click Apply, and then click OK.

5. Go to the SNMP Trap service in the service window and configure the startup to automatic.

Step Three

In the MOM Administrator Console, create a new computer group (called, for example, SNMP Server) and the management server(s) for this group.

Step Four

Create a new rule group following your standard naming convention (e.g., ACME SNMP).

Step Five

Associate the SNMP rule group to the computer group that you have created.

Setting Up an SNMP Rule Group

It takes eight steps to create an SNMP collection event. This is how you do it:

1. Under ACME SNMP in the MOM Administrator Console, right-click Event Rules. From the pop-up menu, select Create Event Rule. This is shown in Figure 3-3.

Figure 3-3. *Selecting the Create Event Rule option*

2. In the Select Event Rule Type window, select Collect Specific Events (Collection), and then click Next. This is shown in Figure 3-4.

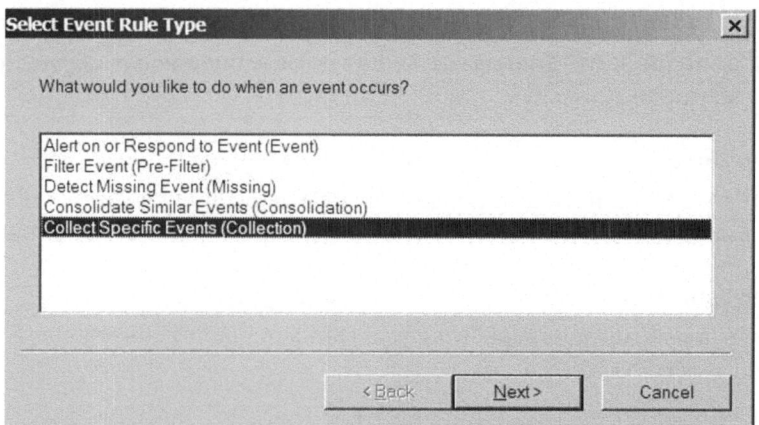

Figure 3-4. *Selecting Collect Specific Events (Collection)*

3. In the Collection Rule Properties - Data Provider window, select SNMP Extended Trap Catcher as the provider, and then click Next. This is shown in Figure 3-5.

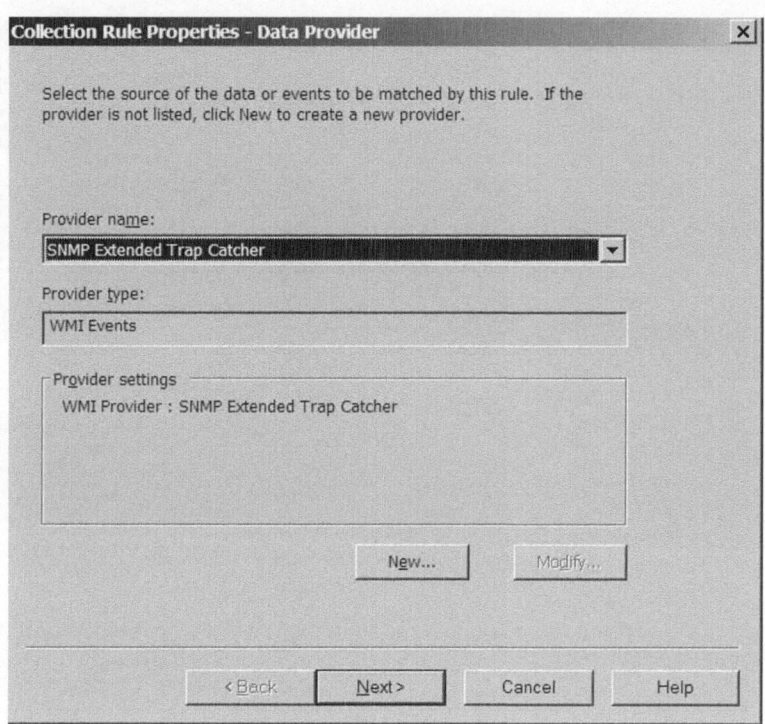

Figure 3-5. *Selecting the provider name*

4. In the Collection Rule Properties - Criteria window, accept the default settings, for which all the Match events boxes are unchecked (as shown in Figure 3-6). Click Next.

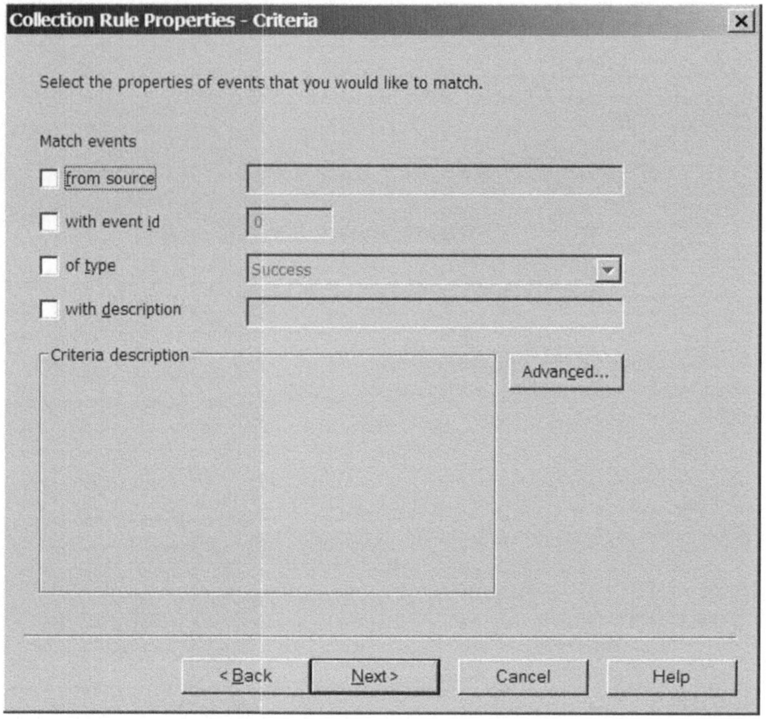

Figure 3-6. *Configuring the criteria*

5. In the Collection Rule Properties - Parameter Storage window, select
   Store all event parameters, and then click Next. This is shown in
   Figure 3-7.

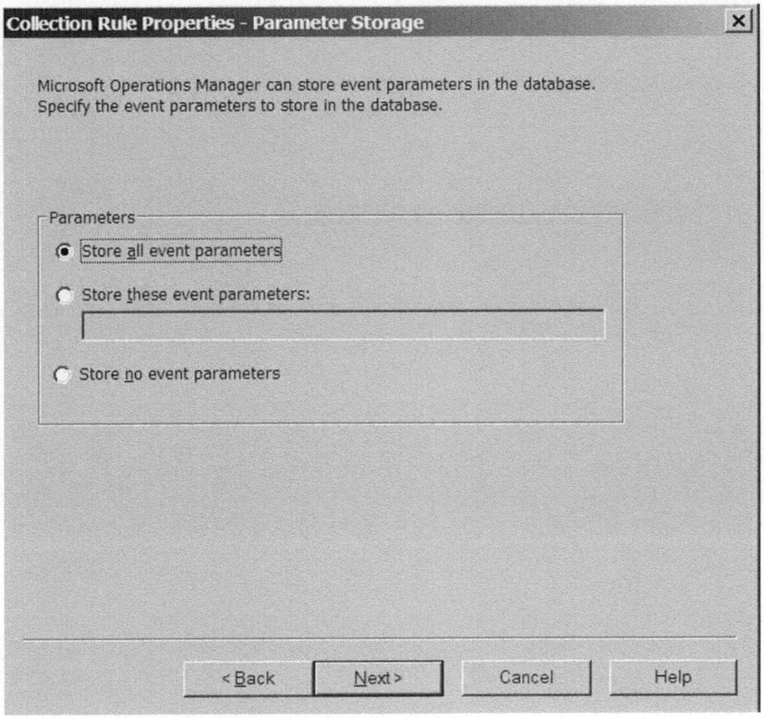

Figure 3-7. *The Parameter Storage window*

6. From the drop-down menu in the Collection Rule Properties - Schedule window, Select Always process data, and then click Next. This is shown in Figure 3-8.

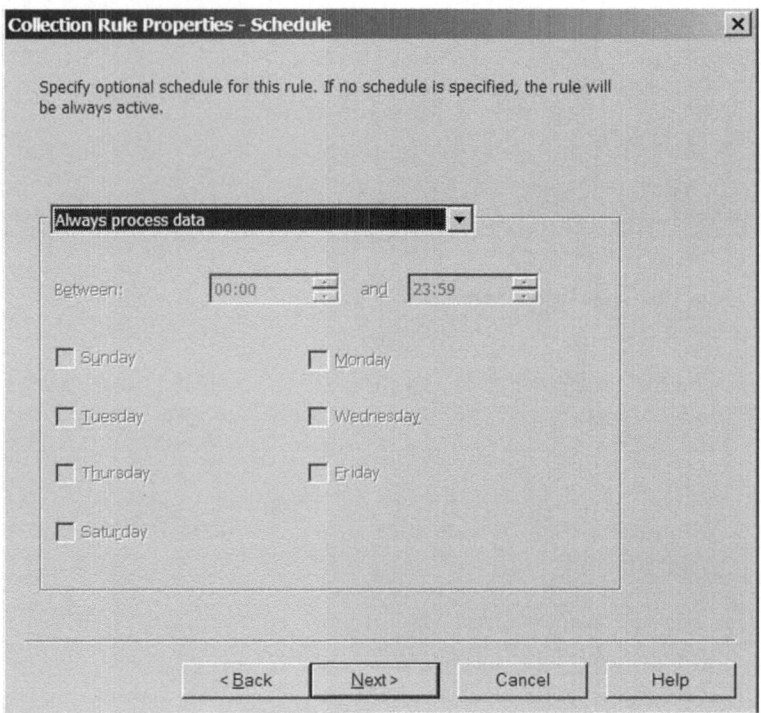

Figure 3-8. *Schedule to process data*

7. In the Collection Rule Properties - Knowledge Base window, enter the knowledge base details on a collection rule. After you have finished entering the details, click Next. This is shown in Figure 3-9.

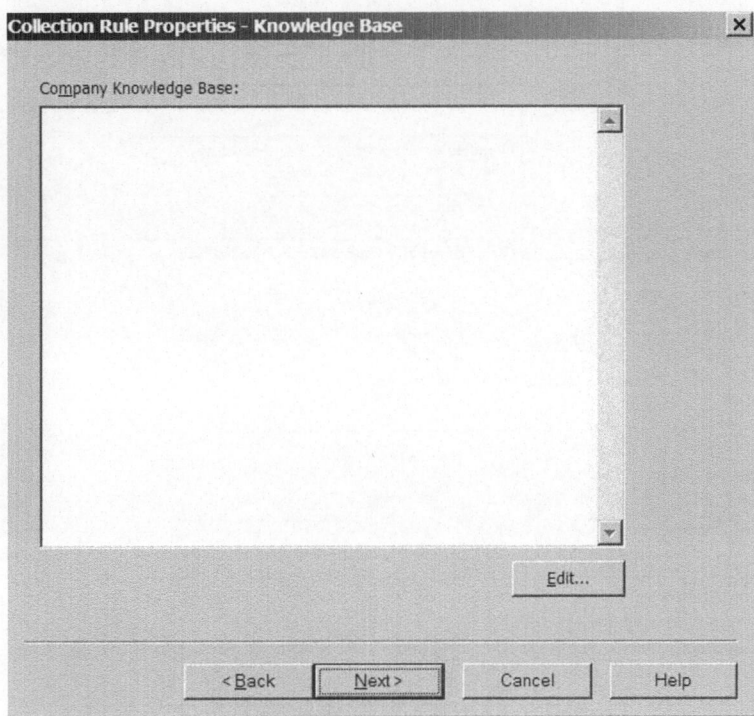

Figure 3-9. *The Knowledge Base window*

8. In the Collection Rule Properties - General window, enter a rule name. Make sure that the rule is enabled. Do not enable rule-disable overrides for this rule. Click Finish. This is shown in Figure 3-10.

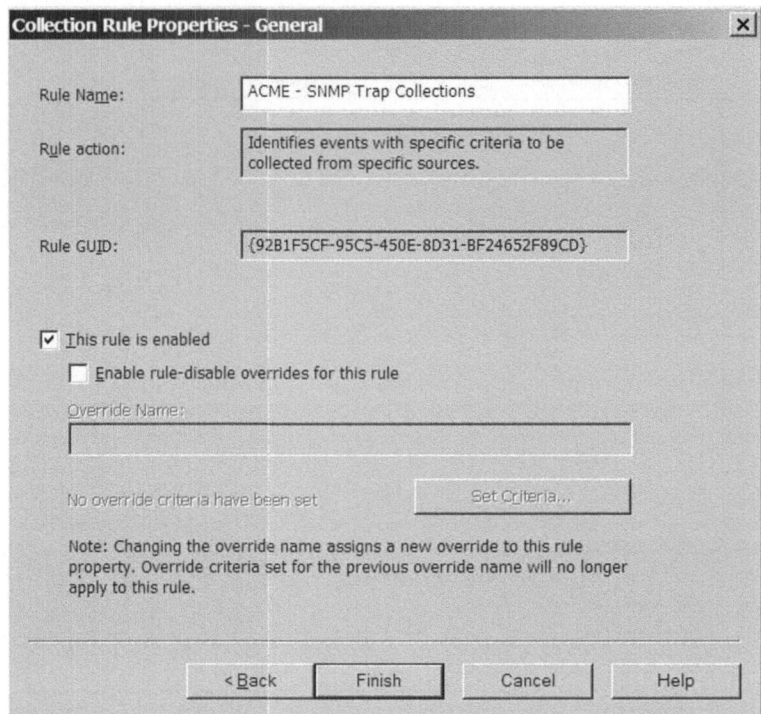

Figure 3-10. *The General window*

Setting Up Alerts for SNMP Traps

It takes 12 steps to set up alerts for SNMP traps. This is how you do them:

1. In the Administrator Console, expand the ACME SNMP rule group and right-click Event Rules. From the pop-up menu, select the Alert on or Respond to Event rule. This is shown in Figure 3-11.

2. In the Event Rule Properties - Data Provider window, select SNMP Extended Trap Catcher as the provider, and then click Next. This is shown in Figure 3-12.

3. In the Event Rule Properties - Criteria window, click Advanced.

Create Event Rule...

Find Rules...

Alert on or Respond to Event...
Filter Event...
Detect Missing Event...
Consolidate Similar Events...
Collect Specific Events...

View   ▶
New Window from Here

Refresh
Export List...

Help

Figure 3-11. *Selecting the Alert on or Respond to Event rule*

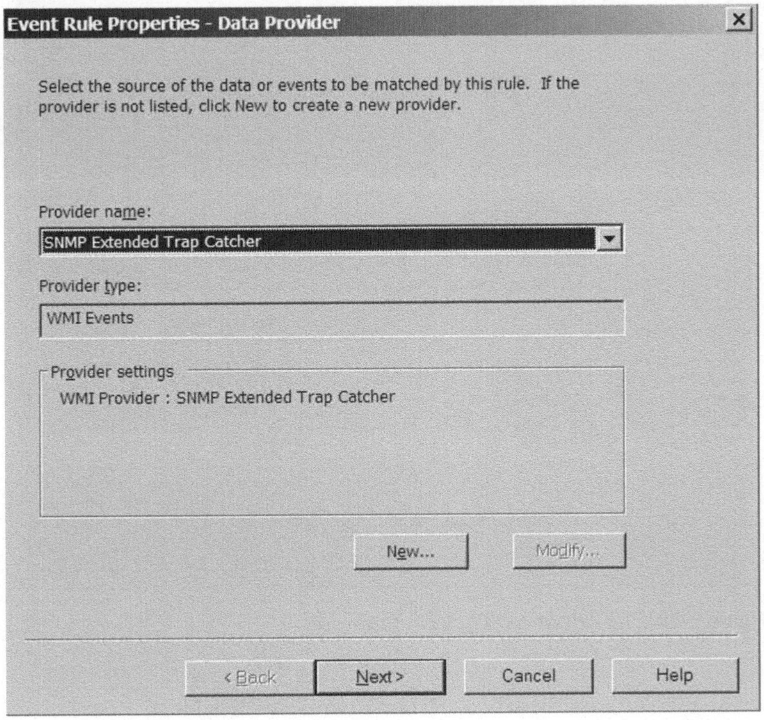

Event Rule Properties - Data Provider   ☒

Select the source of the data or events to be matched by this rule. If the
provider is not listed, click New to create a new provider.

Provider name:

SNMP Extended Trap Catcher   ▼

Provider type:

WMI Events

┌─ Provider settings ───┐
│   WMI Provider : SNMP Extended Trap Catcher   │
│   │
│   │
│   │
│   │
└──┘

                                        New...   Modify...

              < Back   Next >   Cancel   Help

Figure 3-12. *Selecting the data provider*

4. In the Advanced Criteria window, configure the following, and click
   Add to List. This is shown in Figure 3-13.

   - *Field*: Description

   - *Condition*: contains substring

   - *Value*: 1.3.6.1.4.1.14701.6.6.2

5. Configure the following, click Add to List, and then click Close. This is
   shown in Figure 3-13.

   - *Field*: Parameter 17

   - *Condition*: contains substring

   - *Value*: DOWN

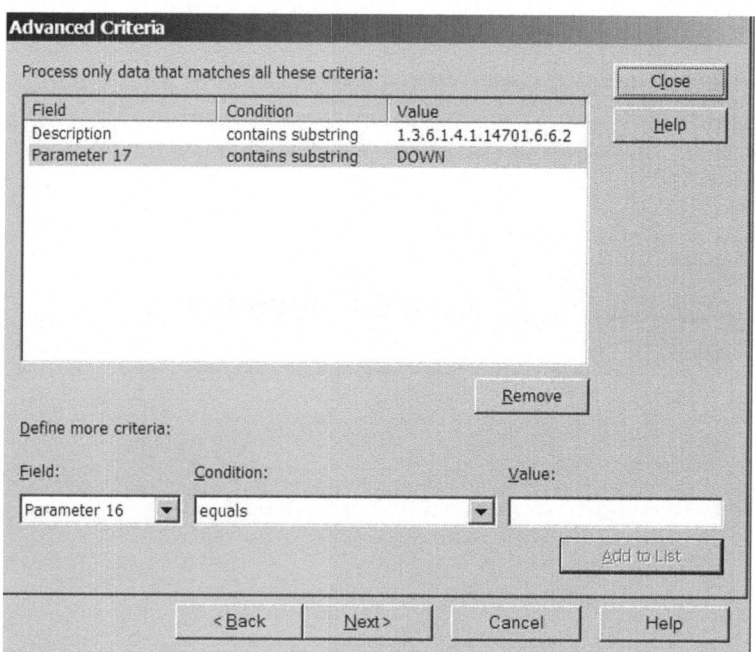

Figure 3-13. *The Advanced Criteria window*

6. In the Event Rule Properties - Criteria window, click Next.

7. In the Schedule window, select Always process data.

8. In the Event Rule Properties - Alert window, check This Rule Generate
   Alerts, and set the alert severity to critical. In the Description field, enter
   RISS host $Parameter 17$, and then click Next.

9. In the Event Rule Properties - Alert Suppression window, uncheck Suppress Duplicate Alerts, and then click Next.

10. In the Event Rule Properties - Responses window, click Next.

11. In the Event Rule Properties - Knowledge Base window, enter the company details, and then click next.

12. In the Event Rule Properties - General window, enter a rule name. Ensure that the rule is enabled. Do not enable rule-disable overrides for this rule. Click Finish.

This information provides the basic steps to configure an alert for the SNMP trap 1.3.6.1.4.1.14701.6.6.2, with a status that the host is down.

You can alter this process to match any SNMP traps that you want to capture in MOM. The parameters for the SNMP traps can be worked out by looking at the events in the Operator Console, and then clicking the Parameters tab. In Figure 3-14, the position number represents the parameter numbers on the alert in the Advanced Criteria window.

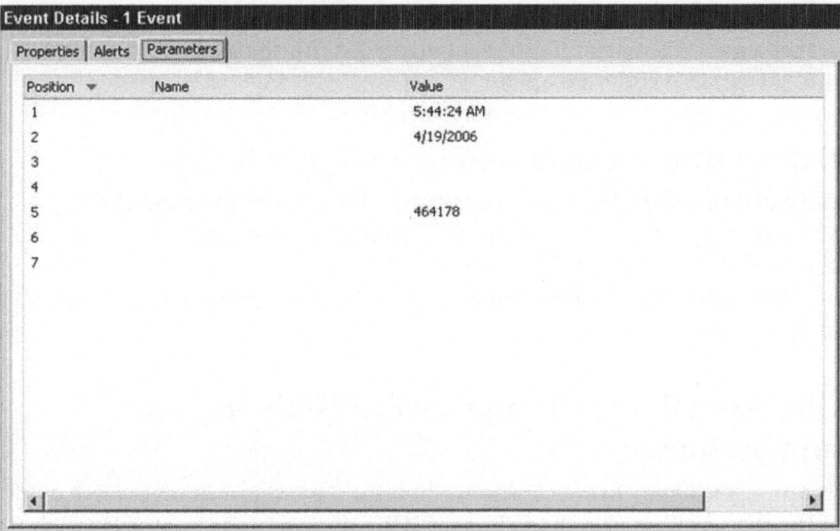

Figure 3-14. *Example of event parameters*

The previous example did not import MIBs, so the meaning of the alert had to be manually added to the Description field. Otherwise, the alert would not be very meaningful to the operations team. If the device that you are going to monitor has MIBs available, it is possible for you to import the MIBs into MOM. This will make it easier to translate the SNMP trap into an alert that you can understand. You can also use the SM12SMIR utility to import the MIBs. This will load the MIB information into the WMI `\\.\root\snmp\smir` namespace and provide SNMP trap translations. Otherwise, you will just receive object identifiers, which are basically strings of numbers (e.g., 1.3.6.1.4.1.9.9.163.2.0.1) and possibly a status value.

Identifying the Rules Assigned to an Agent

When troubleshooting an agent, it is often important to see what rules are assigned to it. There are numerous ways of identifying what rules are assigned to an agent—the following section shows you how you do it.

The Resultant Set of Rules (RSOR) Utility

The resource kit includes the RSOR utility, which will generate a plain text file showing the set of rules that would be deployed to an agent. The syntax is `RSOR.exe <MOMDBServer> <TargetAgent>`. The output is then placed in `C:\ResultantSetOfRules`. If your operations database is a SQL instance, then the syntax would be `RSOR.exe <MOMDBServer\SQL_INSTANCE_NAME> <TargetAgent>`. The text file so created will list the enabled and disabled rules associated with that agent.

Export Rules Associated to an Agent Script

You can download a free script from Huntland Services to export the MOM rules that are associated with an agent from `www.huntland.co.uk/Downloads/MOM/DumpMomRulesForComputerCMD.html`.

The script will export the enabled rules for an agent into a CSV (comma-separated value) file.

Checking When Changes Were Made to Rules and Scripts

At times, it is handy to check when, where, and by whom changes were made to the rules. You can run the following SQL statements against the OnePoint database.

Example 1: This statement will list all rules and show when they were modified and by whom:

```
select  idprocessrule, name, lastmodified, lastmodifiedby,
IsRuleGroup from OnePoint..processrule
```

Example 2: This statement will list a rule identified by its rule GUID:

```
select  idprocessrule, name, lastmodified, lastmodifiedby,
IsRuleGroup from OnePoint..processrule where
idprocessrule ='enter guid here'
```

For example

```
select  idprocessrule, name, lastmodified, lastmodifiedby,
IsRuleGroup from OnePoint..processrule
where idprocessrule ='6C85049A-5F96-48DD-891F-046F3FBEF20F'
```

Example 3: This statement displays a list of scripts sorted by last modified date:

```
select name, isdeleted, lastmodified, lastmodifiedby, timeadded,
description from script
order by lastmodified desc
```

Example 4: This statement lists modification details of global settings:

```
select datacategory + dataname as GlobalSetting, datavalue,
lastmodified, lastmodifiedby from OnePoint..configuration
where lastmodifiedby !='NULL'
```

Third-Party Tools

Numerous third-party vendors have released management packs and tools to manage MOM. The advantages of some of these management packs are that they fill in the gaps in which Microsoft or other vendors have not released a management pack, or extend MOM to monitor non-Windows systems (e.g., UNIX).

These management packs incur a cost, but they can provide a ready-made monitoring solution so that you don't have to develop your own management pack. You can find a list of the main third-party management packs in the Management Pack and Utilities catalog, available on the Microsoft web site at www. microsoft.com/management/mma/catalog.aspx.

■**Note** Not too many third-party tools assist in managing the management pack life cycle. Currently, only Silect Software has products available to help you in this area. You can find more information at www.silect.com/products/products_overview.htm.

Summary

This chapter has explained how to manage the management pack life cycle; this will help to reduce the complexity of managing your MOM environment. The management pack life cycle can be one of the biggest headaches for a MOM administrator, so it is important that you use the information in this chapter to help you define a process that your organization will follow. The chapter has also shown how to extend MOM to monitor SNMP-enabled devices and what management packs you should install to monitor the key components of your infrastructure. Chapter 4 will cover the process you need to follow to ensure that your MOM infrastructure remains healthy.

■ ■ ■

Operational Management of MOM 2005

With MOM monitoring your critical systems, it is important that you keep your MOM infrastructure in working order. As a MOM administrator, you need to monitor the health of the MOM infrastructure to ensure that all the jobs and tasks are functioning as expected.

This chapter will show you to how to maintain your MOM infrastructure, including the changes you need to make to ensure that the required data is getting passed to the Reporting database.

This chapter covers:

- Performance baselines
- Management server management
- Agent management
- Database management

Performance Baselines

Once the management infrastructure has been tuned to your operational requirements, you should carry out a performance baseline of the management server(s) and a typical agent-managed server. This information will be used in performance-related troubleshooting and as part of the process of validating the introduction of new management packs within the managed environment.

The Management Server

A performance monitor log should be configured so that it captures at a minimum the counters listed in Table 4-1 at a 15-minute sample rate over a 7-day period.

Table 4-1. *Management Server Performance Baseline Counters*

Performance Object	Used for Tracking	Counters to Monitor
Disk	Usage	LogicalDisk\% Free Space LogicalDisk\% Disk Time PhysicalDisk\Disk Reads/sec PhysicalDisk\Disk Writes/sec
Disk	Bottlenecks	LogicalDisk\Avg. Disk Queue Length PhysicalDisk\Avg. Disk Queue Length (all instances)
Memory	Usage	Memory\Available Bytes Memory\Cache Bytes
Memory	Bottlenecks or leaks	Memory\Pages/sec Memory\Page Faults/sec Memory\Pages Input/sec Memory\Page Reads/sec Memory\Transition Faults/sec Memory\Pool Paged Bytes Memory\Pool Nonpaged Bytes
Network	Usage	Network Segment: % Net Utilization
Network	Throughput	Network Interface\Bytes total/sec Network Interface\Packets/sec Server\Bytes Total/sec or Server\Bytes Sent/sec and Server\Bytes Received/sec
Processor	Usage	Processor\% Processor Time (all instances)
Processor	Bottlenecks	System\Processor Queue Length (all instances) Processor\Interrupts/sec System\Context switches/sec
MOM Server	Throughput	Db Alert Insert Simple Count
MOM Server	Throughput	Db Disc Insert Simple Count
MOM Server	Throughput	Db Event Insert Simple Count
MOM Server	Throughput	Db Perf Insert Simple Count
MOM Server	Throughput	Queue Process Simple Count
MOM Server	Throughput	Resp Exec Simple Count
MOM Server	Throughput	Task Exec Simple Count
MOM Server	Usage	Db % Free Space Available

You should run the baseline when the management server configuration has been finalized and all installed management pack alert tuning has been completed. You should also run it when new management packs are introduced. This information will help in diagnosing performance-related issues on the management server, as the current performance can be compared to the baseline. This may help highlight the cause of the problem (e.g., if the Physical Disk \%Disk Time counter is consistently high and the disk queue length is greater than 2, your disk may be a bottleneck).

During the management server's day-to-day tasks, there will be occasional performance spikes, which are to be expected.

Tip Once the performance log has been created, save it as an HTML file. This file can be imported to ensure that the settings are consistent. Also, if you use the Use local computer objects option when adding the objects, then the HTML file can be used on other servers, which can save time.

Agent Baselines

The agent baseline is intended to focus on the performance of the MOM agent rather than the full OS. A performance monitor log should be configured so that it captures at a minimum the counters listed in Table 4-2 at a 15-minute sample rate over a 7-day period.

Table 4-2. *Agent Performance Baseline Counters*

Performance Object	Used For Tracking	Counters to Monitor	Comments
Process	Usage	MOM Service Working Set	The working set values should not show a steady increase. The value should be approximately 15 MB. This value can increase if the management pack installed on an agent has a large number of scripts.
Process	Usage	MOM Service Private Bytes	The private bytes values will peak when a new management pack is installed; then it should be a horizontal line on the graph. If the graph after the initial install resembles a stair step followed by a horizontal line, and then repeats with an upward progression, this indicates a possible memory leak, and should be investigated.

Continued

Table 4-2. *Continued*

Performance Object	Used For Tracking	Counters to Monitor	Comments
Process	Usage	MOM Service % Processor Time	The processor time percentage should be between 3 and 10, depending on the server being monitored. If it is a higher value, then the agent could be impacting the performance of the server.
Process	Usage	MOM Service Handle Count	When a script in a management pack runs, the handle count should increase; but it should decrease once the script has finished and the handle is released. If the handle count continues to rise, then there may be an issue with the management pack's scripts not releasing the handle.
Mom agent	Usage	Queue Space Percent Used	This specifies the percent of the workflow queue in use (by data and alerts). The queue percent used should remain low; if it does not, this could indicate that the agent may be overloaded.

The agent baseline is a critical part of the release process of new management packs because the prime goal is to avoid introducing any new issues into the monitored environment.

Management Server Management

The management server is one of the central components of any MOM installation. Any alerts that are generated by the MOM 2005 management pack should be checked and resolved as soon as possible so that you can ensure that the MOM infrastructure is operating correctly. The emphasis should be on ensuring the availability of the management server rather then resolving issues related to performance. The management server ensures that alert data is sent to the Operations database, but event and performance data could be lost. Table 4-3 contains the main alerts that you will see.

Table 4-3. *Management Server Alerts*

Rule/Cause of Failure	Event Id	Probable Cause	Check
Failed to insert events into the database.	25101	The network connection to the Operations database has been lost. The OnePoint database is full.	Check the network connection to the server holding the OnePoint database. Ensure that the OnePoint database has a maximum size of 30 GB, but that it has 40-percent free space for jobs to complete correctly. The database should never be set to grow automatically.
Unrecoverable database error; the system will continue processing events and alerts.	25102	SQL server is running in single user mode.	Make sure that the SQL server is not running in single user mode. The OnePoint database has run out of capacity. Ensure that the OnePoint database has a maximum size of 30 GB, but that it has 40-percent free space for jobs to complete correctly. The database should never be set to grow automatically.
The MOM Server was unable to retrieve data or prepare data for insertion in the database.	25103, 25106, 25107	The OnePoint database has run out of capacity.	Ensure that the OnePoint database has a maximum size of 30 GB, but that it has 40-percent free space for jobs to complete correctly. The database should never be set to grow automatically.
The MOM Server failed to locate any DAS servers.	25105	The database server is not available. The Data Access Service (DAS) account access rights are incorrect.	Check that the server is running and allowing connections, and that the database is online. Check that the DAS account has a db_owner role for the OnePoint database and a SQL Server Security login with permit server access.

Continued

Table 4-3. *Continued*

Rule/Cause of Failure	Event Id	Probable Cause	Check
The MOM service is not available on the management server.	n/a	The server was manually restarted. The MOM Service service was too busy and had to be restarted.	Check the application and Dr. Watson logs to see if the cause of the crash is listed.
The incoming MOM server queue is full.	21268	This can be a sign that the management server is struggling to cope with the load.	Check the Operations database, and that the volume of alerts that the management server is receiving is at an acceptable level.
The outgoing MOM server queue is full.	220061, 220062, 21269	The database server is not available.	Check that the server is running and allowing connections, and that the database is online. Check that the server is running and allowing connections and that the database is online. Check the network connections between the management server and the database server.

It is highly recommended that you upgrade the MOM 2005 infrastructure to MOM 2005 SP1 as soon as possible as the SP1 upgrade resolves the majority of the common errors.

You should define a process of managing the alerts that the MOM management pack generates. Experience has shown that alerts from the other management packs tend to take priority. If the alerts from the MOM management pack are not acted upon, it could cause a loss of service on the management server(s).

Regular capacity reviews should be carried out to ensure that the management servers are sized to cope with the current load, and for any envisaged growth in the environment that is managed.

Agent Management

This section concentrates on the common issues that you'll encounter on an agent-managed system and what hotfixes you need to use as possible resolutions to the symptoms. Table 4-4 shows the common alerts on agents and recommends hotfixes for each.

Table 4-4. *Common Alerts on Agents*

Symptom	Information	Knowledge Base Article ID/Hotfix
The following entry appears in agent's event log: Event Type: Error Event Source: Microsoft Operations Manager Event Category: None Event ID: 21293 User: NT AUTHORITY\SYSTEM Description: The agent was unable to send data to the MOM Server at Management ServerName. The error code is 10054. An existing connection was forcibly closed by the remote host. Event Type: Information Event Source: Microsoft Operations Manager Event Category: None Event ID: 26021 User: NT AUTHORITY\SYSTEM Description: The agent has restored communication to ManagementServerName	This is normally encountered when monitoring agents over slow networks. A good value for the ServerIOTimeoutMS registry key entry is 45000.	885416

Continued

Table 4-4. *Continued*

Symptom	Information	Knowledge Base Article ID/Hotfix
Event IDs 21246 or 21245 are logged in the application event log on an agent. The agent also has McAfee VirusScan Enterprise 8.0i installed.	This problem occurs because McAfee VirusScan replaces the Windows Script Host component with the ScriptScan proxy component. This can cause `Momhost.exe` to have memory leak.	891605 McAfee Patch 11
The agent's state does not change in the Operator Console even after all alerts have been resolved.	The issue is caused by computer and domain names left unselected in alert rule suppression fields.	891200
After creating rule overrides, alerts are still being received from agents for which the rule override criteria has been applied.	This problem can occur if rule overrides are not committed after they are created.	898466
The DNS discovery script fails and alerts are raised in the Operator Console.	This issue may be caused by a resource leak in the WMI DNS provider, which builds up over time and causes the DNS discovery scripts to fail.	906515
Numerous instances of event ID 9122 are logged in the application log, and the management server's last heartbeat time is blank.	This issue occurs if you use a NetBIOS domain name containing a period, or if the agent's computer name is in lowercase in the registry.	889187
You see the following alerts: `The script 'AD Replication monitoring' encountered a runtime error. Failed to determine whether the WMI replication provider is installed. The error returned was 'Invalid Parameter' (0x80041008)` `AD Remote Topology Discovery cannot determine whether the WMI Replication Provider is installed. The error returned was: 'Invalid Parameter' (0x80041008).`	There is a problem with the `replprov.dll` file, which is part of the WMI replication provider. This is installed by default on Windows 2003 systems and manually on Windows 2000.	889054

The agent status should be monitored closely. If the MOM agent is not working correctly, then alerts may be missed, since the agent may not be communicating or the management pack may not be functioning correctly.

When troubleshooting agents, you should consider the following valuable resource kit tools.

`MOMInfo.exe` allows you to do the following:

- Export the rules, responses, and `VarSet` values at the MOM agent into an XML file.

- Clear the queues on the agent.

- Place the agent into maintenance mode. This has to be run locally on the agent.

- Enable script debugging.

`RSOR.exe` allows you to create a text file showing the set of rules that would be deployed to an agent. This will not show any overrides that my be applied.

`MOMClusterTool.exe` helps diagnose why a Windows Server cluster virtual server cannot be detected by MOM.

`CleanupMOM.exe` will remove the MOM installation on the agent. This will not remove the details of the agent on the management server.

Database Management

A typical MOM 2005 implementation is made of two SQL databases: the Operations database and the Reporting database. The Operations database contains all the configuration details for the MOM installation, so it must be monitored closely, and any alerts must be resolved as soon as possible.

The Operations Database

This is also known as the OnePoint database. It has a maximum size of 30 GB, and 40-percent free space must be available to allow the indexing jobs to complete correctly. The database should never be configured to grow automatically because during the growth process, all operations on the database are suspended. When MOM 2005 is installed, a number of SQL jobs are created, as follows:

- MOMX Partitioning And Grooming
- OnePoint - Update Statistics
- OnePoint - Update Database
- OnePoint - TodayStatisticsUpdatePerfmonRulesKB
- OnePoint - TodayStatisticsUpdateEvents
- OnePoint - TodayStatisticsUpdateComputersAndAlerts
- OnePoint - Reindex

- OnePoint - Computer Maintenance
- OnePoint - Check Integrity

These keep the database operational; you should change them only if you are very familiar with SQL and understand the role that each job carries out. If you are changing the default times of the SQL jobs, make sure that they do not conflict with any other scheduled MOM tasks (e.g., computer discovery).

Configuring the Grooming Settings

You can configure default grooming settings via the MOM Administrator Console. The default settings are shown in Table 4-5.

Table 4-5. *The Default Database Grooming Settings*

Auto-Resolution Settings	Older Than
Automatically resolved critical error alerts	90 days
Automatically resolved error alerts	2 days
Automatically resolved inactive alerts	1 hour
Automatically resolved informational alerts	4 hours
Automatically resolved security issue alerts	90 days
Automatically resolved service unavailable alerts	90 days
Automatically resolved success alerts	4 hours
Automatically resolved warning alerts	1 day

If you run into a situation in which you need to quickly free up space, you should manually run the grooming job.

If you get alerts or become concerned about the size of the Operations database, then you should review these settings and change them as appropriate.

■**Note** The grooming job will only remove alerts that are resolved. The acknowledged alerts will not be automatically resolved and deleted from the database. The acknowledged alerts need to be manually set to `resolved` for the grooming jobs in order for them to be deleted from the database. The Microsoft Operations Manager 2005 Operations Guide, which is available from the Microsoft web site, has a detailed overview of the SQL jobs that are configured by default.

Reindexing

The OnePoint - Reindex job runs each Sunday at 3 a.m. This locks the tables. As the database gets larger, it takes longer to run the reindexing jobs, which can impact performance. It can also take longer for an event to be written to the database and for an alert to be generated. If the index job continues to fail, data read operations will take longer to complete. This is most noticeable in the Operator Console because refresh speeds get considerably slower. The most common cause of failure of this job is that there is less than 40-percent free space in the Operations database.

Tip Change the schedule for this job so that it runs daily, as it can help improve the response time of the Operator Console.

Backups

You should fully back up the OnePoint database every day. The backup job should not overlap with any of the following jobs:

- MOMX Partitioning And Grooming
- OnePoint - Reindex
- OnePoint - Update Database
- OnePoint - Check Integrity
- SystemCenterDTSPackageTask

These jobs read and write to the OnePoint database. If a backup is run at the same time, this can cause either the SQL job or the backup to fail.

Tip The restore process should be tested in a test environment and documented fully. This will ensure that you have tested that your backup process is working correctly, and that you have a backup of everything required to restore the MOM infrastructure. You should also ensure that you back up your management packs. If you ever need to roll back a change, it is easier to just import your management pack backup than to try to restore the database. There is a command-line tool that you can use, `ManagementModuleUtil.exe`, which allows you to back up the management packs (e.g., `ManagementModuleUtil.exe -O MomServer "Microsoft Windows DNS Server" "C:\Export\ Microsoft Windows DNS Server" -W`).

The Reporting Database

The reporting database holds the historical alert, event, and performance data from the OnePoint database. By default, the date is retained for 395 days (13 months). The data in this database is invaluable for capacity management and problem management because trends and potential future capacity issues can be quickly identified with the predefined reports that come with the different management packs.

Specifying the Data Retention Period

The Reporting database size can grow rapidly, so careful planning must be carried out on how much data you actually want to retain. Microsoft has released a MOM 2005 Sizer spreadsheet, available from www.microsoft.com/downloads/details.aspx?FamilyID=93930640-FA0F-48B3-8EB0-86836A1808DF&displaylang=en. Using the spreadsheet can help you estimate the capacity you will need. To find what your current data retention period is, run the following SQL command against the SystemCenterReporting database:

```
select cs.cs_tablename 'Table Name', wcs.wcs_groomdays 'Groom Days'
from warehouseclassschema wcs
join classschemas cs
on cs.cs_classID = wcs.wcs_classID
where cs.cs_tablename = 'SC_AlertFact_Table'or
cs.CS_TableName = 'SC_AlertHistoryFact_Table' OR
cs.CS_TableName = 'SC_AlertToEventFact_Table' OR
cs.CS_TableName = 'SC_EventFact_Table' OR
cs.CS_TableName = 'SC_EventParameterFact_Table' OR
cs.CS_TableName = 'SC_SampledNumericDataFact_Table'
AND wcs.WCS_MustBeGroomed = 1
```

This will return the retention period—for example:

```
SC_EventParameterFact_Table   395
SC_AlertFact_Table   395
SC_SampledNumericDataFact_Table   395
SC_AlertToEventFact_Table   395
SC_EventFact_Table   395
SC_AlertHistoryFact_Table   395
```

To change the retention period, run the following SQL command:

```
Declare @DataRetention int
Select @DataRetention = 180

exec p_updateGroomDays 'SC_SampledNumericDataFact_Table',
@DataRetention
exec p_updateGroomDays 'SC_AlertFact_Table', @DataRetention
exec p_updateGroomDays 'SC_EventParameterFact_Table', @DataRetention
exec p_updateGroomDays 'SC_AlertToEventFact_Table', @DataRetention
exec p_updateGroomDays 'SC_EventFact_Table', @DataRetention
exec p_updateGroomDays 'SC_AlertHistoryFact_Table', @DataRetention
```

■**Tip** When planning the capacity of the Reporting Server database, ensure that you factor in the capacity on the drive for the backup of the SQL database to disk.

Specifying the Data Transformation Services (DTS) Latency Parameter

If you install MOM Reporting Services after the management server has been running for a while, you may encounter an issue with reports that are empty or incomplete. You may also encounter some of the following symptoms:

- The OnePoint database size suddenly increases.
- The application log on the MOM Reporting Server displays the following events:

  Event ID 1001:

  Source: MOM.Datawarehousing.DTSPackageGenerator.exe

  Description: MOM Reporting DTS Job failed to complete successfully

  Event ID 81:

  Event Source: DataTransformationServices

  Description: The execution of the following DTS Package failed

The normal reasons for the DTS job to fail are that the DTS package is trying to copy a large amount of data to the Reporting Server database, or the Reporting Server database has insufficient free space to complete the copy task. You will need to increase the size of the SystemCenterReporting database and the SystemCenterReporting log. We recommend that you use the latency parameter, which lets you specify the age of the data to transfer to the SystemCenterReporting database. To configure the latency parameter, open a command prompt and go to the MOM reporting server's reporting folder, which is by default `C:\Program Files\Microsoft System Center Reporting\Reporting`. Enter the following command:

`MOM.Datawarehouse.DTSPackageGenerator.exe /latency:6.`

This will only copy data that is more than 6 days old. You can alter the latency period to meet your own requirements.

Tip If the DTS job fails for more than 4 days, you should use the latency parameter.

Changing the Time of the DTS Job

One common issue that you will encounter with the Exchange MP is that DTS is scheduled to run every day at 1:00 a.m. However, the Exchange 2003 - Collect Database Size per Server script is scheduled to run every day at 1:55 a.m. Also, the Exchange 2003 - Collect Server Information script is scheduled to run every day at 2:30 a.m. Because DTS runs before the scripts, the data that the scripts collect is not transferred to the Data Warehouse database until DTS runs the next day at 1:00 a.m. In this case, the data that the MOM scripts collect is not added to the Data Warehouse database until 1 day after the scripts run. The DTS job should be changed to run at a different time; however, you need to check your jobs on the Operations and Reporting databases to ensure that there will not be a conflicting schedule.

Summary

This chapter has given you an overview of how to manage your MOM infrastructure. If your MOM infrastructure is not healthy, then you may miss alerts or find that some reports do not have data.

In Chapter 5, we will show you how to create custom rules to monitor events in your environment.

CHAPTER 5

■ ■ ■

Rule Creation

MOM is a rule-based application. In this chapter, we will show you how to configure MOM to react if the conditions in a rule are met or not met, or even if the conditions in the rule don't occur within a certain amount of time. Rules are also used to collect data for reporting and for the measuring of performance data and the monitoring of thresholds. Rules launch scripts, send e-mails, execute responses, and basically carry out every task in MOM. Therefore rule creation deserves particular attention. In this chapter, we will show you how to create rules.

Types of Rules

There are three main types of rules that make up the rule base in MOM 2005. Contained within these rule types are a number of different rules that carry out the various tasks in MOM. The rule types are listed following, and will be covered in more detail in this chapter:

Event rules: These rules consolidate, filter, and react to events in the MOM database. They can also launch scripts and collect event parameters.

Performance rules: These rules are used to collect performance data and can also be configured to alert when performance thresholds are exceeded.

Alert rules: These rules react to alerts in the MOM database and are used to launch responses, such as sending e-mail alerts to notification groups.

Custom Rule Creation

The main reason for creating custom rules is to monitor an application or a specific event that is not monitored by any of the available MOM 2005 management packs. You may also wish to create custom rules and scripts to allow MOM to perform specific tasks that it would not usually perform, such as clearing log files or counting files in a directory. Custom rules may also be created to collect performance counter data that is not collected by MOM by default.

You can also copy the default management pack rules and customize them to suit your infrastructure, allowing the rules and scripts to be updated without modifying the original copy of the default management pack. This method is recommended, since you may lose all customizations in the event that the management pack is reimported.

In this chapter, we will show you how to create different types of rules and the best method for grouping a number of rules into a custom management pack. We will also briefly mention custom script creation, but scripts will be covered in more detail in Chapter 13. We will also cover creation of custom computer groups, providers, and computer attributes to augment your custom management pack.

First, we will cover how you can create some custom event rules. As mentioned earlier, event rules can be used for a variety of different functions, and we will cover these functions in the following section.

Event Rules

These rules are the bread and butter of MOM. They are responsible for processing all events that enter the MOM data stream and generate the majority of alerts that are shown in the Operator Console. Basic event rules are also used to initiate scripts and launch custom responses (e.g., command-line code, batch files, and scripts)—these responses are launched every time the rule they exist in is initiated.

You can configure event rules to monitor for events in a Windows event log, an application log file, a MOM event generated by a script and placed in the MOM data stream, and an internally generated event (one generated by the MOM Management Server components). You can also configure an event rule as a *timed event*, which runs a script or triggers a response at a certain time or according to a schedule.

Next, we will look at the different types of event rules, the process for creating them, and the options that can be configured.

Event Rule Options

When you create an event rule, there are many options to choose from that allow you to tailor the rule specifically to your needs. We will spend some time now looking at the different sets of options for the following tabs in the Event Rule Properties dialog:

- General
- Data Provider

- Criteria
- Schedule
- Alert
- Alert Suppression
- Responses
- Knowledge Base

You will see these tabs after you select Alert on or Respond to Event (Event) as the rule type to use when an event occurs (see Figure 5-1).

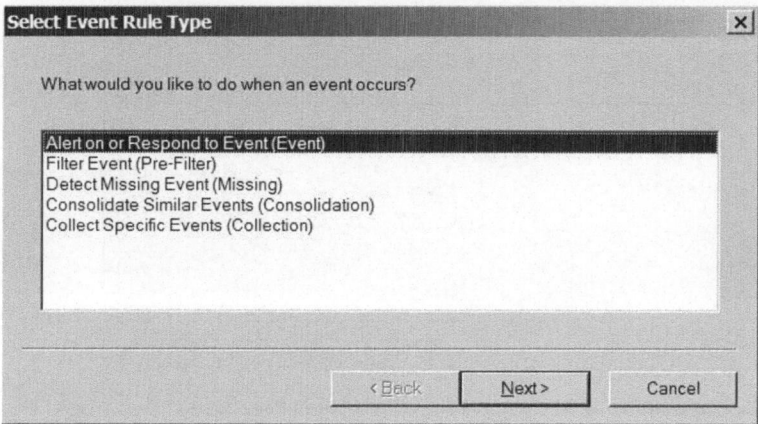

Figure 5-1. *Event rule types*

While we will examine the tabs individually, it is important to note that when you create a new event rule, the option screens may not appear in the same order as we examine them here. For this reason, familiarize yourself with each tab and the associated options.

The General Tab

Figure 5-2 shows the General tab. This tab contains the basic information for the rule, such as the rule name, description, location in the rule base, and rule GUID (unique ID). There is also an option to disable the rule, a check box to enable the rule-disable override function, and a Set Criteria button, which takes you to the Set Override Criteria dialog box (see the "Rule Overrides" section later in this chapter). This function allows you to disable the rule for a single agent or a number of agents without disabling it for all monitored machines. You will notice that some of the options on this tab are grayed out and therefore cannot be changed.

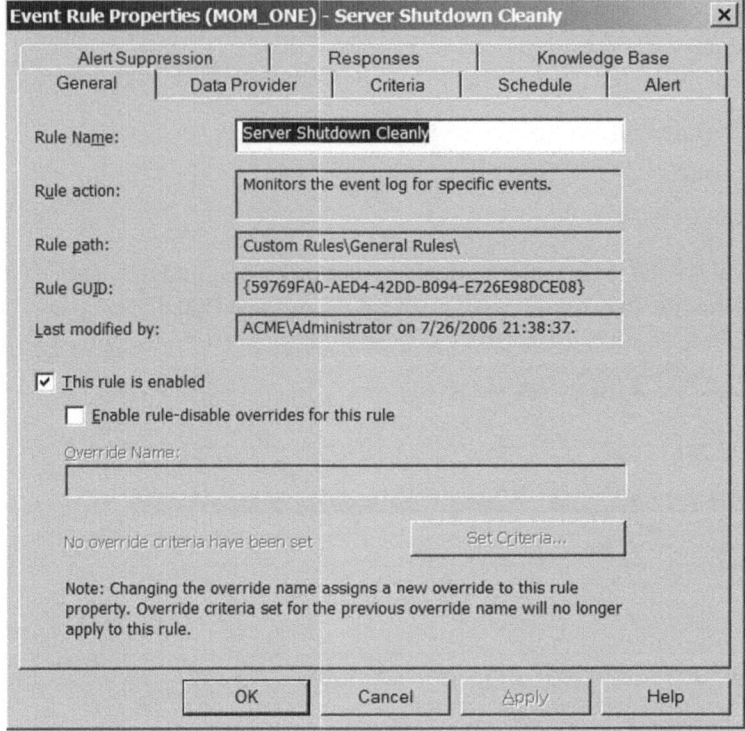

Figure 5-2. *The General tab of the Event Rules Properties dialog*

The Data Provider Tab

The Data Provider tab is shown in Figure 5-3. You use this tab to specify the source of data, such as an event log. You can also select timed events from the list (providers are methods for obtaining data such as event logs, log files, and timed events) to allow you to use the rule to start a script or initiate a response to an event according to a schedule.

Note If you select a timed event as the data provider, the available tabs will be limited, since tabs such as Criteria will not be required.

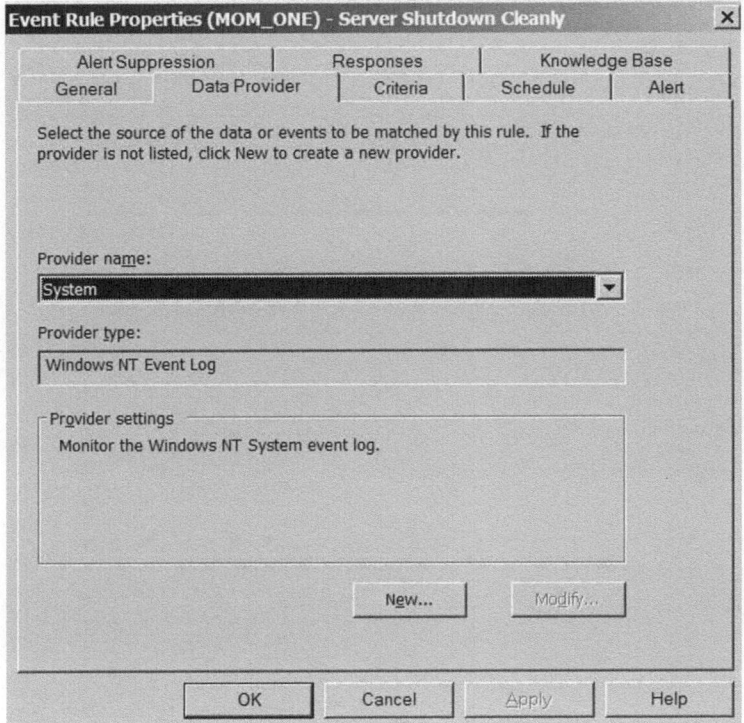

Figure 5-3. *The Data Provider tab of the Event Rule Properties dialog*

The Criteria Tab

Figure 5-4 shows the Criteria tab. You use this tab to select the options you need to trigger an alert in MOM (e.g., based on the data from an event found in an event log).

From the initial screen, you can specify a number of different options that you can use to match the properties of events against source, event ID, event type, and description. However, in certain circumstances, these options may not be specific enough to enable the rule to function correctly. If this is the case, you can click the Advanced button to add details to make further comparisons to help to make the match more specific.

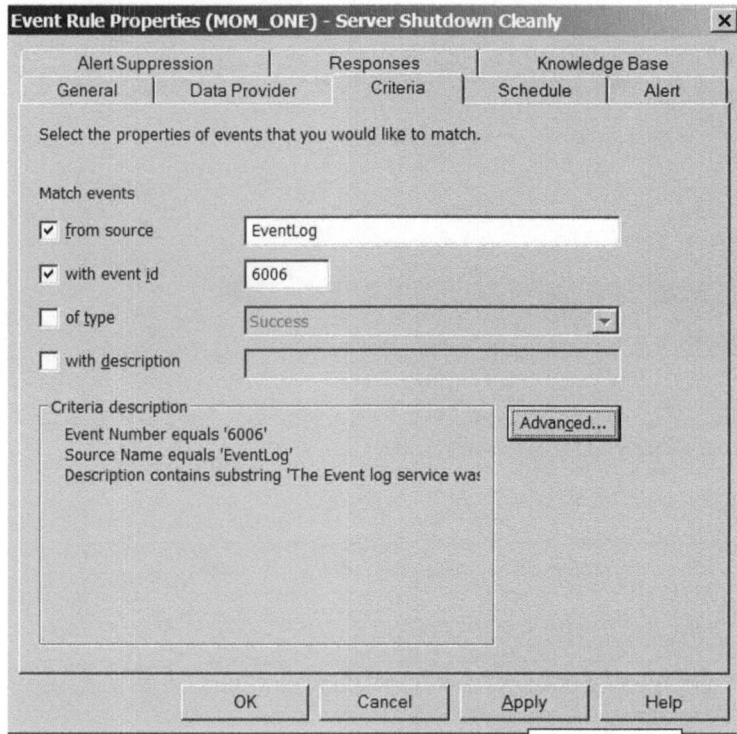

Figure 5-4. *The Criteria tab of the Event Rule Properties dialog*

After clicking the Advanced button, you will be presented with the screen shown in Figure 5-5.

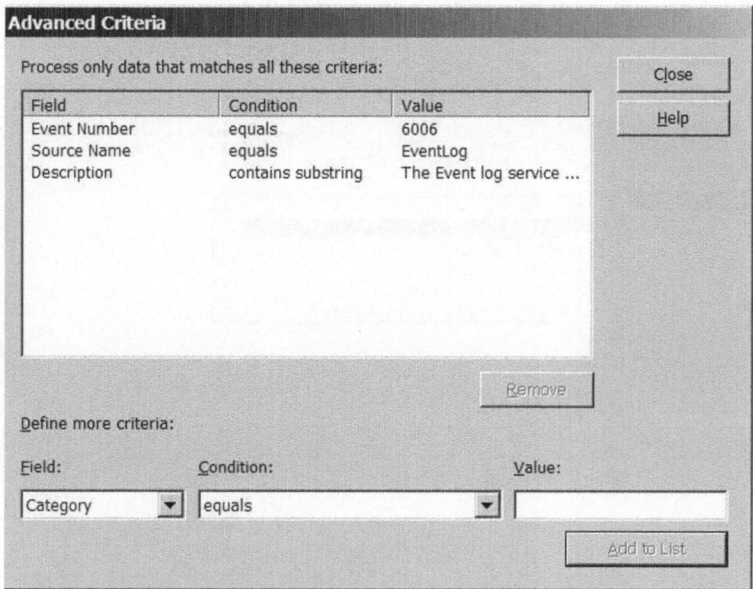

Figure 5-5. *The Advanced Criteria dialog for the Criteria tab*

From this screen, you can specify query values to match an event against. To get a list of field criteria, click the down arrow in the Field text box. From the drop-down list, select a field. To get a list of matching conditions, click the down arrow in the Criteria text box. From the drop-down list, select a condition. The values that you can select are shown in Figure 5-6.

You can combine the field, condition, and value criteria to create a custom template that you can use to match events against. A common field-condition combination to use would be the Description field and the "contains substring" condition. You would then enter a value that you expect to see in the event description. The "matches wildcard" condition is also very useful, since you can use standard wildcard values such as * and # to make your query more specific. You can also use multiple criteria in one query. For example, you might use the Event Number field, the "matches wildcard" condition, and the value 600#; or you might use the Description field, the "contains substring" condition, and the value Event Log. The first query, for example, would match any events with event number 600x and a description that contains the text "Event Log." For each field, condition, and value that you see in the list, click the Add to List button. Here you can see how powerful MOM rules can be when you use the options in the Advanced Criteria dialog.

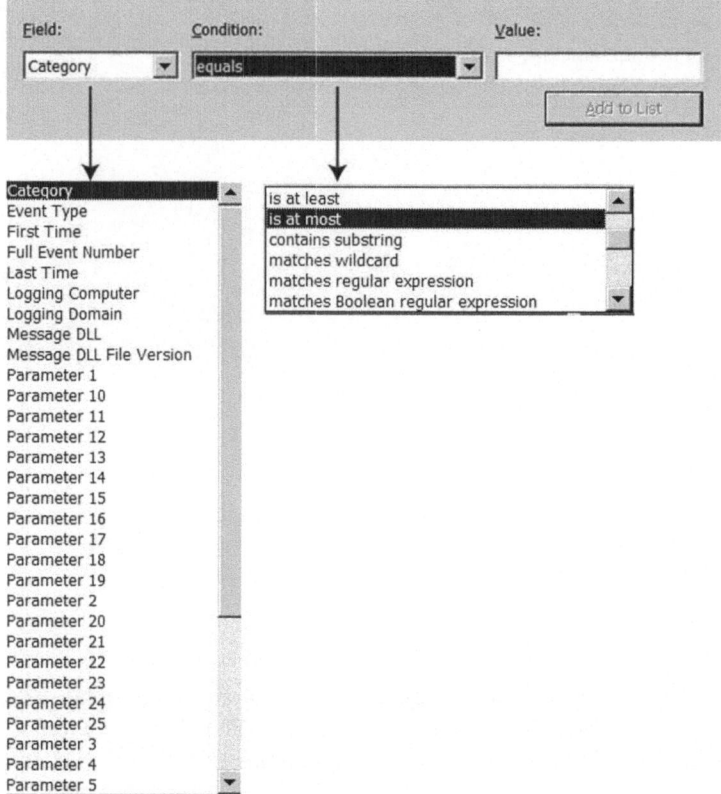

Figure 5-6. *Selection lists in the Advanced Criteria dialog*

The Schedule Tab

The Schedule tab, shown in Figure 5-7, allows you to choose one of the following schedules for the event rule: "Only process data during the specified time," "Process data except during the specified time," and "Always process data." The most common setting is "Always process data," but you can use the other values if you expect a particular event to occur only during a specified time.

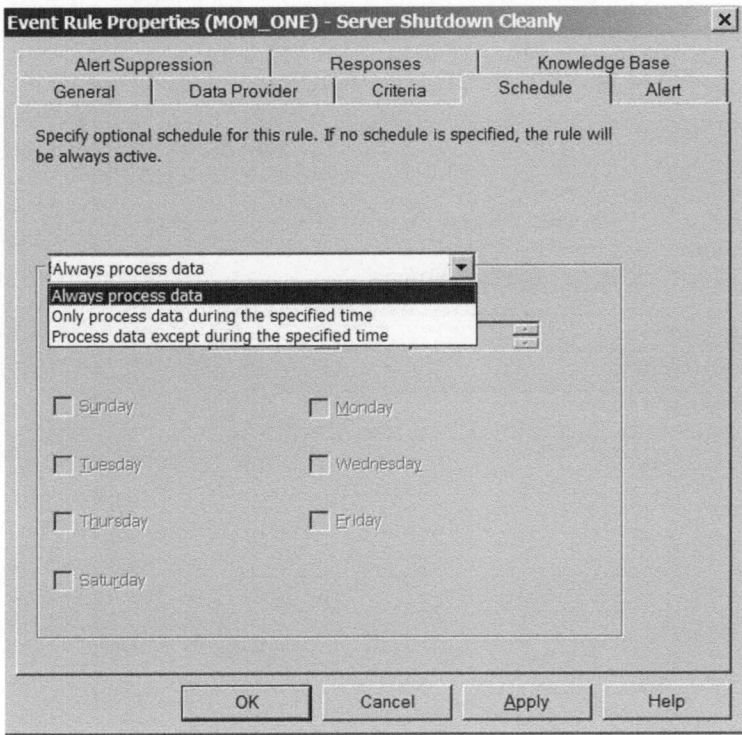

Figure 5-7. *The Schedule tab of the Event Rule Properties dialog*

The Alert Tab

The Alert tab, shown in Figure 5-8, allows you to specify whether an alert (displayed in the Operator Console) is generated when the criteria for the event rule are met. From this tab, it is possible to customize the way an alert message and related information are displayed. You can also modify the state alert properties. The state alert properties feature allows you to create a formula which will update the State view in the MOM Operator Console. By selecting the 'Enable state alert properties' radio button, the grayed out options in Figure 5-8 become available. Here you can select the individual Server Roles and Components that will be affected by the formula you specify in the State view formula dialog. This dialog is accessible by clicking the Edit button from the Alert tab of the Event Rule Properties dialog. This is covered in more detail in the "Advanced Rule Configuration" section later in the chapter.

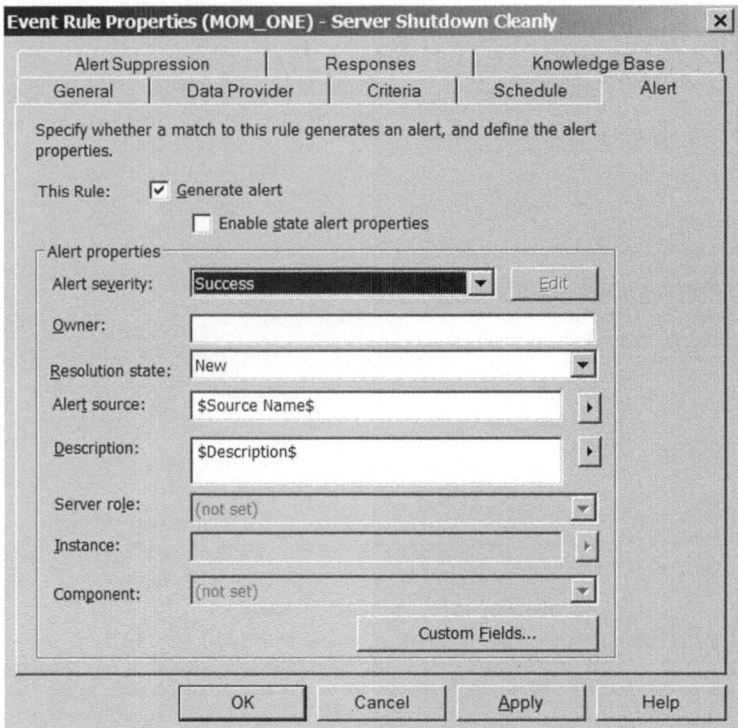

Figure 5-8. *The Alert tab of the Event Rule Properties dialog*

Figure 5-9 shows the drop-down lists containing the Alert severity and Resolution state options.

Figure 5-10 shows the options that are available when you click the arrow next to the Alert Source or Description text box. From the drop-down list, select Source Name, and then prepend and append a dollar sign ($) to the selected field (if it isn't created automatically). Click the arrow to the right of the Description text box. From the drop-down list, select Description, and then prepend and append a dollar sign to the selected field.

Clicking the Custom Fields button opens a dialog that allows you to modify the alert's custom fields. These custom fields are user-defined fields that can be used if you need to store data required for custom views in the Operator Console, or specific data required by any third-party applications that may be utilizing the MOM connector framework to connect to MOM.

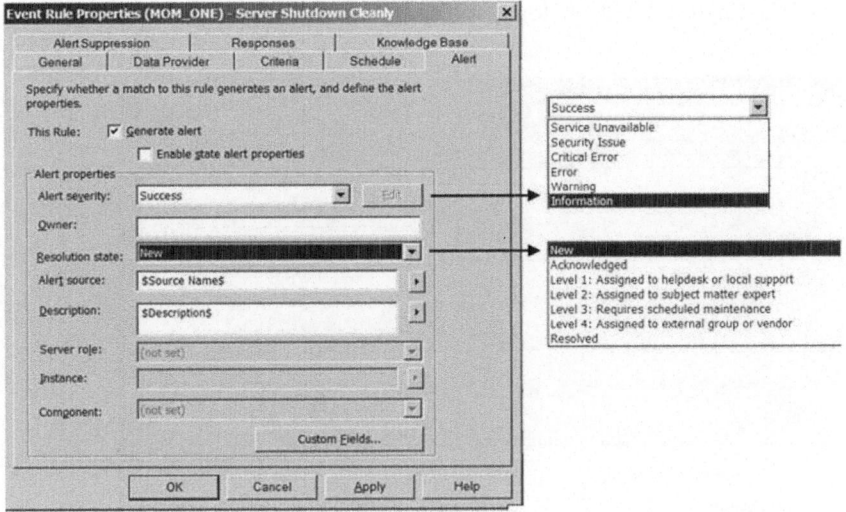

Figure 5-9. *The Alert severity and Resolution state options on the Alert tab*

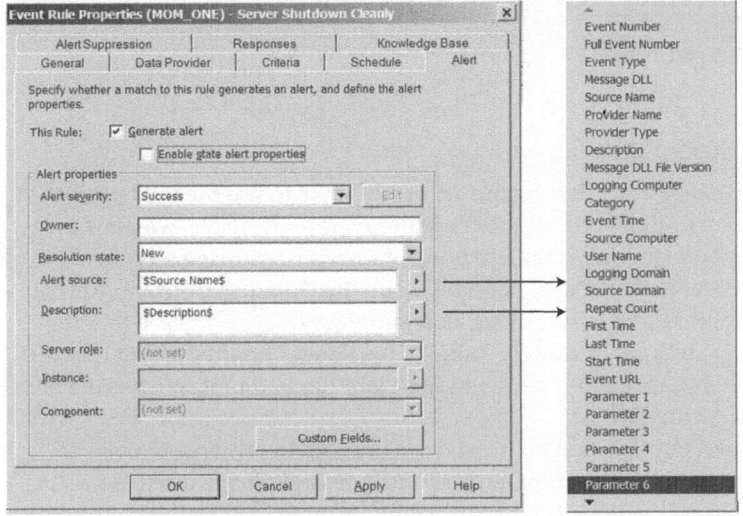

Figure 5-10. *The Alert tab, showing the Alert source and Description options*

The Custom Fields dialog is shown in Figure 5-11.

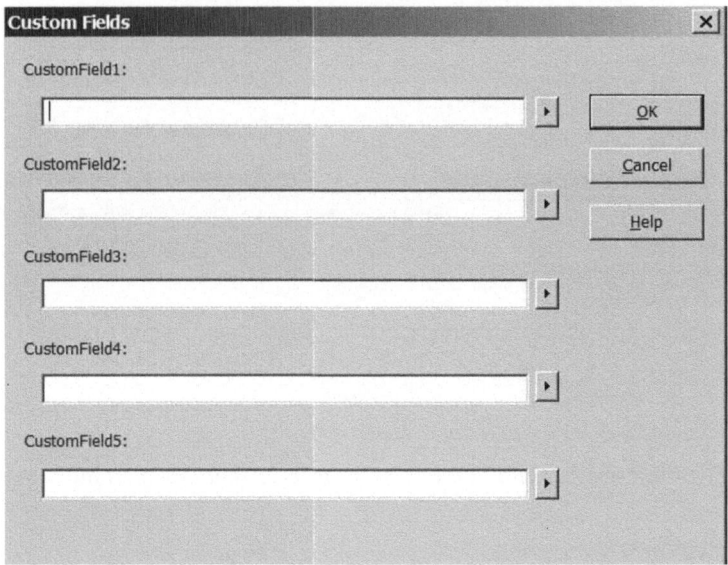

Figure 5-11. *The Custom Fields dialog*

The Alert Suppression Tab

Figure 5-12 shows the Alert Suppression tab. You can use the tab options to prevent recurring alerts from flooding the Operator Console, which sometimes happened in MOM 2000. To prevent seeing a recurring alert being generated over and over again and filling up the Operator Console, you can use alert suppression. When using alert suppression, you will see that the alert appears only once, and the value of the Repeat Count field on the alert is increased by one every time a new alert is generated that satisfies the alert suppression criteria.

The Alert Suppression tab contains a number of options that can be included to further customize a rule. To suppress duplicate alerts, select Computer and Domain. (This is the default setting.)

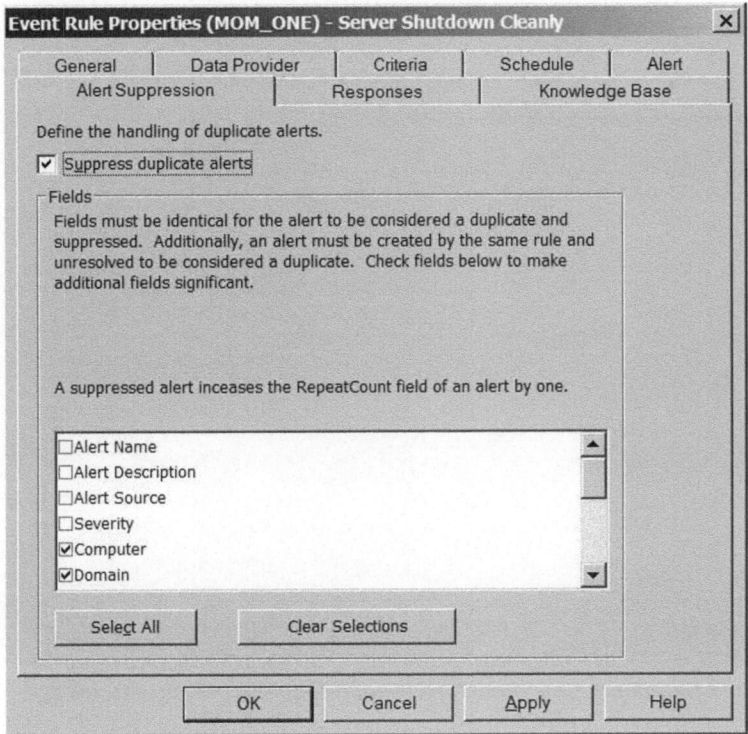

Figure 5-12. *The Alert Suppression tab of the Event Rules Properties dialog*

The Responses Tab

The Responses tab is shown in Figure 5-13. This tab is used to configure any responses that the event rule will execute when an event that matches the rule is detected. These responses can carry out a variety of different functions, but the most commonly used responses are "Launch a script," "Send a notification to a Notification Group," and "Execute a command or batch file." These responses will be covered in the "Advanced Rule Configuration" section later in this chapter.

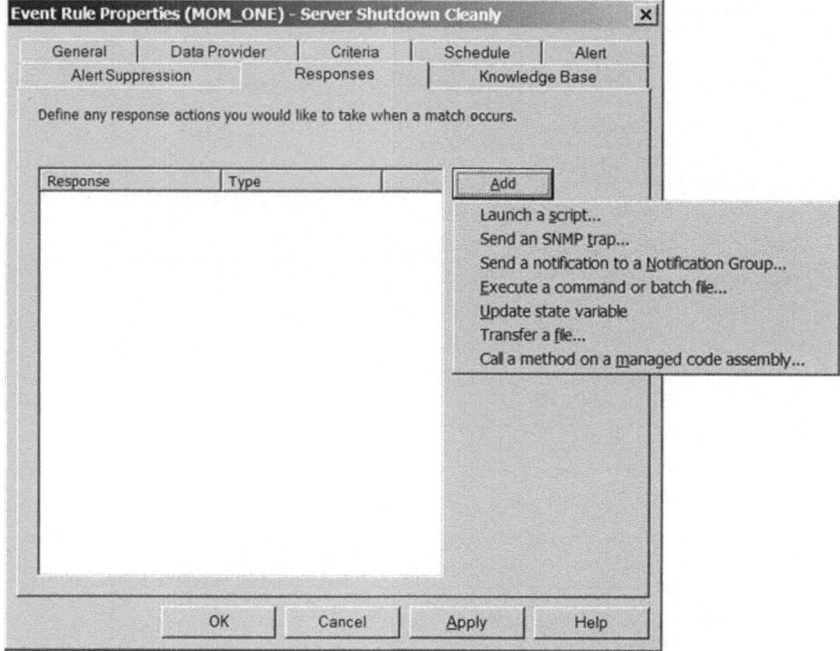

Figure 5-13. *The Responses tab, showing a list of response types you can select*

The Knowledge Base Tab

You can use the Knowledge Base tab (Figure 5-14) to provide a complete
knowledge base of issues, troubleshooting steps, and resolutions for the
alerts that are generated. The vendor-created rules (those that are part of
a vendor-downloaded management pack) will already come complete
with a comprehensive knowledge base. This knowledge base will help you
to understand what the alert means and troubleshoot the issue that triggered the alert.

From time to time, however, a knowledge base article may not match
your particular issue, or the resolution offered in the knowledge base article
may not function as expected. In these cases, you typically employ your own
troubleshooting methods until a resolution is found. This is where the Company Knowledge Base section comes in. This section allows you to add
custom knowledge base information into an alert, so that if the same issue
occurs again, the troubleshooting steps that you took to resolve the issue can
be made available to anyone who has access to MOM. You can update the
company knowledge base section from the Administrator Console in the rule
properties; you can also update in the Operator Console by clicking the Edit
button at the bottom of the Knowledge Base tab.

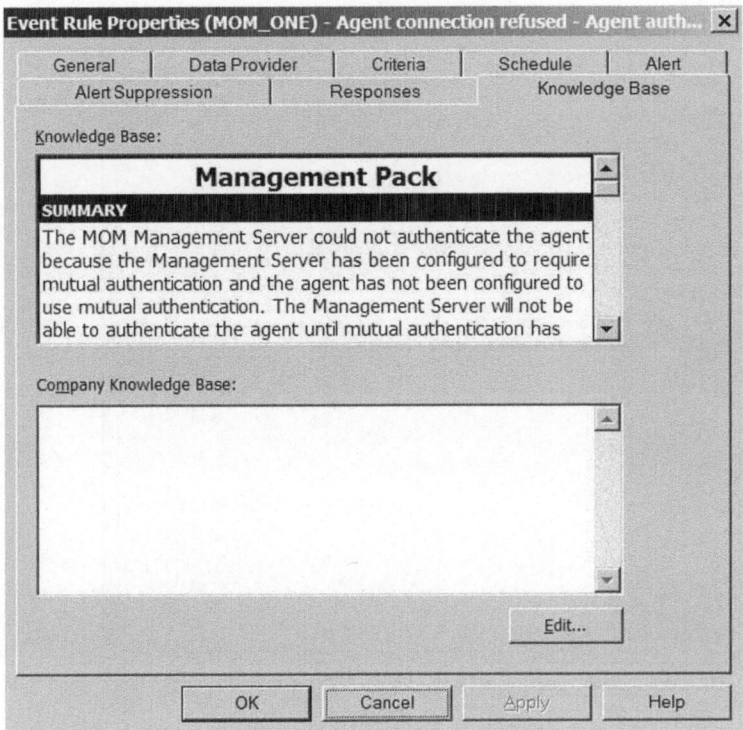

Figure 5-14. *The Knowledge Base tab, showing vendor-created knowledge*

This Company Knowledge Base section is also useful when you create custom rules to populate your newly created rules with knowledge base entries.

In the "Event Rule Options" section earlier in the chapter, we showed you how to use the tab options after creating an Alert on or Respond to an Event (Event) rule. We will now show you how to use the options of other tabs that are displayed when you create other types of event rules.

The Filter Tab

You will see the Filter tab (shown in Figure 5-15) after creating the Filter Event (Pre-Filter) rule.

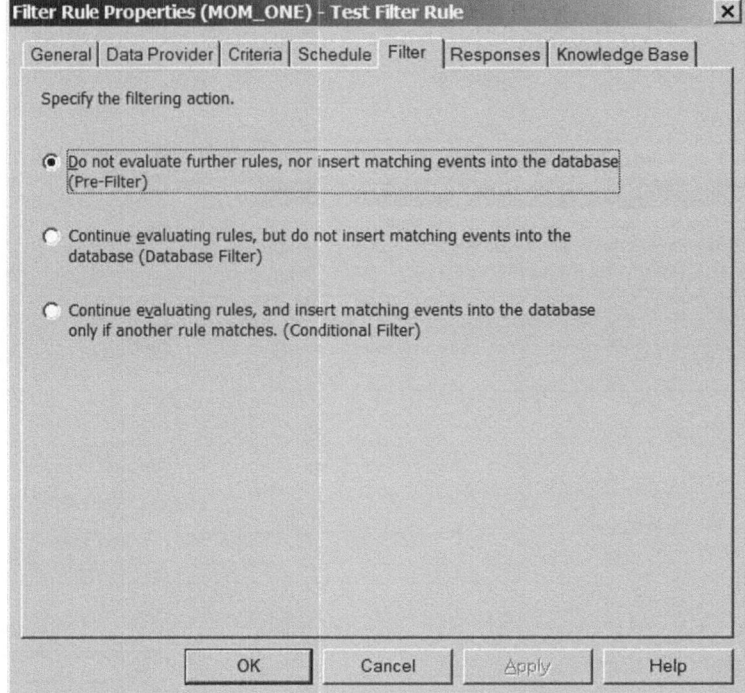

Figure 5-15. *The Filter tab of the Filter Rule Properties dialog*

On this tab, you can choose one of the three event filter types, as follows:

Pre-filter: The pre-filter is the highest level of filter. If an event match occurs with the criteria specified in a Pre-Filter rule, the event will be completely removed from the workflow, and thus will not be transferred to the management server and will not be stored in the database.

Database filter: The database filter allows the event to stay in the MOM workflow, but none of the matching events or their parameters or data will be stored in the MOM database.

Conditional filter: This filter is similar in nature to the database filter, with the exception that if an event is already marked for collection, it will be written to the database. If the event is not marked for collection, it will not be collected and written to the database.

The Consolidate Tab

You can use the Consolidate tab (Figure 5-16) after selecting the Consolidate Similar Events (Consolidation) rule type. You use consolidation rules to gather and consolidate events that are very similar or the same. Consolidation rules are particularly useful when you are expecting a large number of similar events to be generated and only want to raise a single alert (e.g., on security events). In Figure 5-16, the Event Number and Source Names fields are selected from the list of event fields that must match with the events to be consolidated. All selected events must occur within 1 second.

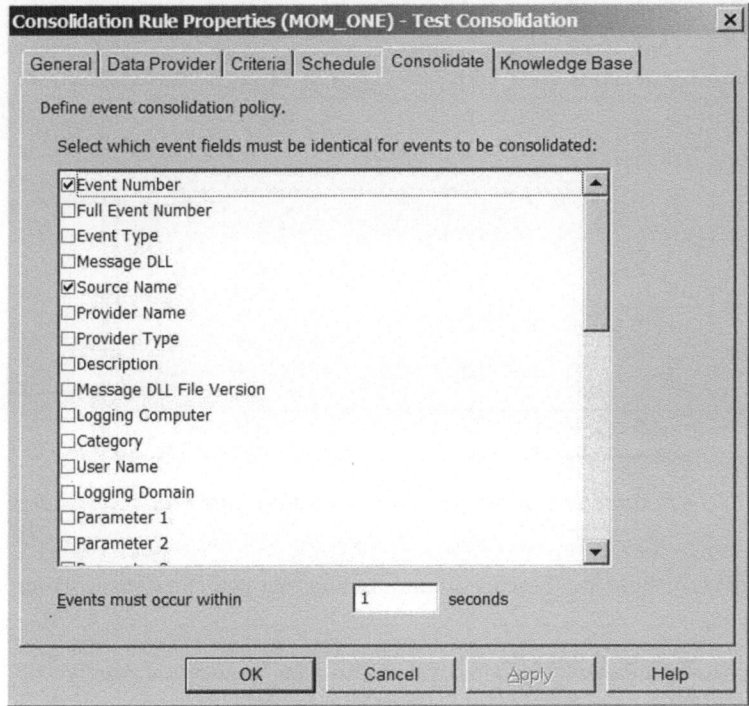

Figure 5-16. *The Consolidate tab of the Consolidation Rule Properties dialog*

The Parameter Storage Tab

You can use the Parameter Storage tab (shown in Figure 5-17) to display the options for the properties for Collect Specific Events (Collection) rules. You use these rules to collect data from an event and store it in the database for use by other rules and in report generation.

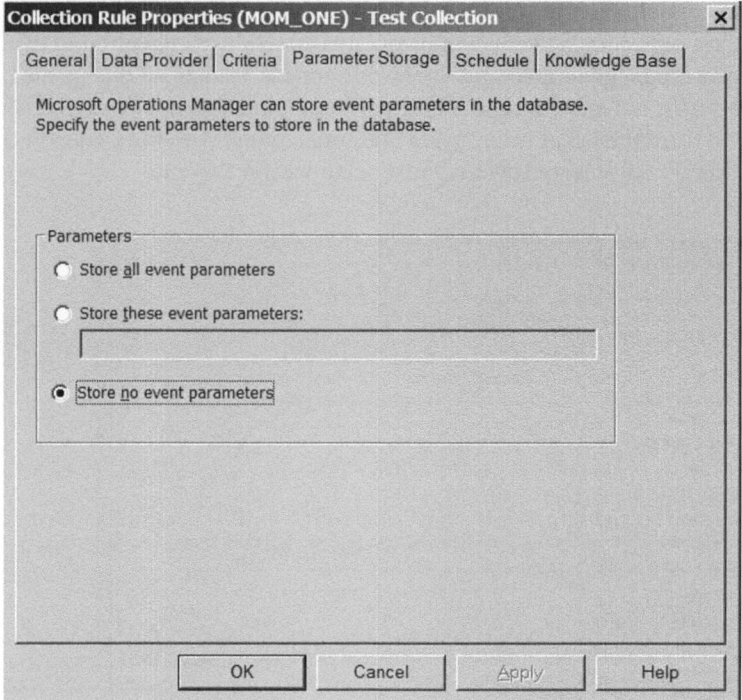

Figure 5-17. *The Parameter Storage tab of the Collection Rule Properties dialog*

On this tab, there are three event parameters that you can choose from, as follows:

Store all event parameters: This option is self-explanatory; it simply collects all the parameters from a matching event. This is particularly useful if the event you are collecting data from only has a small number of parameters. If the event, however, has a large number of parameters, the next option would be better suited to conserve space in the OnePoint and SystemCenterReporting databases.

Store these event parameters: This option is used to control the specific event parameters that are collected from matching events. It is useful if you are collecting data from an event with a large number of parameters and your requirement is only for a small number of these. The parameter numbers for the collection should be added in the option box, with a comma separating them (i.e., to collect parameters 5 and 14, you would type **5,14**).

Store no event parameters: This option allows the event to be collected and stored in the database with none of the parameters. This is useful if there is a requirement to collect the event but there is no requirement to store any of the event parameters. Figure 5-17 shows this option being selected.

Common Custom Event Rules

This section looks at some of the custom event rules that we always create when deploying MOM. We use the three rules described in the following sections to monitor for server shutdowns and reboots. We use a rule to trigger a success alert when the MOM Reporting DTS package completes successfully.

We will now show you how to create the three rules to help in gathering information regarding server shutdowns and restarts. The three event rules will detect if a server has been 1) shut down cleanly, 2) shut down unexpectedly, and 3) started correctly. From these three rules, you should be able to keep track of scheduled and unscheduled reboots of your monitored servers. We will not go through rule creation step by step; instead, we will show you how you should specify the settings for the rule.

The Clean Shutdown Rule

This rule is used to identify when a server has been cleanly shut down or shut down properly. This might have been initiated by an administrator logged into a Terminal Services session or logged directly to the console, or even by an administrator executing tsshutdn from the command line.

This rule looks for an event that will appear in the system log on a server every time a server is shut down. This event is well documented, and you will find information at http://support.microsoft.com and www.eventid.net. Figure 5-18 shows an example of the use of the Clean Shutdown rule to match an event.

The event shown in Figure 5-18 originates from a source of EventLog, and has an event ID of 6006. We will use these values together with part of the event description to match against our rule.

This rule is an Alert on or Respond to Event (Event) rule (see Figure 5-1) with a data provider of System (since that is the event log file in which we expect the event to appear). On the Criteria tab, we need to specify Source as EventLog and Event ID as 6006. We also need to use the Advanced option, since we are only using a portion of the event description.

From the Advanced Criteria dialog, select the Description field and the "contains substring" condition, and then enter the value **The Event log service was stopped**. You will need to click the Add to List button once you have made your selections and entered the value.

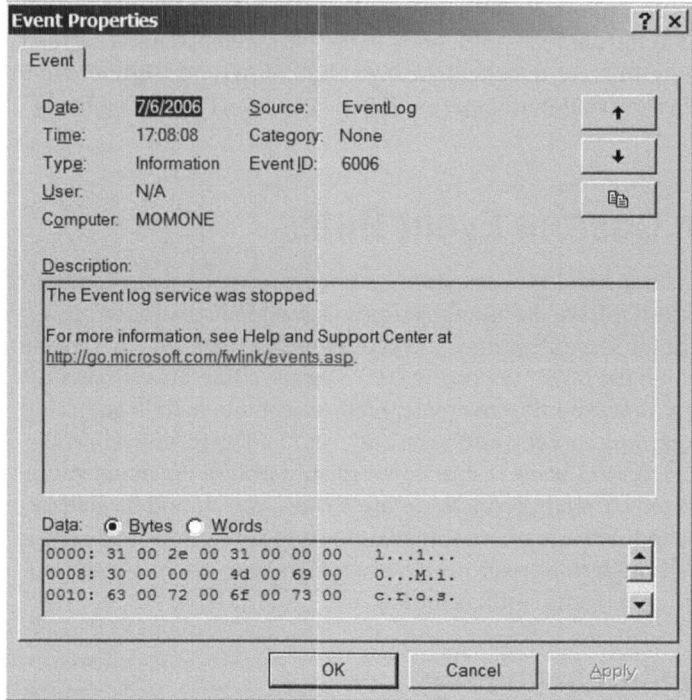

Figure 5-18. *The Event tab of the Event Properties dialog, showing that the event log service was stopped (server shutdown)*

Leave all other options as the defaults. You can add a knowledge base entry if you like—we will show you how to structure knowledge base entries later in the chapter.

The Unexpected Shutdown Rule

You use the Unexpected Shutdown rule to detect when a server crashes.

This rule looks for an event that will appear in the system log on a server once the server has restarted after a crash or blue screen dump. This event is well documented, and you will find more information at http://support. microsoft.com and www.eventid.net. Figure 5-19 shows the Windows event that indicates that a server was unexpectedly shut down. This is the event that we will match the MOM rule to.

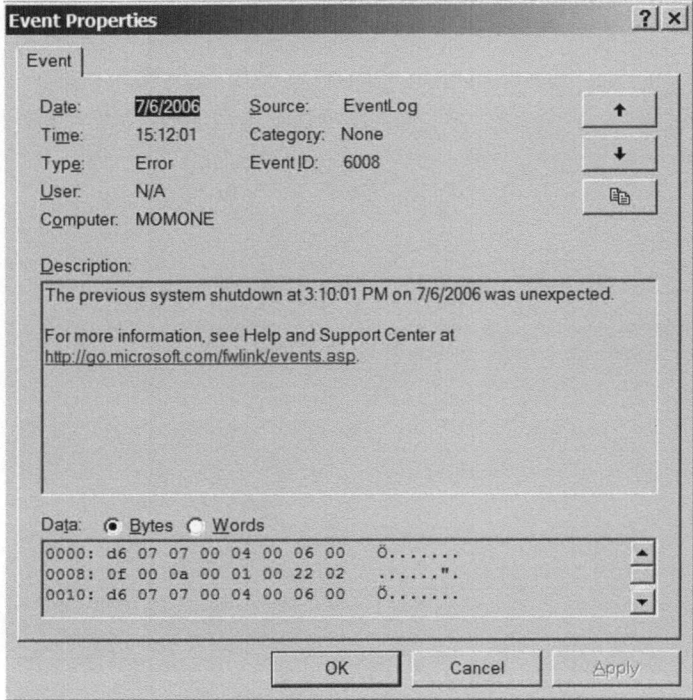

Figure 5-19. *The Event tab of the Event Properties dialog, showing that the previous system was shut down unexpectedly*

The event monitored by this rule originates from a source of EventLog, with an event ID of 6008. You can configure the rule in the same way as the Clean Shutdown rule: using the details of the preceding event in the Criteria tab. Again, use the Advanced button on the Criteria tab (see Figure 5-4) to specify the description, but this time select the "matches wildcard" condition and enter the value **The previous system shutdown * was unexpected**. Again you can create a custom knowledge base entry if needed.

The Server Started Correctly Rule

The Server Started Correctly rule detects the event that is generated when a server boots to the operating system correctly. This helps to determine when a server that has been shut down or crashed has started back up.

It matches an event that appears in the system log once the server has started up. This event is well documented, and you will find more information at http://support.microsoft.com and www.eventid.net. Figure 5-20 shows the results after the values are matched up against the rule to start the event log service.

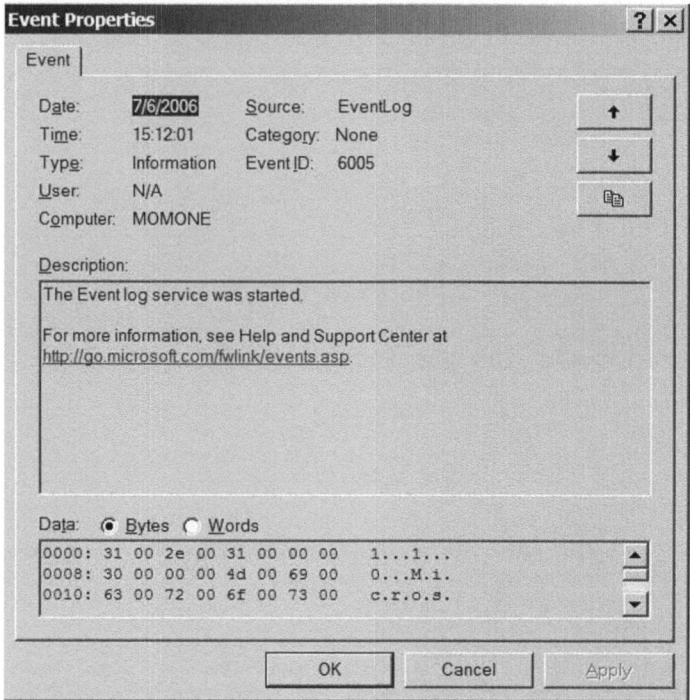

Figure 5-20. *The Event tab of the Event Properties dialog, showing that the event log service was started (server booted)*

The event monitored by this rule originates from a source of EventLog with an event ID of 6005. You can configure this rule in the same way as the Clean Shutdown rule, using the details in the preceding event in the Criteria tab. Clicking the Advanced button on the Criteria tab will take you to the Advanced Criteria dialog, where you select a description field from the list, use the "contains substring" condition, and then enter the value **The event log service was started**. Create a custom Knowledge Base entry as required.

Finally, we will show you how to use a rule that can detect events indicating that the MOM DTS package has completed successfully. You can configure the rule to generate an alert if an event that matches the rule is detected.

The MOM DTS Package Completed Successfully Rule

You use this rule to generate a success alert when an event is detected in the application log indicating that the MOM DTS package has completed successfully. This alerts you to a successful completion of the DTS package (in addition to the indication of a failure given by the default rule).

This event is generated by the MOM DTS Package executable. We will talk more about the MOM DTS package in Chapter 9.

Figure 5-21 shows an example of an event that we are looking to match.

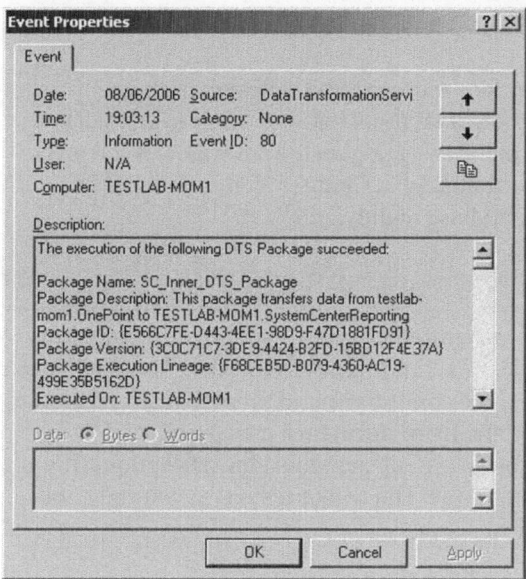

Figure 5-21. *Event indicating the successful completion of the DTS package*

The event originates from a source of DataTransformationServices with an event ID of 80. We will use these values together with part of the event description to match against the rule we have created.

This rule is an Alert on or Respond to Event (Event) rule (see Figure 5-1), with a data provider of Application. On the Criteria tab, we need to specify the source as DataTransformationServices and the event ID as 80. We need to click the Advanced button on the Criteria tab (see Figure 5-4) to get to the Advanced Criteria dialog to see the portion of the event description. You can see the rest of the description by moving the separator between the Condition and Value separators in the header with your mouse.

From the Advanced Criteria dialog, select the Description field and the "matches wildcard" condition, and enter the value *** DTS Package succeeded * SC_Inner_DTS_Package ***. Leave all other options as their defaults, and add a knowledge base entry if required.

Performance Rules

We will now look at the second type of MOM rule, the performance rule. You can use performance rules to collect performance data (Measuring rule) and also to monitor for performance thresholds being exceeded (Threshold rule).

Measuring Rules

Measuring rules allow performance metrics to be collected from agent machines and stored in the MOM database. This allows you to view all performance data in a single place and to aggregate the data. Also, if you are using the Reporting database (discussed in Chapter 7), this data will be archived off to the Reporting database nightly.

Threshold Rules

Threshold rules allow performance thresholds to be set. You can configure the rules to generate an alert if a threshold value is exceeded. This facilitates the monitoring of key performance counters on the agents, which will generate an alert if an agent is experiencing performance problems.

When first creating a performance rule, we consider two options: the measuring rule and the threshold rule. The two options that you can choose from are shown in Figure 5-22.

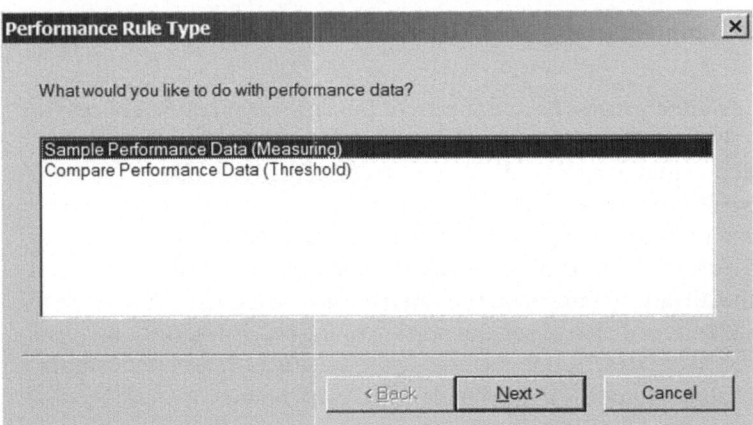

Figure 5-22. *The Performance Rule Type dialog*

As with the event rules, we'll look at all the tabs in turn, but we'll focus only on the tabs not yet discussed. The General, Schedule, Alert, Alert Suppression, Reponses and Knowledge Base tabs are not specifically covered in this section, as they are addressed in the earlier "Event Rule Options" section.

The Data Provider Tab

The Data Provider tab (shown in Figure 5-23) contains the same options as the Data Provider tab of the Event Rule Properties dialog. The difference to note is with the actual provider itself. Whereas with the event rules, the providers were log files and timed events, with performance rules, they are operating systems and their associated application performance counters, which have been previously added into the providers container in the Administrator Console.

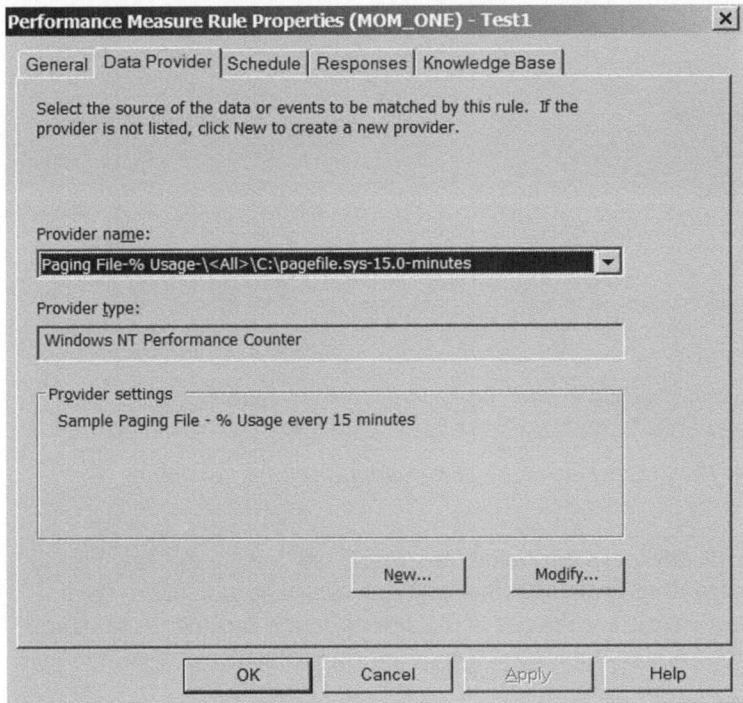

Figure 5-23. *The Data Provider tab of the Performance Measure Rule Properties dialog*

The Criteria Tab

You use the Criteria tab (shown in Figure 5-24) to specify a particular performance counter, instance, or agent to collect the data from. This tab is not often used since most performance rules are configured to apply to all agents.

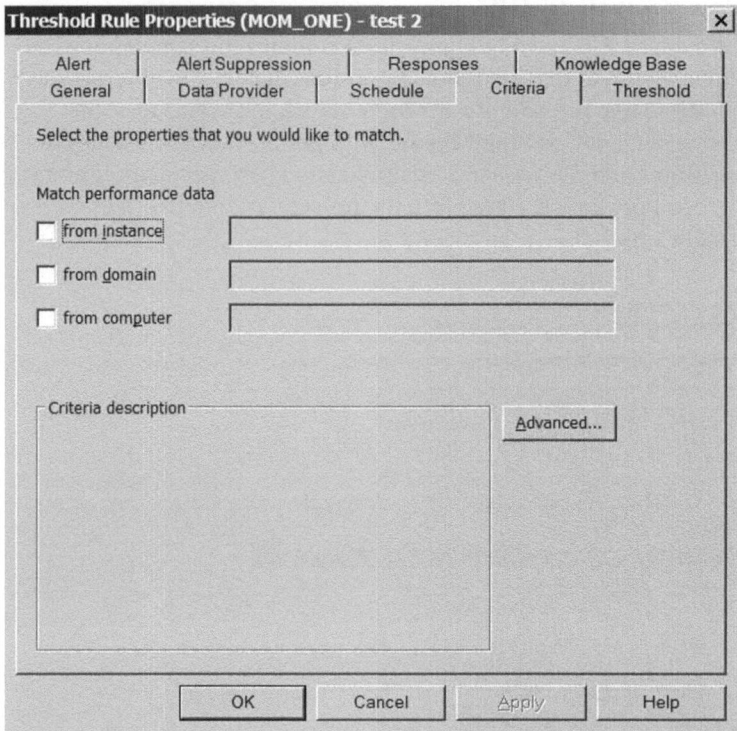

Figure 5-24. *The Criteria tab of the Threshold Rule Properties dialog*

Click the Advanced button on the Criteria tab (see Figure 5-4) to get to the Advanced Criteria dialog, which will show you a portion of the event description. You can see the rest of the description by moving the separator between the Condition and Value separators in the header with your mouse.

The Threshold Tab

Figure 5-25 shows the options on the Threshold tab that you can use to create threshold rules. You can specify options such as threshold values and the number of samples to average against. You can also specify overrides for the threshold values (rule and threshold overrides are explained in the Rule Overrides section later in the chapter).

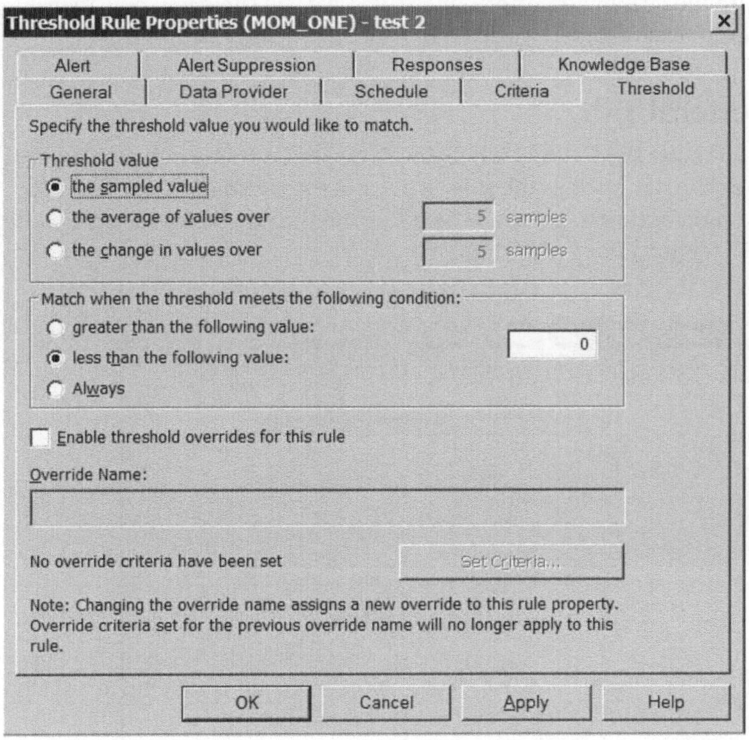

Figure 5-25. *The Threshold tab of the Threshold Rule Properties dialog*

Alert Rules

Now that we have looked at event and performance rules, we will focus attention on the third type of MOM rule: the alert rule.

You use the alert rule to monitor for alerts that appear in MOM (generated either by event rules, performance rules, or directly by a MOM script). These rules are most commonly used to send an SMTP mail response or paged response to a notification group for alerts generated by rules in a specific rule group. The reason for using alert rules is to maintain manageability within MOM. Configuring each event and performance rule to send an SMTP mail or page is entirely possible, but not particularly easy to manage, since every rule would need to be configured individually. For this reason, alert rules are used. As mentioned previously, a single alert rule can be configured to send SMTP mails or paged responses for many individual event or performance rules, making the MOM rule base far easier to manage (especially when you consider that a large rule base can easily have in excess of 5,000 active rules).

As with the event and performance rules, we will show you how to use the options in each tab.

The General Tab

Figure 5-26 shows the General tab. This tab mostly contains information that cannot be changed, such as the rule GUID and the rule path. You must click the Set Criteria button to get to the Set Override Criteria dialog (see the "Rule Overrides" section later in the chapter).

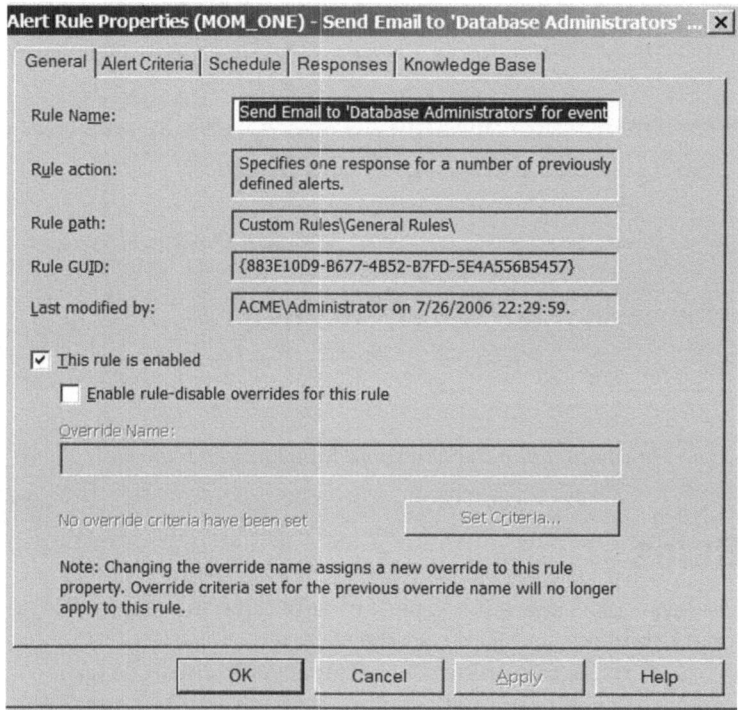

Figure 5-26. *The General tab of the Alert Rule Properties dialog*

The Alert Criteria Tab

The Alert Criteria tab (shown in Figure 5-27) is the most important tab of the Alert Rule Properties dialog. You can use it to configure which rule groups the alert rule applies to. You can also use it to specify the severity and source of the alert to be matched by the rule.

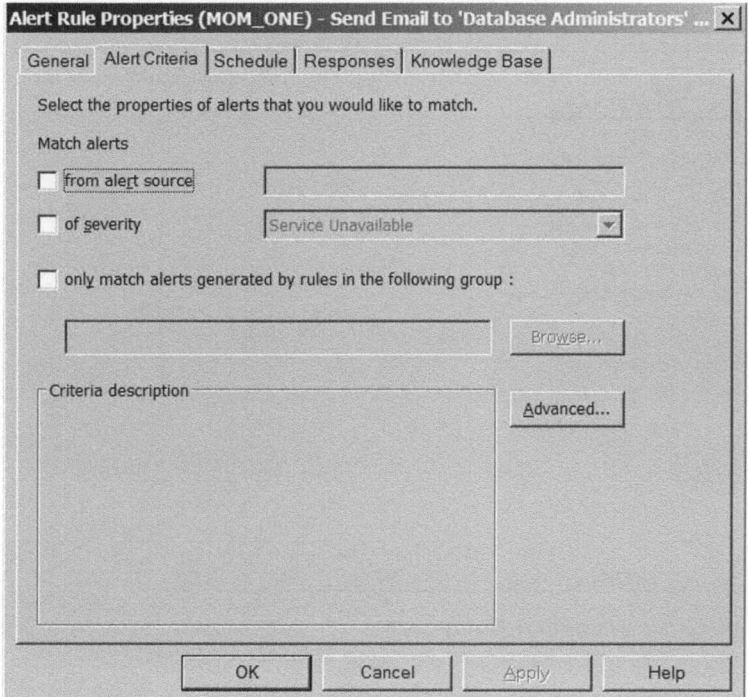

Figure 5-27. *The Alert Criteria tab of the Alert Rule Properties dialog*

The most common setting for this rule is to leave the "from alert source" check box unchecked. Doing so allows you to catch alerts from all sources and simply use the severity to match.

The alternative approach is to check the "only match alerts generated by rules in the following group" box while leaving the boxes for the first two Match alerts options blank. Clicking the Browse button will take you to the Select Rule Group dialog, as shown in Figure 5-28. In this figure, the branch tree for Operations Manager 2005 has been expanded into a subtree. Choose an item for further expansion to make your selection.

You can click the Advanced button on the Alert Criteria tab (see Figure 5-27) to get to the Advanced Criteria dialog, in which you can specify more advanced and specific criteria. Figure 5-29 shows the Advanced Criteria dialog.

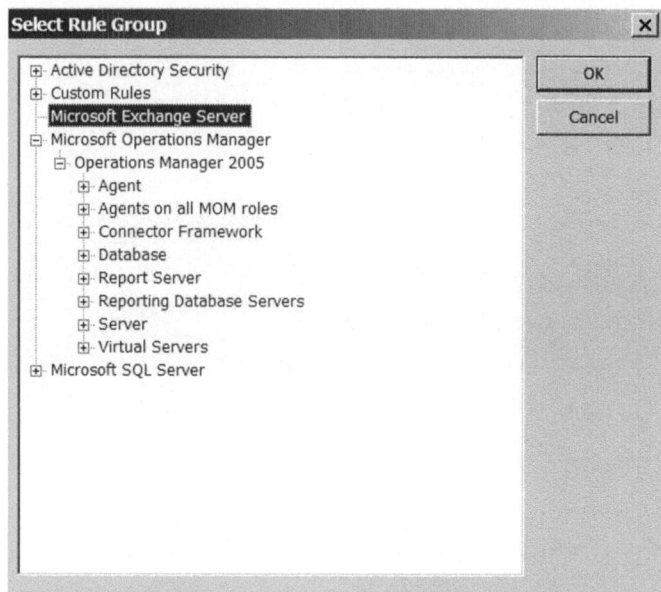

Figure 5-28. *The Select Rule Group dialog*

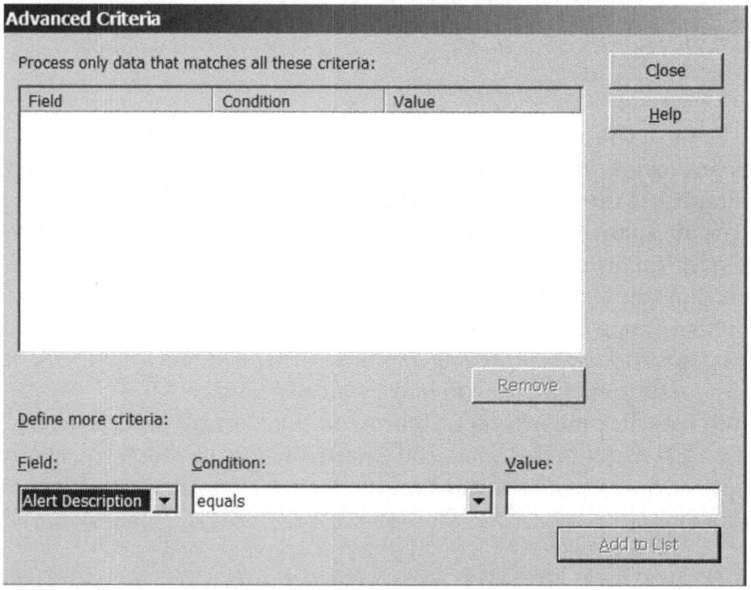

Figure 5-29. *The Advanced Criteria dialog*

The Responses Tab

You use the Responses tab (see Figure 5-30) to configure a response that executes when a match to the rule is found. This tab offers the same options as those of the Responses tab of the Event and Performance Rules dialog, but is more commonly used in Alert rules. It is most often used to execute responses that send SMTP e-mails or paged responses. We will look at those responses now.

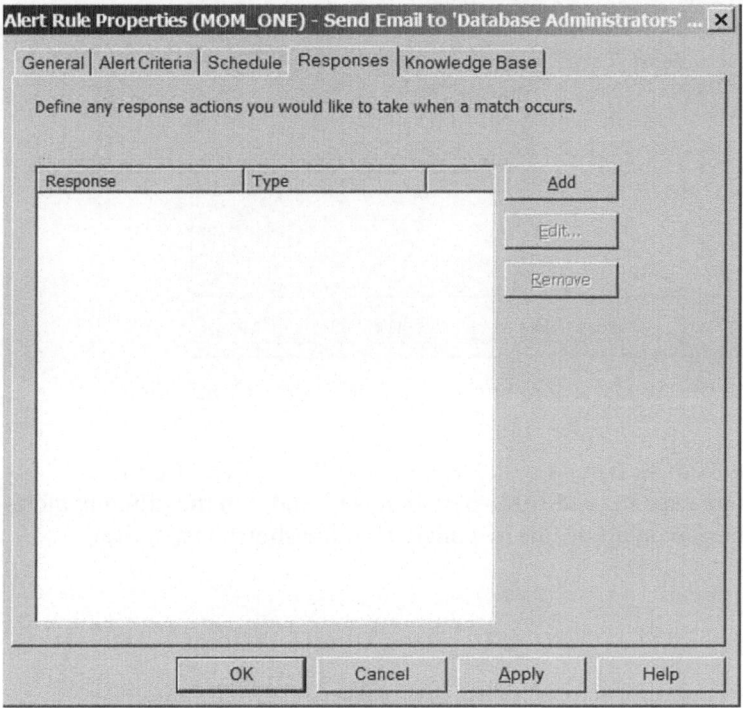

Figure 5-30. *The Responses tab of the Alert Rule Properties dialog*

After clicking the Add button and selecting "Send a notification to a Notification Group," you will see Figure 5-31.

From the dialog, you can select which notification group you want to send the e-mail or paged response to. You can also choose to create a new notification group or modify an existing one from here. Finally, this dialog displays a check box that reads "Run this response before duplicate alert suppression." You use this option if you are using alert suppression on a rule, but would like the alert rule to process for every instance of an alert—even those that have been suppressed.

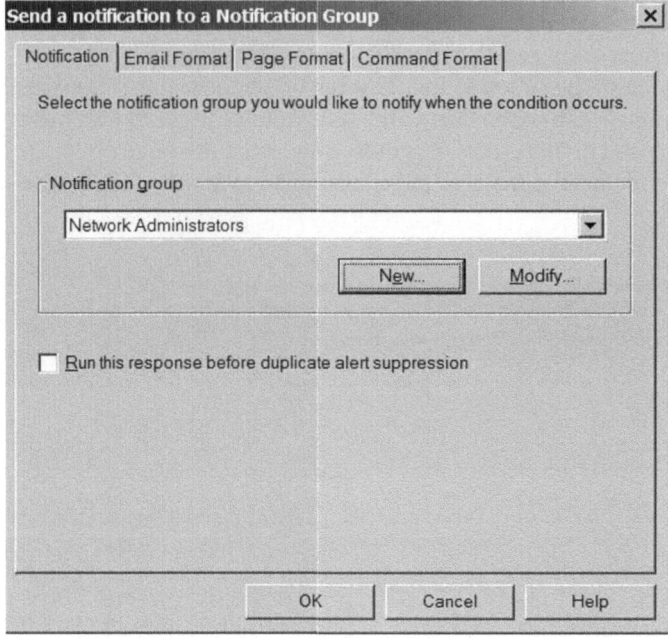

Figure 5-31. *The "Send a a notification to a Notification Group" dialog*

The next three tabs—Email Format, Page Format, and Command Format—are used to modify the data that is placed into the different alerts that can be generated by this response. They are shown respectively in Figures 5-32 to 5-34.

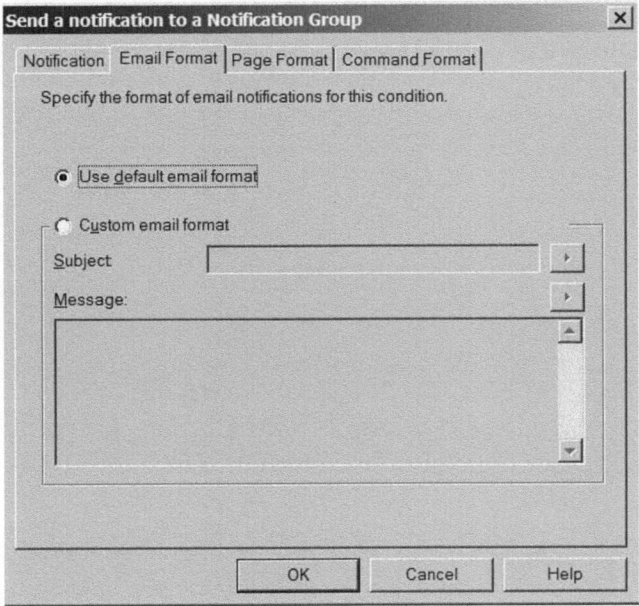

Figure 5-32. *The Email Format tab of the "Send a notification to a Notification Group" dialog*

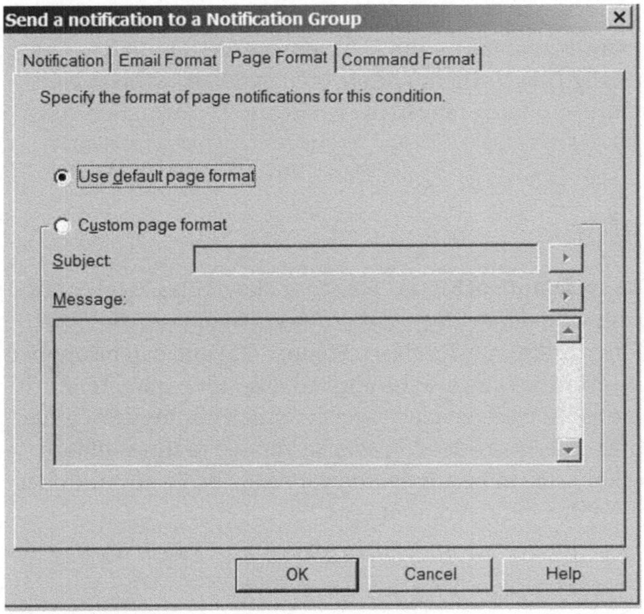

Figure 5-33. *The Page Format tab of the "Send a notification to a Notification Group" dialog*

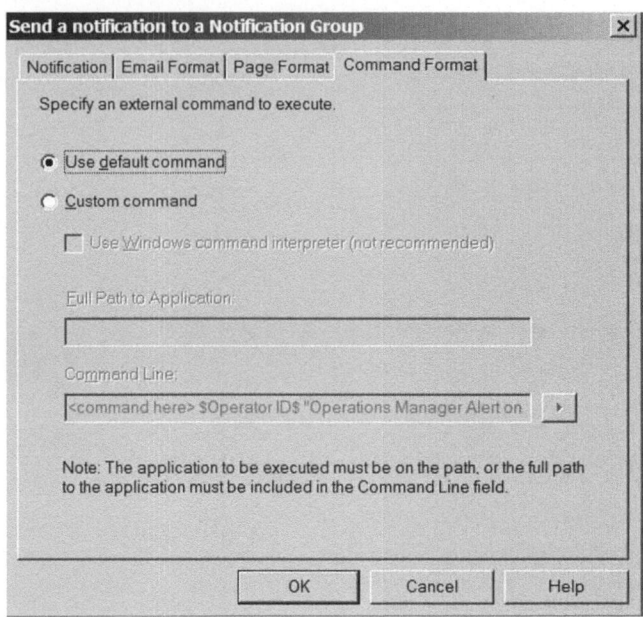

Figure 5-34. *The Command Format tab of the "Send a notification to a Notification Group" dialog*

The remaining tabs that make up the Alert Rule Properties dialog (Schedule and Knowledge Base) will not be covered in detail, as we already have discussed the corresponding tabs in the Event and Performance Rules dialog.

Rule Overrides

Rule overrides are a new feature of MOM 2005; they allow rules to be configured specifically to individual machines and groups of machines. Rule overrides are configured at the rule level (see Figure 5-35) and can be applied to all rule types. Rule overrides can also be applied to script parameters, meaning that a single script rule can cover servers with a multitude of different parameter settings. Rule overrides can also be applied to thresholds to enable a single threshold rule to be configured very specifically to a number of agents with different threshold requirements.

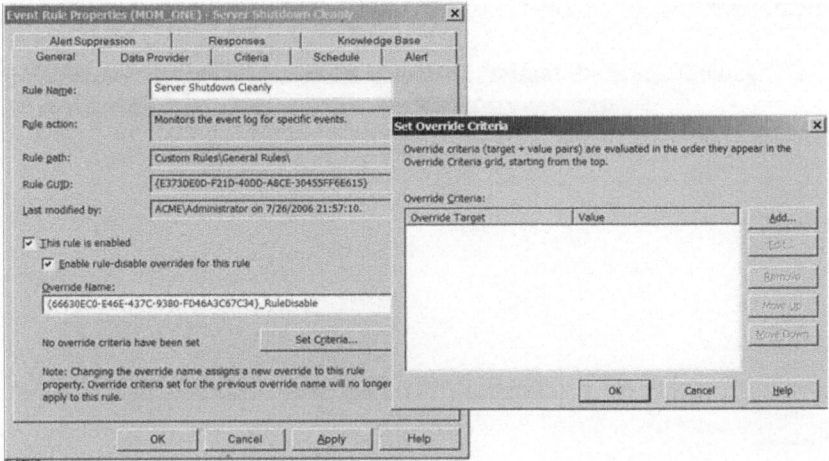

Figure 5-35. *Set Override Criteria dialog*

Rule overrides can be configured to enable or disable a rule for a specific computer or computer group, change parameter values for scripts, and specify individual threshold values. This feature makes the MOM rule base very versatile, and allows a single rule to apply to many different agents that would usually require separate rules. This allows you to minimize the size of the rule base and reduce the number of rules to be applied to the agents, thus reducing the footprint of the MOM agent on the monitored machines.

Advanced Rule Configuration

In addition to the standard configuration options, there are some advanced options that can be used. The main advanced features we will cover in this section are state alert variables and custom responses. You can use state alert variables to update the state of an agent and a service on that agent in the State view in the MOM Operator Console. You can use custom responses to launch scripts, batch files, send e-mails, and execute other tasks at the same time a rule executes.

State Alert Properties

The State view in MOM allows you to see the current state of the components residing on a MOM agent. The MOM State view is shown in Figure 5-36.

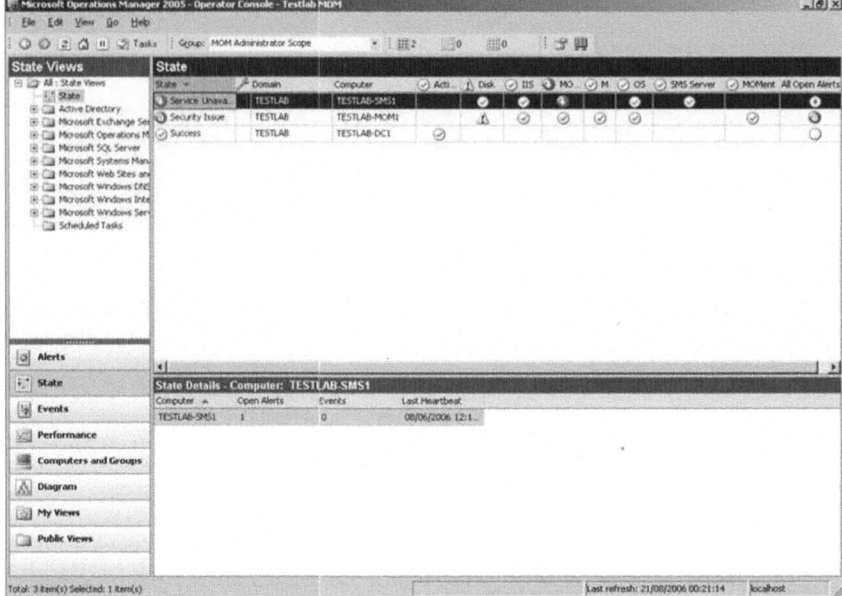

Figure 5-36. *State view in the MOM Operator Console*

The rule properties necessary to update the State view are usually configured by default in MOM 2005 management packs. If you wish to update components yourself, you can use state alert variables. To access these, open the Properties dialog of a rule and navigate to the Alert tab. When you check the "Enable state alert properties" check box, the Server role, Instance, and Component options become available, as does the Edit button (as shown in Figure 5-37).

Click the Edit button to change the formula, which will update the State view. When you click the Edit button, the Alert Severity Calculation for State Rule dialog will be displayed. This will show the conditions that affect the State view. Select the condition that you want to change and click Edit; or, if you wish to create a condition, click Add. Once you have clicked one of these options, the Edit Alert Severity Condition dialog will be displayed (as shown in Figure 5-38).

An example of a state alert condition would be `AttributeValue(Event Number) > "10" AND AttributeValue(Parameter 5) = "9"`, which will look for matches with an event number greater than 10 and with parameter 5 equal to 9. Once you have created the condition, you can select the alert severity that will be set when the condition is met from the drop-down list below the Condition box.

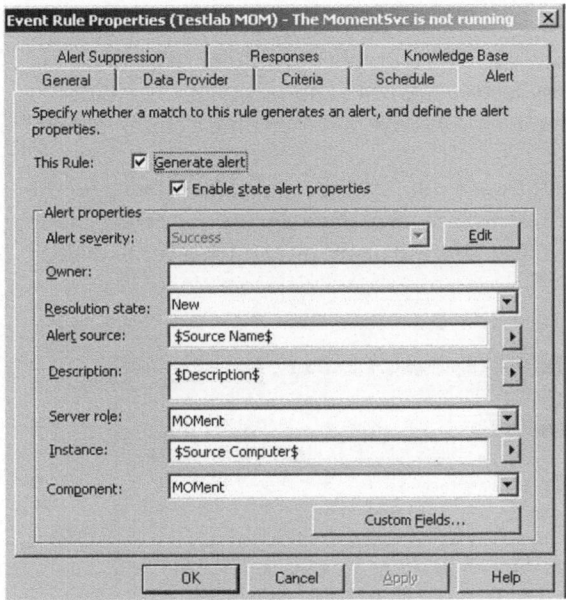

Figure 5-37. *The Alert tab of the Event Rule Properties dialog, with the "Enable state alert properties" check box selected*

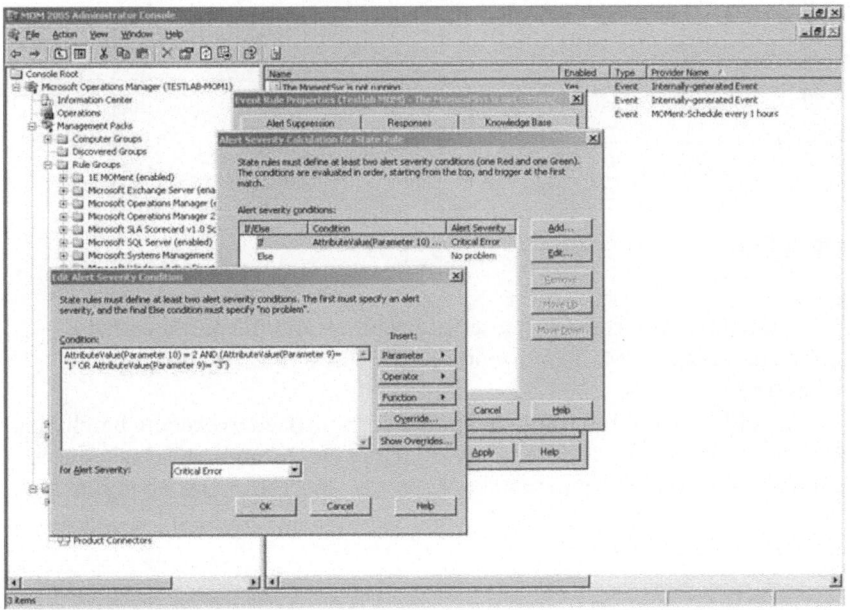

Figure 5-38. *The Edit Alert Severity Condition dialog*

Custom Responses

MOM rule responses provide you with a number of options in addition to sending notifications. In this section, we will examine the most commonly used responses—such as launching a script and executing a command or batch file.

To launch a MOM script from a rule, open the Properties dialog for the rule, navigate to the Reponses tab (shown in Figure 5-13), and select Launch a script from the drop-down list. This will open the Launch a Script dialog (shown in Figure 5-39).

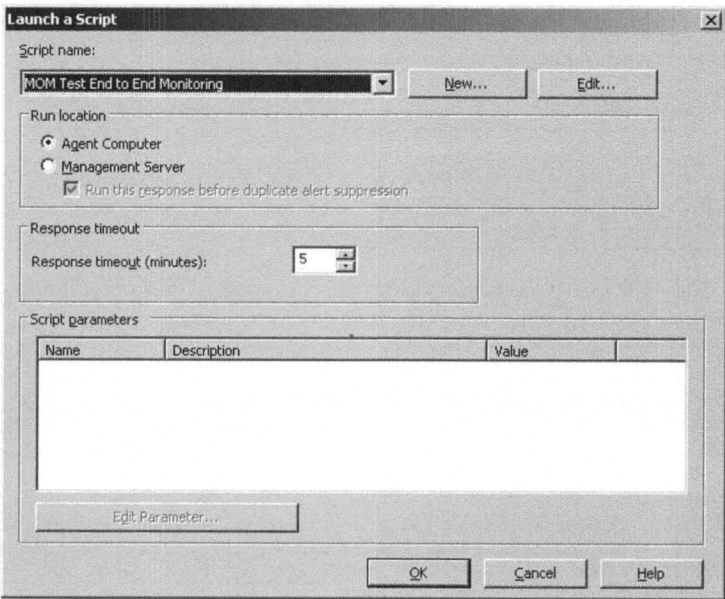

Figure 5-39. *The Launch a Script dialog*

From here, you can select a script to launch and the parameters to attach to the script. More information on MOM scripts can be found in Chapter 13.

In addition to other things, responses can be used to execute batch files. We will now show you how to execute a batch file through MOM responses. From the drop-down list in the Reponses tab, select "Execute a command or batch file." This will display the Configure Response Command dialog shown in Figure 5-40.

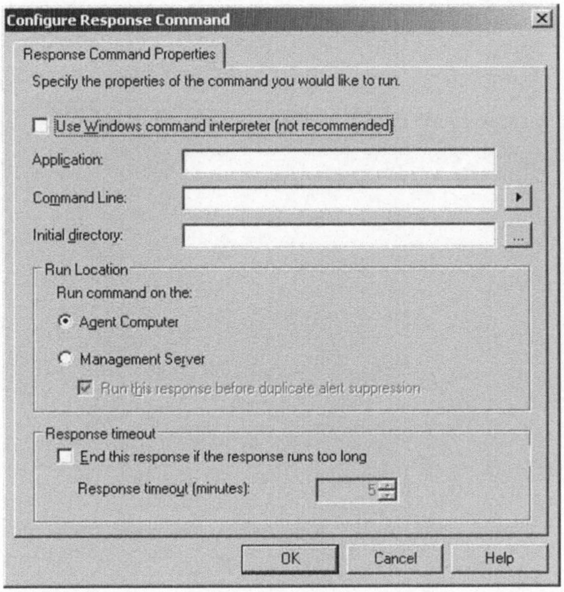

Figure 5-40. *The Configure Response Command dialog*

From here, you can select the batch file or command to run from the rule. I find it is a good idea to use the cmd.exe /c command to launch the script, which executes the command and then exits. An example of a command to run might be restarting a service, which might look something like this: cmd /c net stop MOM & net start MOM.

Summary

In this chapter, we have looked at the creation of the different types of MOM rules, including event rules, performance rules, and alert rules, and we have explored the options that are available to configure each of the rules. We have also looked at some common rules that augment the default rules for server startups, server shutdowns, and the MOM DTS package.

Chapter 6 will cover MOM alerts, which are generated by the event rules you have created in this chapter. We will also make recommendations for alert tuning, which will help to reduce the number of spurious alerts that appear in the Operator Console.

CHAPTER 6

■ ■ ■

Alerts

In Chapter 5, we looked at the different types of rules in MOM, including how to create them. We will now look at alerts, which are generated by the rules created in Chapter 5.

Alerts are used to notify the IT team or MOM operator of issues detected by MOM. Alerts are displayed in the Alert Views section of the Operator Console and used by the operator to locate and troubleshoot issues. Alerts contain Windows event information and product knowledge (containing information dedicated to the methods to troubleshoot and resolve an issue), as well as information from any custom fields that may have been created.

Out of the box, MOM does a very respectable job of monitoring hardware, operating systems, and applications; but without some configuration, the number of alerts received by the operator will be very high. It is for this reason that alert tuning and threshold customizations are necessary.

In this chapter, we show you how to take advantage of the general alert tuning information and settings for the most common Microsoft management packs, as well as provide advice on carrying out alert tuning on management packs not covered by this book. Alert threshold customizations for the common management packs will also be covered in this chapter.

On completion of this chapter, you will be able to carry out alert tuning on the most common management packs, including triaging of alerts and customization of thresholds to ensure that the monitoring carried out by the management packs is appropriate for your environment.

Alert Tuning and Threshold Customization Basics

The default alerts that you see in the Alert Views section in the Operator Console are not always relevant to the infrastructure that MOM is monitoring. In some environments, these spurious and unnecessary alerts may need to be filtered out. The process of filtering these alerts is referred to as alert tuning, and will be covered in this section. It is also necessary to tweak alert thresholds to meet the requirements of your monitoring infrastructure. Alert threshold customization will be covered later in the chapter.

Alert Tuning Basics

In this section, we will look at the basics of alert tuning and point out any issues to be aware of when carrying out alert tuning. We will also show you how to carry out alert tuning in the fastest and most efficient and reliable way.

Note Alerts are generated by event rules, so bear in mind that when this chapter refers to rules, unless otherwise specified, it is referring to event rules.

With alert tuning, it is important to remember that it is easier to disable a rule that generates an alert than it is to locate and reenable it. Therefore, it is essential that before disabling a rule, you ensure that the alert is not required and will not be required in the foreseeable future.

In cases where an alert is not necessary, you can disable the rule that generates the alert by right-clicking in the Alert Details section of the Operator Console, as shown in Figure 6-1.

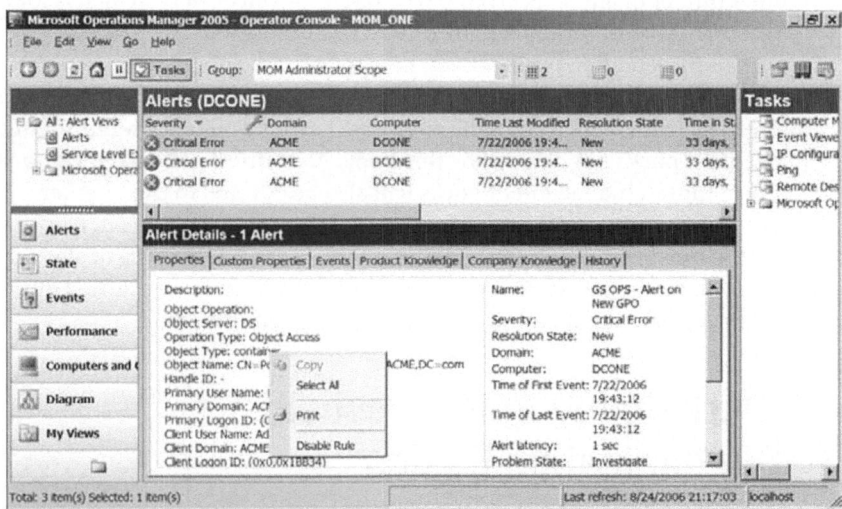

Figure 6-1. *Rule disabling from the Operator Console*

Other rules will need to be modified so that the alerts they generate are appropriate to your environment. To modify the rules, you may need to change the scripts, script parameters, or thresholds, which are discussed later in the chapter.

Before disabling rules and customizing thresholds, you must identify the appropriate alerts for alert tuning. It should be noted that this can take considerable time. While this chapter aims to reduce the time required for alert tuning, it will always be necessary to carry out alert tuning, even after the MOM installation is well established, as IT infrastructures, by design, change frequently due to hardware refreshes, software updates, and additions to the environment.

To identify alerts for tuning, you may need to troubleshoot the problems identified by the alerts. This can be accomplished by using the product knowledge for the alert in question (located on the Product Knowledge tab in the Operator Console).

The alerts that need to be tuned may require some changes in the configuration. As all infrastructures are configured differently, some best practice configurations may not be appropriate to your environment. These rules will need to be disabled to prevent unwanted alerts from being displayed.

Threshold Customization Basics

While still remaining in the enabled state, some rules in MOM require that the threshold values contained within them be modified to suit the performance thresholds in the environment. The default threshold values have been defined by the appropriate product teams that created the product, and therefore are reasonably accurate. However, due to hardware differences, configuration, or load on the environment, these values may need to be changed.

The first stage of modifying threshold values is to baseline the server or application in question to determine the average operating values. This can be done using Performance Monitor (perfmon), or more likely, with MOM itself using the Performance View in the Operator Console, and/or the MOM Reporting web console and archived data. Once you have a clear baseline defined, you will be able to formulate the threshold values that will give you the greatest visibility of issues within your environment without creating a large number of spurious alerts.

After baselining has been completed and your threshold values have been defined, you can make the necessary rule changes.

Note It is recommended that you continue to baseline the server(s)/application(s) for at least 7 days after making the threshold change in MOM to ensure that the new value you have defined is accurate. If this continued monitoring is not carried out, it is possible that critical performance alerts will not appear, and an impact on the monitored computer will result.

Alert Tuning and Threshold Customization for Common Management Packs

This section will look at alert tuning and threshold customizations for the most common Microsoft management packs.

Microsoft Exchange Server Management Pack for MOM 2005

When you configure the Exchange Server management pack, it is critical that you use the Microsoft Exchange Server Management Pack Configuration Wizard. This can be downloaded from www.microsoft.com/downloads.

You may need to make some additional changes to the management pack to enable the automated logon testing scripts to work. We will talk about them in this section.

Alert Tuning

The Exchange Server management pack is one of the biggest and most complicated MOM management packs and therefore, in some environments, requires heavy tuning. In this section, we will take a look at the most common alerts that require tuning in the Exchange Server management pack.

The rules shown in Table 6-1 generate alerts. Since not all alerts are required in all environments, you may need to disable some of the rules. In addition to preventing unwanted alerts from being displayed, this will also free up resources on the MOM agent machines by limiting the active rules on the agent. The rules that require threshold changes will be covered in the next section.

Table 6-1. *Exchange Server Management Pack Rules*

Rule Name	Location	More Information
SSL should be required to secure HTTP access to the Exchange server.	`Microsoft Exchange Server\Exchange 2003\Health Monitoring and Performance Thresholds\Server Configuration and Security Monitoring\`	This rule detects whether HTTP access to the Exchange server is secured in IIS. If you aren't using HTTPS to secure this (and don't intend to), this rule should be disabled.
Disabled user does not have a master account SID.	`Microsoft Exchange Server\Exchange 2003\Exchange Event Monitoring\ Information Store service\`	This is a common issue if a user account is disabled without the msExchMaster AccountSID Active Directory attribute set. This can cause performance issues on Exchange servers if there are a lot of these alerts but this rule can be disabled providing you have a process in place for dealing with disabled Active Directory user accounts
Synthetic Outlook Web Access logon.	`Microsoft Exchange Server\Exchange 2003\Availability and State Monitoring\Verify Outlook Web Access Front-End Availability\`	This rule runs the script that performs a synthetic logon to Outlook Web Access (OWA), and verifies that OWA is working correctly. This rule should only be disabled if you have no requirement to monitor OWA. This rule requires some configuration in most environments; this configuration is detailed later in this section.

As you may notice, despite the complexity of the management pack, there are very few rules that actually require disabling and modifying. This is due to the fact that the management packs are written by the product teams themselves, and so are fairly accurate out of the box.

Modifying the script that is initiated by the Synthetic Outlook Web Access logon rule is often required to enable it to function correctly in some Exchange environments. The default script (Exchange 2003 - OWA logon verification) uses the IIS configuration and the `CustomUrls` registry keys on the front-end servers to identify the websites for monitoring. These registry keys are not created by default, but can be added if you are using a custom URL for your Outlook Web Access (OWA)/Outlook Mobile Access (OMA) or Exchange ActiveSync (EAS) access.

Note For more information on the `CustomUrls` registry keys, refer to the Exchange Server management pack deployment guide, which can be downloaded from www. microsoft.com/mom/techinfo/productdoc/default.mspx.

In some infrastructures in which HTTPS certificates are used, this feature does not function correctly. This will cause spurious MOM alerts if not addressed. The reason for this issue is that the HTTPS certificate issued to the OWA web page does not match the page collected from IIS by the script, as the script often collects the IP address of the script rather than the DNS name as defined on the certificate.

You can modify the script to prevent it from checking IIS for this information. We will now show you how to do this.

Note The best practice for modifying a script in MOM is to create a copy of the script and make changes to the copy. That way, the modified script will not be lost in the event of reinstalling the management pack, and the original script will still exist for reference.

---

1. Locate lines 720 through 723 in the Exchange 2003 - OWA logon verification script (shown in the following code snippet).

```
if (OWALogon(strMailbox, TIME_OUT_THRESHOLD, "",
objLogonResult) == "Quit")
break MainRoutine;
bAllLogonsSucceed = objLogonResult.value;
```

2. Comment out the lines, as shown in the following code:

```
// if (OWALogon(strMailbox, TIME_OUT_THRESHOLD, "",
objLogonResult) == "Quit")
// break MainRoutine;
// bAllLogonsSucceed = objLogonResult.value;
```

Note By adding the `//` symbols at the beginning of the line, you are telling the script that this line can be ignored. Since these lines of code are the ones that pass the data from the lookup in IIS to the script, they should be ignored by the script.

Once the copied script has been modified, best practice dictates that you should create a custom rule to launch the newly modified script. When creating the new rule, make sure to locate it in a custom management pack, as explained in Chapter 5. Disable the original Exchange Management Pack rule to prevent the old script from running.

You may need to carry out additional customizations to rules that we have not yet talked about. Here is one example of a rule:

Microsoft Exchange Server\Exchange 2003\Health Monitoring and Performance Thresholds\Server Configuration and Security Monitoring\ Exchange Transaction Log files are equal to or older than the maximum days allowed

You use the preceding rule to detect when Exchange transaction logs are not purged by Exchange backups. The number of days set as maximum by default is 2. Depending on your Exchange backup schedule, you may need to increase the maximum number of days. The number of days is a script parameter, and is therefore changed in the Responses tab of the Event Rule Properties dialog, as shown in Figure 6-2 (for more information, see Chapter 5).

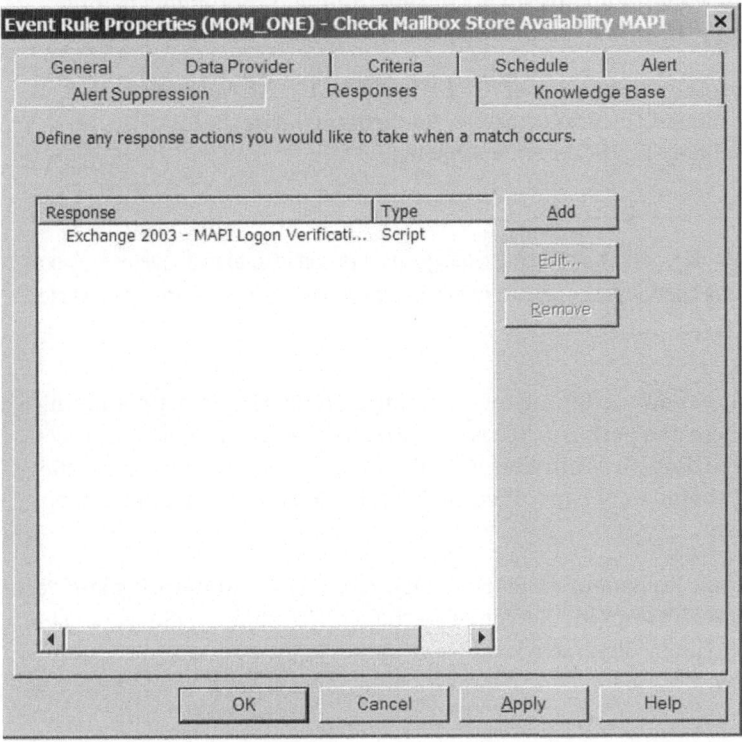

Figure 6-2. *The Responses tab of the Event Rule Properties dialog*

Threshold Customization

A number of the rules in the Exchange Server management pack contain thresholds that often require modification. This section will look at these rules and explain the best way to obtain recommended settings for these rules.

Here are two common rules that often require threshold modification:

Microsoft Exchange Server\Exchange 2003\Health Monitoring and Performance Thresholds\Server Performance Thresholds\Disk Write Latencies > 20 msec

Microsoft Exchange Server\Exchange 2003\Health Monitoring and Performance Thresholds\Server Performance Thresholds\Disk Read Latencies > 20 msec

These rules may require modification depending on the disk performance of the Exchange server(s). The need to increase the thresholds in these rules indicates that you may be experiencing poor disk performance on the Exchange server(s) and should immediately investigate.

The rule shown following can also be affected by disk performance issues, but may also indicate Active Directory communication problems. Once again, you should investigate the environment thoroughly before increasing the threshold on this rule.

Microsoft Exchange Server\Exchange 2003\Health Monitoring and Performance Thresholds\Server Performance Thresholds\ MSExchangeIS:RPC latency > 200 ms

---

■**Note** Poor disk performance on Exchange servers can lead to mail queue problems and poor e-mail performance. Issues of this nature should be investigated immediately.

The rule shown following may indicate an Active Directory communications problem or a performance issue with one or more domain controllers. One or more domain controllers may also be unavailable. Once again, this is a rule that should not be modified without thorough investigation of the environment.

Microsoft Exchange Server\Exchange 2003\Health Monitoring and Performance Thresholds\Server Performance Thresholds\DSAccess:LDAP Search Time > 50 ms avg. over 5 minutes

Active Directory (AD) Management Pack for MOM 2005

The Active Directory management pack requires alert tuning for some environments due to the way Active Directory is implemented in different environments. This section looks at the different rules that require tuning, configuration, and threshold customization to ensure that your Active Directory installation is correctly monitored by MOM.

First, ensure that the Active Directory management pack has been correctly configured, that the Active Directory management pack helper objects file (oomads.msi) has been installed on the domain controllers, and that the necessary Active Directory MOMLatencyMonitors container has been created and all required permissions applied. Instructions on carrying out this configuration can be found in the Active Directory management pack deployment guide, downloadable from www.microsoft.com/mom/techinfo/productdoc/default.mspx.

Alert Tuning

The Active Directory management pack, while not the biggest, does require some level of alert tuning. However, there are no rules that require immediate threshold customization in most environments.

The rules shown in Table 6-2 generate alerts that are not required in all environments. These rules may be disabled if necessary. The rules that require threshold changes will be covered in the next section.

Table 6-2. *Active Directory Management Pack Rules*

Rule Name	Location	More Information
Script - AD Monitor Trusts	Microsoft Windows Active Directory\ Active Directory Monitor Trusts\	This rule is used to launch the AD Monitor Trusts script. Unless you have a specific requirement to monitor Active Directory trusts, this rule should be disabled, as the script is known to generate errors if no trusts are found.
The AD Machine Account Authentication Failures Report has data available.	Microsoft Windows Active Directory\ Active Directory Windows Server 2003\ Active Directory - NetLogon\	This rule can usually be disabled, as it provides information that is not required, provided that you correctly configure a subscription to the report (covered in Chapters 7 and 8).

In addition to the rules in Table 6-2, the following rules may need to be modified for them to work in your environment.

You use the AD Replication Monitoring script rule (shown following) to launch the AD Replication Monitoring script, which monitors Active Directory replication both within the local site and the enterprise.

> Microsoft Windows Active Directory\Active Directory Windows 2000 and Windows Server 2003 \Active Directory Availability\ Script - AD Replication Monitoring

The script parameters found on the Responses tab in the Event Rule Properties dialog can be changed to reflect the expected total replication time within your infrastructure, since this differs across different environments. The default values are listed alongside the parameters in Table 6-3.

Table 6-3. *Parameters and Values*

Parameter Name	Description	Default Value
IntersiteExpectedMaxLatency	Value for replication across all domain controllers in the Enterprise	15 minutes
IntrasiteExpectedMaxLatency	Value for replication across all domain controllers in the local site	5 minutes

■**Note**   More information on configuring these values can be found in the Active Directory management pack deployment guide, downloadable from `www.microsoft.com/ mom/techinfo/productdoc/default.mspx`.

The following rule launches the AD Remote Topology Discovery script: Microsoft Windows Active Directory\ Replication Topology Discovery (Connection Objects)\ Script - AD Remote Topology Discovery

There is a known issue with this script that is caused by a table in the OnePoint database not being populated correctly. There are two methods for resolving this issue. One is to modify the database directly, and the other is to change the script. Since modifying the OnePoint database is not recommended, modifying the script is the preferred option.

The script change that is necessary is to locate the `TargetFQDNComputer` object and replace it with the `TargetNetbiosComputer` object. You should copy the script before you make the change, and then modify the copy of the script. This is to ensure that you have a reference script in the event that you need to revert back to the default setting.

The following AD Client GC Availability script rule checks the number of global catalog servers available and responding in the local site, and generates an alert if the number is less than the default of three. This value can be changed in the script parameters from the Reponses tab of the Event Rule Properties dialog if necessary.

> Microsoft Windows Active Directory\Active Directory Client Side Monitoring\Script - AD Client GC Availability - script

---

Note Exchange requires at least one global catalog server to be available at all times in the local site. The recommendation is that there should be *at least* two for fault tolerance, and as many more as are required depending on the size of the Exchange infrastructure and the number of Active Directory and Exchange users in the local site.

Threshold Customization

There are no rules in the Active Directory management pack that require specific threshold customization. However, you may need to make some changes to thresholds depending on your environment. Since there are no specific changes that we would recommend, we will not cover threshold customization of the Active Directory management pack in detail.

Microsoft Windows Server Base Operating Systems Management Pack for Microsoft Operations Manager 2005

The Windows Server Base Operating Systems management pack will require some degree of alert tuning in all environments, as it monitors the operating system environment, which differs greatly across infrastructures and even between servers in the same infrastructure.

The rules that are most likely to require threshold customization are the rules that monitor the operating system performance.

Alert Tuning

By default, the Windows Server Base Operating Systems management pack requires very little alert tuning. Most of the changes required are threshold changes. However, it is recommended that you disable the rule groups and computer groups for operating systems that are not present in your environment to prevent any spurious alerts being generated, and also to make administration of the rule base easier.

Threshold Customization

The rules shown in Table 6-4 may require threshold changes in your environment. To determine the correct values to specify in the rules, baselining your environment will be required.

Table 6-4. *Windows Base OS Rules*

Rule Name	Location	More Information
Performance Threshold: Processor\ % DPC Time threshold exceeded.	Microsoft Windows Servers Base Operating System\Windows 2003\ State Monitoring and Service Discovery\	This rule monitors the Processor % DPC Time performance counter. A requirement to set a high threshold value here could indicate processor performance issues on one or more of your servers.
Performance Threshold: Memory\ % Committed bytes In Use threshold exceeded.	Microsoft Windows Servers Base Operating System\Windows 2003\ State Monitoring and Service Discovery\	This rule monitors the Memory % Committed bytes in use performance counter. A requirement to set a high threshold value here could indicate memory usage issues on one or more of your servers.
Performance Threshold: PhysicalDisk\Avg. Disk sec/Write threshold exceeded.	Microsoft Windows Servers Base Operating System\Windows 2003\ State Monitoring and Service Discovery\	This rule monitors the Physical Disk Avg. Disk Writes/sec performance counter. A requirement to set a high threshold value here could indicate disk performance issues.
Performance Threshold: Processor\ % Interrupt Time threshold exceeded.	Microsoft Windows Servers Base Operating System\Windows 2003\ State Monitoring and Service Discovery\	This rule monitors the Processor Interrupt Time performance counter. A requirement to set a high threshold value here could indicate performance issues on one or more of your servers.

Rule Name	Location	More Information
Performance Threshold: PhysicalDisk\Avg. Disk sec/Read threshold exceeded.	Microsoft Windows Servers Base Operating System\Windows 2003\ State Monitoring and Service Discovery\	This rule monitors the Physical Disk\Avg. Disk sec/Read performance counter. A requirement to set a high threshold value here could indicate processor performance issues on one or more of your servers.
Performance Threshold: Processor\ % Processor Time threshold exceeded.	Microsoft Windows Servers Base Operating System\Windows 2003\ State Monitoring and Service Discovery\	This rule monitors the Processor % Processor Time performance counter. A requirement to set a high threshold value here could indicate processor performance issues on one or more of your servers. It may also indicate that an application or process is utilizing a large amount of processor time.
Performance Threshold: Memory\ Available MBytes threshold exceeded.	Microsoft Windows Servers Base Operating Servers Base Operating xState Monitoring and Service Discovery\	This rule monitors the Memory Available Mbytes performance counter. A requirement to set a high threshold value here could indicate a requirement to upgrade memory on one or more of your servers.

Microsoft SQL Server Management Pack for MOM 2005

The SQL Server management pack is the final management pack that will be addressed in this chapter. This management pack contains a number of rules with thresholds to be customized, as well as some additional configuration to suppress alerts for databases that are not required for monitoring.

Alert Tuning

There are no specific recommendations on rules that should be disabled in the SQL Server management pack. However, once again, rule groups for components of SQL that do not need to be monitored can be disabled for tidiness and ease of manageability. A common component that will not need to be monitored in some environments is the SQL Replication component. If this is the case, you can disable the SQL Replication rule group.

In some environments, there will be a requirement to monitor a SQL server, but not necessarily all the databases resident in the SQL instance hosted by the server. In this case, there is a way to configure the management pack to remove individual databases from monitoring. In order to remove a database from monitoring, create a text file on the root of the system drive (usually `C:`) on the agent called `SQLExclude.txt`. Populate the file with the names of the databases that you want to remove from monitoring with a single database name on each line.

For example, enter the data in the `SQLExclude.txt` file, like this:

```
Database1
Database2
Database3
```

Threshold Customization

The rules shown in Table 6-5 have thresholds that you can configure as needed.

Table 6-5. *SQL Management Pack Rules*

Rule Name	Location	More Information
Locks : Number of deadlocks > 1 for 15 minutes	`Microsoft SQL Server\ Server Performance Thresholds\`	This rule detects SQL deadlocks. A deadlock occurs when two users (or sessions) have locks on separate objects and each user wants a lock on the other's object. Each user waits for the other to release their lock. If this threshold needs to be increased, the affected SQL database should be investigated, as this condition can cause a performance impact on the database.
SQLSERVR Process > 90% CPU for 15 minutes	`Microsoft SQL Server\ Server Performance Thresholds\`	This rule monitors the CPU time used by the sqlservr process. If there is a requirement to increase the threshold in this rule, this indicates that the SQL server affected may be overutilized and may need to be upgraded.

Rule Name	Location	More Information
Cache Hit Ratio < 90% for 15 minutes	`Microsoft SQL Server\ Server Performance Thresholds\`	This rule monitors the hits on the SQL cache. A cache hit occurs when the server requests data pages that are stored in a memory buffer pool. If the threshold for this rule needs to be increased, it may indicate that the memory in the SQL server is not sufficient and should be increased.
SQL Server User Connections > 500	`Microsoft SQL Server\ Server Performance Thresholds\`	This rule is the most likely rule to require changes, as it monitors the number of SQL users concurrently connected to the database. If you have a SQL server that is configured to accept more than 500 connections, this threshold may need to be increased to prevent spurious alerts.
SQLAGENT Process > 90% CPU for 15 minutes	`Microsoft SQL Server\ Server Performance Thresholds\`	This rule monitors the CPU time used by the SQLAgent process. If there is a requirement to increase the threshold in this rule, this indicates that the affected SQL server may be over-utilized and may need to be upgraded.

One final point to reiterate is the fact that once initial alert tuning and threshold customization have taken place, it will still be necessary to carry out additional alert tuning and threshold customization in the future, since IT infrastructures are constantly changing.

Summary

In this chapter, we have looked at the basics of alert tuning and threshold customizations for the most common Microsoft management packs. We have also looked at some generic alert tuning steps that may be carried out against any management pack.

In the next chapter, we will look at the basics of MOM reporting, including installing and configuring the product, and importing and generating basic reports.

CHAPTER 7

■ ■ ■

Reporting

MOM Reporting consists of the SystemCenterReporting SQL database and a web console built on SQL Server Reporting Services. It is used to store archived data that is transferred from the MOM Operational (OnePoint) database.

MOM Reporting is a separate component of MOM that can be installed using the MOM Reporting setup wizard or the command line. MOM Reporting takes the form of the SystemCenterReporting database and the Reporting web console, hosted by SQL Server Reporting Services.

MOM Reporting allows long-term data storage of MOM data for all monitored systems and provides trend analysis, issue tracking, and configuration monitoring. The reports viewable through the MOM Reporting web console augment the MOM operational data. This allows the status and configuration of all monitored machines to be viewed over a long period of time. Leveraging SQL Server Reporting Services technology, MOM Reporting offers automated generation of reports, batch reporting, and a rich, graphical report output.

Once MOM Reporting is installed, you can access the MOM Reporting web console (shown in Figure 7-1) using the following URL: `http://<SQL RS Web Server>/Reports/Pages/Report.aspx`.

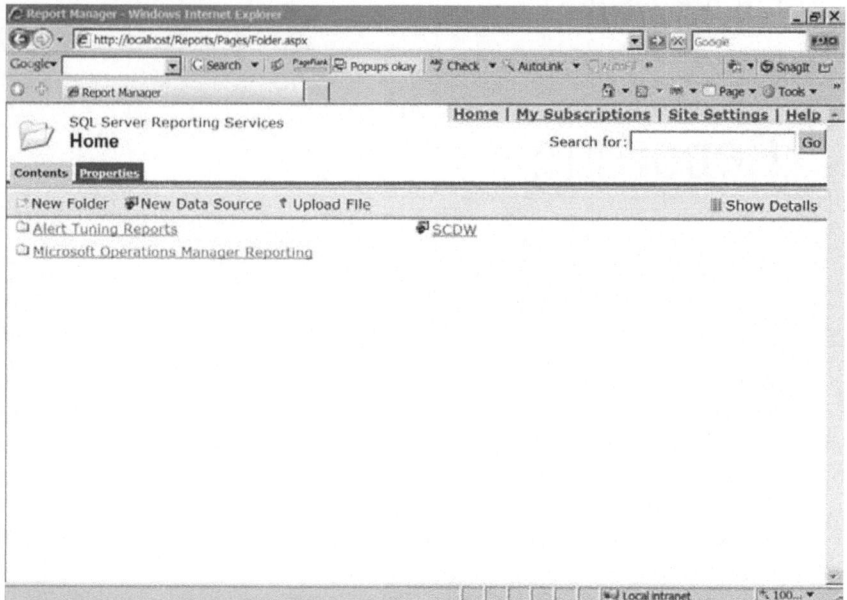

Figure 7-1. *The MOM Reporting web console*

MOM Reporting Setup

After MOM has been installed, you can install MOM Reporting separately to enable archival data storage and reporting. Before you do so, you must install and configure SQL Server 2000 or 2005 Reporting Services.

■Note Information about installing MOM 2005 and MOM Reporting onto SQL Server 2005 and Reporting Services 2005 can be found in Appendix A.

Installing and Configuring MOM Reporting

Once SQL Server Reporting Services is installed and configured, you can install MOM Reporting. You can install MOM Reporting from either the MOM setup wizard or the command line. This section will not cover the setup wizard in detail, but will highlight the points you need to be aware of when installing MOM Reporting, and will also examine the command-line installation parameters of MOM Reporting, including an example of a completed command line.

When you install MOM Reporting from either the wizard or the command line, it is always a good idea to run the MOM Reporting prerequisite checker to verify that you are installing MOM Reporting onto a server that meets the necessary software and hardware requirements to support MOM Reporting. You can execute the prerequisite checker by running setup.exe from the MOM 2005 installation CD and selecting the Check Prerequisites option, as shown in Figure 7-2.

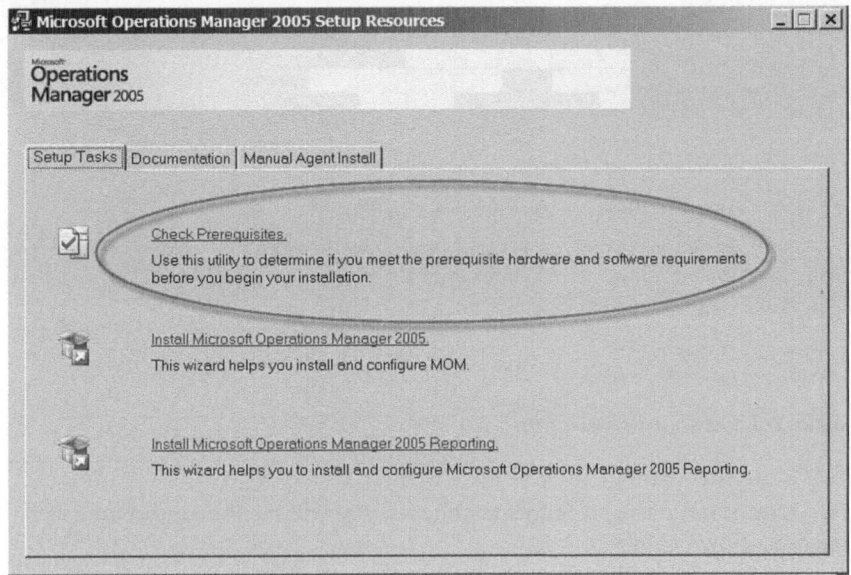

Figure 7-2. *The setup screen*

Once you have selected the Check Prerequisites option, you will see the component selection screen, as shown in Figure 7-3. Here, you need to select MOM 2005 Reporting, and also enter the name of the web server hosting the SQL Server Reporting Services web components if you have not installed them locally.

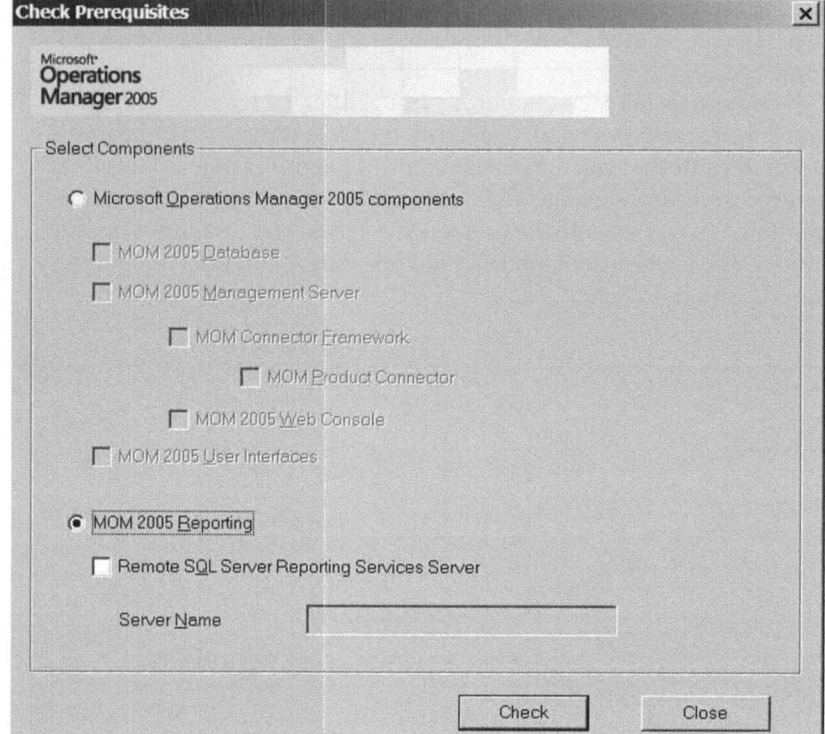

Figure 7-3. *Component selection*

After you run the prerequisite checker, you will see the output on a web page, as shown in Figure 7-4.

After you verify that the prerequisites have been met, you can install MOM Reporting.

As mentioned earlier in the chapter, MOM Reporting can be installed from either a graphical wizard or the command line. Installing from the wizard is straightforward, and therefore we will not cover it in greater detail in this chapter. However, since installing from the command line is my preferred method of installing MOM Reporting in most environments, especially advanced configurations (discussed later in the chapter), we will look at the parameters necessary to install MOM Reporting from the command line.

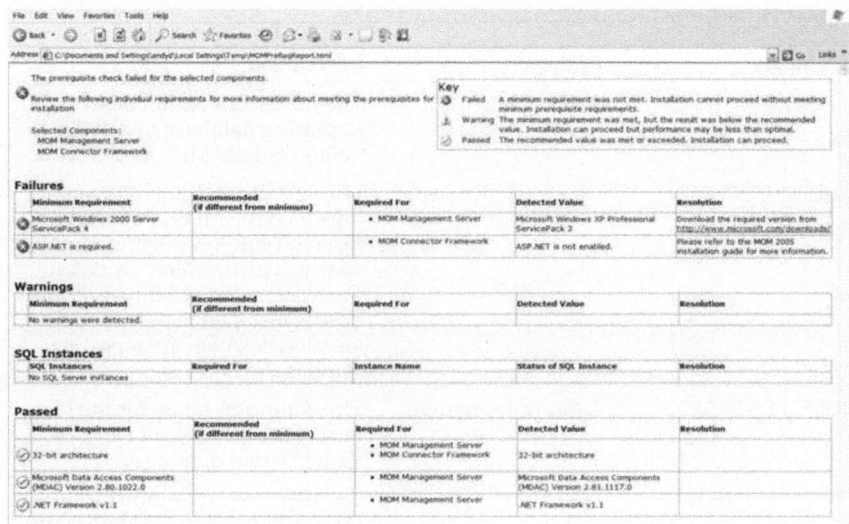

Figure 7-4. *The prerequisite web page*

To install MOM Reporting from the command line, I use the `msiexec` command and the `MOMReporting.msi` file. Table 7-1 shows the list of available command-line parameters for `MOMReporting.msi`, with a short description for each parameter.

Table 7-1. *Parameters for MOMReporting.MSI*

Parameter	Values	Description
DB_SIZE	Size in MB	The initial size of the MOM Reporting database in MB. The default is 1000 MB.
SQLSVR_INSTANCE	SQL instance name	The specific SQL Server instance on which the MOM Reporting (SystemCenterReporting) database will be installed. By default, the SystemCenterReporting database is installed locally to the location at which the reporting setup is run.
ROSETTA_SERVER	Computer name	The computer name for the location of the SQL Server ReportServer database.
TASK_USER_ACCOUNT*	User name	The user account name for the DTS task that imports data from the MOM database to the Reporting database.
TASK_USER_PASSWORD*	Password	The DTS account's password.
TASK_USER_DOMAIN*	Domain name	The DTS account's domain.
REPORTING_USER*	User name	The user account name for the MOM Reporting service (the DAS account).
REPORTING _PASSWORD*	Password	The MOM Reporting service account's password.
REPORTING _DOMAIN*	Domain name	The MOM Reporting service account's domain.
MOM_DB_SERVER	Computer name\ instance name	The DNS or fully qualified domain name (FQDN) of the MOM database server (and when applicable, the SQL Server instance name) from which data will be imported.
DATA_DIR	Default: SYSTEMDRIVE\SQL Server install path\MSSQL$ InstanceName\Data	The directory in which the SQL Server OnePoint database file (EeaData) should be stored (valid only during database installation).

* *In my experience, when I specify the DTS task and Reporting user accounts, I find it is best to use the MOM DAS account. There are two reasons for this: first, it is much quicker and more practical from an administrative perspective to use an account that already has the majority of the SQL permissions necessary to carry out the tasks. Second, from a security perspective, there is no sense in creating an additional account with the same or very similar permissions as an existing account. If you do create such an account, you are simply creating an additional opportunity for a determined hacker to access your systems.*

Parameter	Values	Description
LOG_DIR	Default: SYSTEMDRIVE\SQL Server install path\MSSQL$ InstanceName\Data	The directory in which the SQL Server OnePoint database log file (EeaLog.ldf) should be stored.
AUTOMATICALLY_ DETECT_ROSETTA_ VDIRS**	0: Check prerequisites 1: Do not check prerequisites Default: 0	Determines whether a prerequisite check has already been run (1) or needs to be run (0). Note that if you set this to 1, you must also include the REPORT_ SERVER_URL and REPORT_URL parameters.
REPORT_SERVER_URL**	Default: ReportServerVRoot	Name of the virtual directory hosting the report server.
REPORT_URL**	Default: Web ApplicationVRoot	Name of the virtual server hosting the reports.

** *When installing MOM Reporting using either the wizard or the command line, I have found it to be more reliable to* not *set the installation procedure to automatically detect virtual directories. The reason for this is that when I install SQL Server Reporting Services in an advanced configuration (which will be explained later in the chapter), I find this feature to be unreliable. It is therefore a good idea to set these manually to ReportServer (the default location for the report manager web page) and Reports (the default location for the web page hosting the reports).*

An example of a MOM Reporting installation command line is as follows:

```
msiexec /i <path>\MOMReporting.msi DB_SIZE=2000
SQLSVR_INSTANCE=<MOM Reporting DB Instance Name>
ROSETTA_SERVER=<ReportServer DB Server>
TASK_USER_ACCOUNT=<DTS Task User>
TASK_USER_PASSWORD=<DTS account password>
TASK_USER_DOMAIN=<DTS account domain>
REPORTING_USER=<Report Server user account>
REPORTING_PASSWORD=<Report Server user password>
REPORTING_USER_DOMAIN=<Report Server user domain>
MOM_DB_SERVER=<MOM DB Instance Name>
DATA_DIR=<database location>
LOG_DIR=<log file location>
AUTOMATICALLY_DETECT_ROSETTA_VDIRS=0
REPORT_SERVER_URL=ReportServer
REPORT_URL=Reports
```

As you can see, the command line is very long. It is recommended that you copy this and break it into sections to make reading and interpreting it easier.

Importing MOM Reports

After MOM Reporting has been installed, it is necessary to import MOM reports for the management packs that you have installed. This can be accomplished using the MOM Administrator Console.

MOM reports are among the extracted files that form the management pack download. They are in the form of an XML file found in the same folder as the management pack (.akm) file.

To import the reports, open the Administrator Console, right-click Management Packs, and select Import/Export Management Pack. Follow the wizard and browse to the folder in which the XML file is located. Once the wizard has completed, the management pack reports will be imported and can be viewed from the MOM Reporting web console.

■**Note** Be aware that when you have imported a new management pack and associated reports, it can take up to 24 hours for the reports to generate correctly. This is due to the fact that the reporting data is only archived to the reporting database every 24 hours (at 1 a.m. by default) by the MOM DTS package.

Using MOM Reports

In this section, we will look at the basics of report generation, from creating a data source to running a report. Finally, we will look at the process for exporting MOM reports. Topics will include data selection for reports, the most common reports and their functions, the basics of data sources, and exporting reports to different data formats to be e-mailed or copied.

Data Sources

All SQL Server Reporting Services reports, and hence all MOM reports, require a data source, which is a connection to the database. This data source provides all the information necessary for the report to connect to the database and retrieve data. The default data source that is created by management pack reports as they are created is the SCDW data source, which connects to the SystemCenterReporting database.

When you look at the MOM Reporting home page, you will see the SCDW data source. You may also see a data source in some of the management pack report folders. These data sources are all configured in exactly the same way as the data source you would see on the home page with the same settings.

The SCDW data source is shown in Figure 7-5.

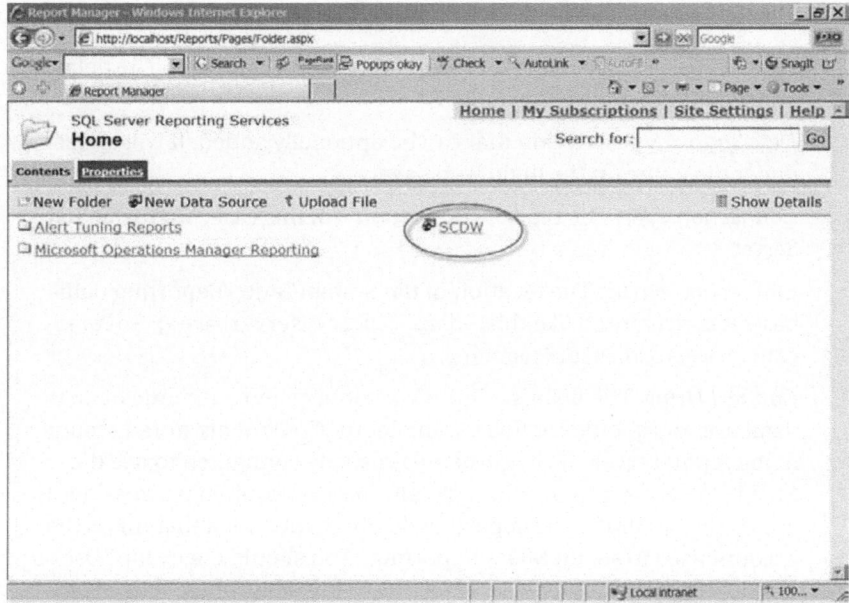

Figure 7-5. *The SCDW data source*

The SCDW data source (which is the data source used by all the MOM reports) shown in Figure 7-5 is configured with the parameters shown in Figure 7-6, and should be re-created in the event that it is mistakenly deleted or fails to function correctly.

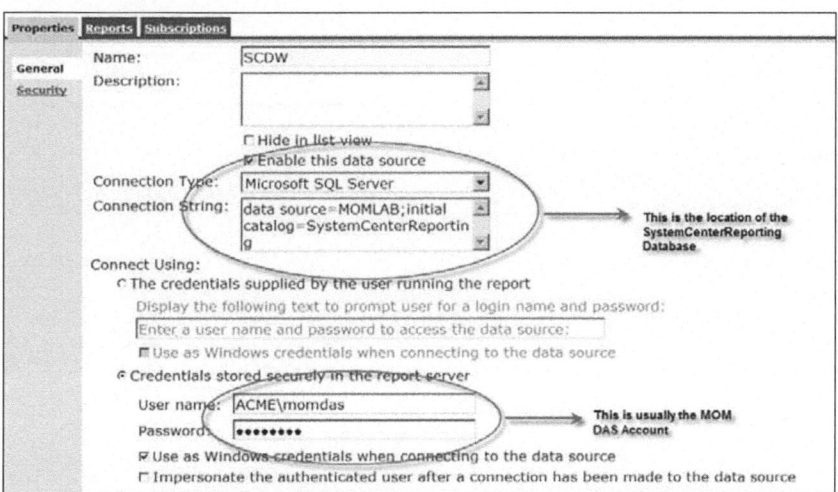

Figure 7-6. *The SCDW properties window*

The parameters shown in Figure 7-6 are explained in the following list.

Name: A descriptive name for the data source you created. The default and recommended setting is SCDW.

Description: A description that can be optionally added. It will appear under the name on the main web page.

Connection Type: The type of connection—in this case, Microsoft SQL Server.

Connection String: The location of the SystemCenterReporting database; it is structured like this: `'data source=<servername>; initial catalog=SystemCenterReporting`.

Connect Using: The details required to connect and authenticate to the database. You should set this parameter to "Credentials stored securely in the report server." The username is usually configured to use the MOM DAS account since this typically has the required permissions to access the SystemCenterReporting database (provided that this is the account used to set up MOM Reporting). You should check the "Use as Windows credentials when connecting to the data source" check box.

As explained, the SCDW data source should only need to be created if it is deleted or becomes corrupted. However, the process of creating the data source is generic and can be followed when creating additional data sources.

If you are creating custom reports or reimporting existing reports, it may be necessary to attach a data source to a report. This should be done from the Data Sources tab of the Report Properties screen, as shown in Figure 7-7.

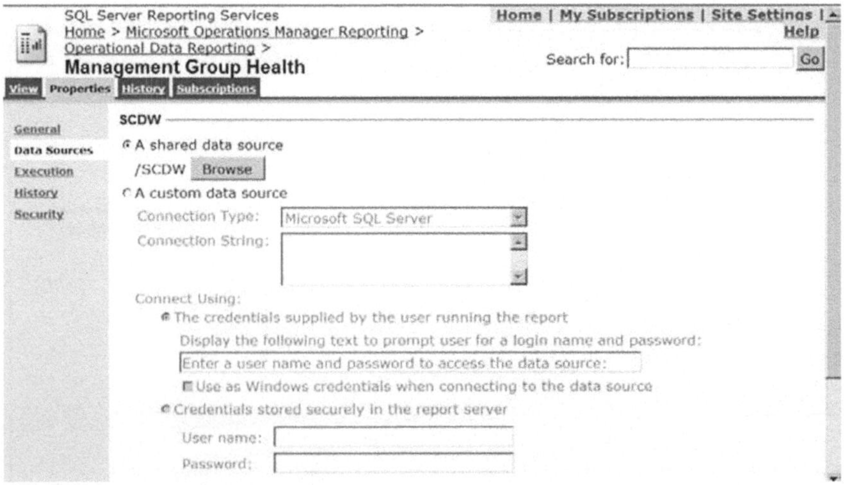

Figure 7-7. *The Data Sources tab*

As shown in Figure 7-7, the "A shared data source" option is used, since the data source we are using already exists in the report server.

In order to configure the report to use the data source, click the Browse button. As shown in Figure 7-8, a screen will be displayed, on which you can select the data source from the top of the folder tree.

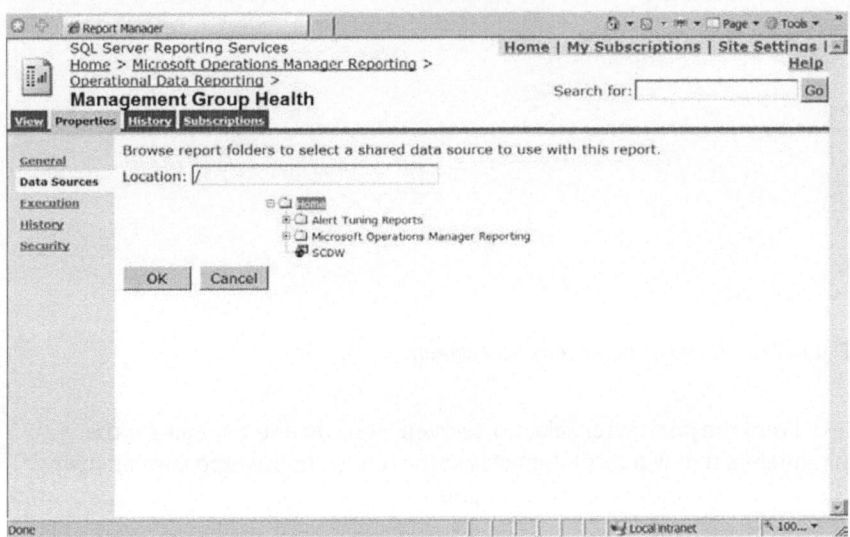

Figure 7-8. *The data source selection screen*

Once the report data sources have been verified and created as necessary, MOM reports can be generated. This will be covered in the next section.

Report Generation

When you load the MOM Reporting web console, you will be presented with a view of all the applications that have reports available (this is dependent on which management pack reports you have imported). To generate a report, first navigate to the report in question. For this example, we will use the Most Common Events by Computer report. Navigate to this report by clicking the Operational Health Analysis folder, and then clicking the report. Once the report has loaded, you will be presented with the parameter selection screen shown in Figure 7-9.

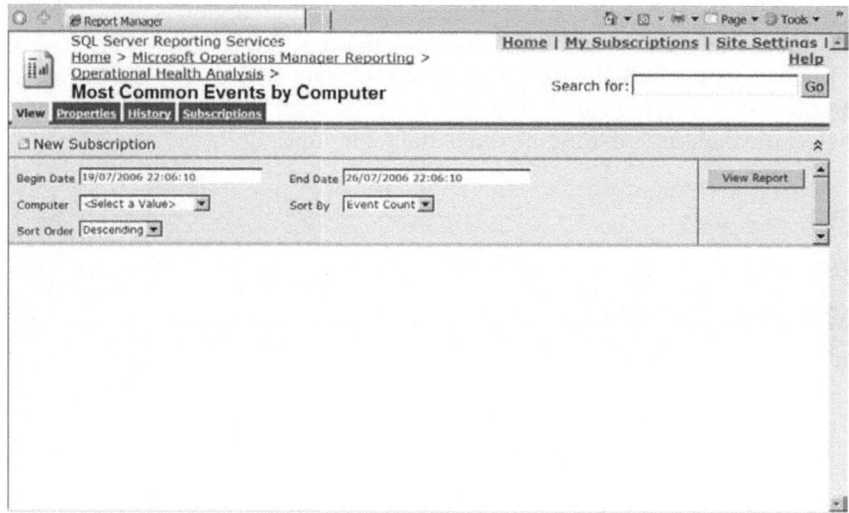

Figure 7-9. *The parameter selection screen*

From the parameter selection screen, you can enter values for the parameters that will form the basis of the report. In the report we are using, the following parameters are available:

Begin Date: Specify the start date for the data in the report.

End Date: Specify the end date for the data in the report.

Computer: Select a value for the computer that the report will generate data against (<All> is a valid selection to generate the report for all computers).

Sort By: Select how you want to sort the data in the report.

Sort Order: Select either Ascending or Descending.

Once you have selected the appropriate parameters for the report, click the View Report button to generate the report.

The Most Common Events by Computer report is shown in Figure 7-10.

The report shown in Figure 7-10 is only an example of a MOM report; different reports will have different parameters to be configured (e.g., some of the performance reports will have computer groups and performance counter names). However, the principle for report generation is the same for all reports; you enter the required parameters and click the View Report button.

Once you have generated the MOM report, you may choose to export the report to a file or configure the report to e-mail to a recipient. The report can then be viewed offline. We will be looking at the process of exporting a MOM report in the next section.

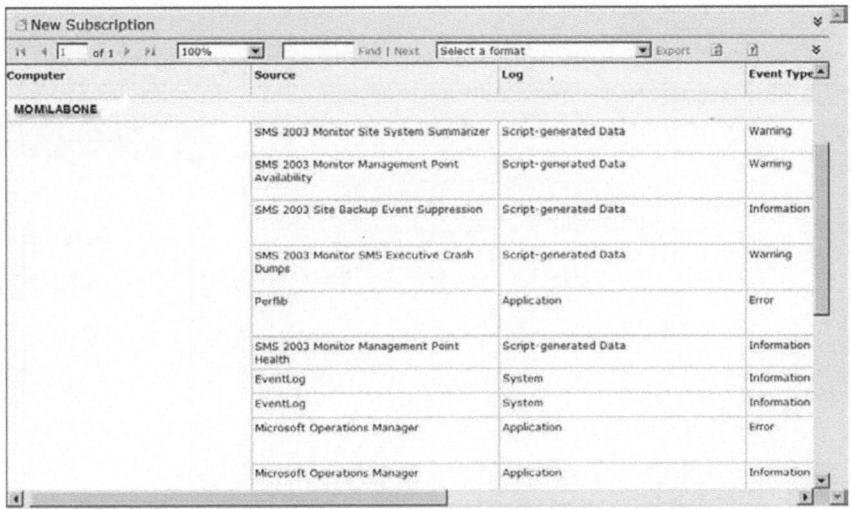

Figure 7-10. *The MOM Most Common Events by Computer report*

Exporting MOM Reports

MOM reports can be exported into any one of several formats. Following is the list of formats, with an explanation for each.

HTML with Office Web Components: For web display

Excel: For raw data in a table format

Web archive: For web display

Acrobat (PDF) file: For printing/distributing

TIFF file: For printing/distributing

CSV (comma delimited): For raw text data separated with a delimiter (not often used)

XML file with report data: For raw XML data (not often used)

In order to export a report, click the down arrow next to the field showing a default value of "Select a format," and then select the desired format from the drop-down list.

After you click the icon next to the Export label, you will be prompted to save or open this file, as shown in Figure 7-11.

Of course, being able to export reports by hand is a nice feature, but it does involve some manual intervention. The next section of the chapter will look at how you can get the best out of SQL Server Reporting Services by using report subscriptions to generate MOM reports automatically.

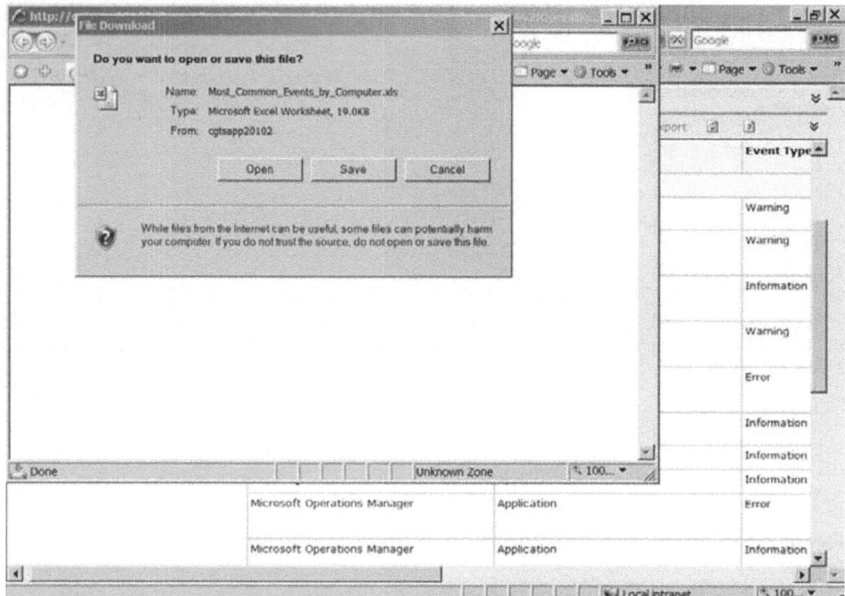

Figure 7-11. *Exporting a MOM report*

Report Subscriptions

Report subscriptions are SQL Server Reporting Services features that allow reports to be generated automatically according to a schedule using the SQL Server Agent and SQL Agent jobs. Reports can be configured not only to generate automatically, but also to send the generated files to a location on disk or an e-mail recipient, for example.

■**Note** The report e-mail subscriptions will only work correctly provided that SQL Server Reporting Services is configured to send SMTP e-mails. This is covered in this section.

Configuring Reporting Services to Send SMTP E-mails

In order for report subscriptions to be configured for sending reports to an e-mail address, you must configure the SMTP server address for SQL Server Reporting Services. You can configure that address during Reporting Services setup, or you can configure it later using the process described in this section.

If the SMTP server settings have not been configured during setup, you will need to configure them manually in the report server configuration file. This file is called RSReportServer.config, and can be found in the C:\Program Files\Microsoft SQL Server\MSSQL\Reporting Services\ReportServer directory.

Open the file using WordPad, and you will be presented with an XML-based configuration file.

Find and take a look at the following code section:

```
<RSEmailDPConfiguration>
    <SMTPServer>192.168.150.11</SMTPServer>
    <SMTPServerPort></SMTPServerPort>
    <SMTPAccountName></SMTPAccountName>
```

The server address of the SMTP server should be input between <SMTPServer> and </SMTPServer>. The SMTPServerPort does not need to be entered unless it is different from the default port (25). The SMTPAccountName value will need to be added if there is a particular account that is required to authenticate to the SMTP server—provided that the MOM Reporting server is allowed to relay SMTP e-mails through the SMTP e-mail server. In most environments that I have come across, it is not necessary to enter this value.

Edit the file, enter your settings, and then simply save the file and restart the ReportServer service.

Using Report Subscriptions

In order to configure a report subscription, open a report and navigate to the Subscriptions tab. You are shown two options: New Subscription and New Data Driven Subscription. We will look at data-driven subscriptions in more detail in Chapter 8.

Click New Subscription, and you will be presented with the screen shown in Figure 7-12. This screen applies to report subscriptions configured to e-mail. The screen is different for report subscriptions configured to send to a network location. We will look at this is greater detail later on.

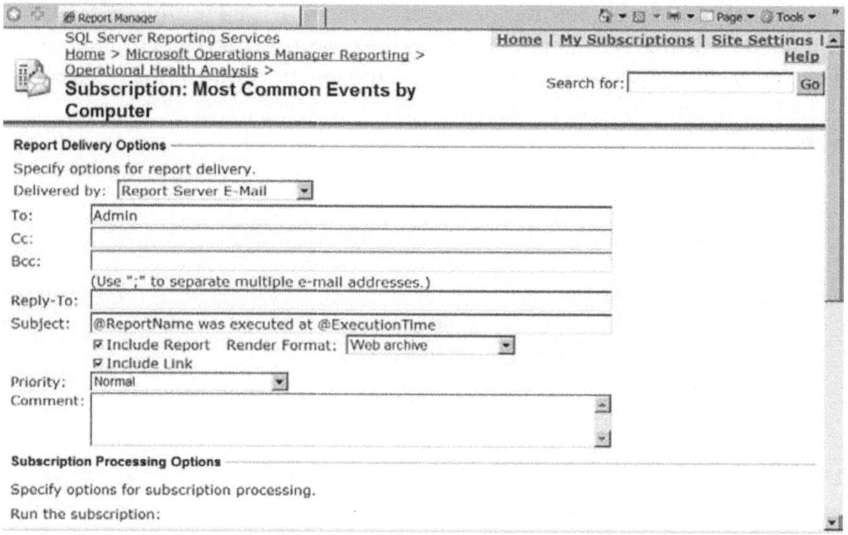

Figure 7-12. *Report subscription properties (e-mail subscription)*

Following is the list of report delivery options, subscription processing options, and report parameter values. Each option comes with a brief explanation on what it is or does. The report delivery options are as follows:

Delivered by: The delivery method for the report. Set to Report Server E-mail. It can also be set to Report Server File Share. (This option will be discussed later in the section.)

To, Cc, Bcc: Enter the recipient addresses for the e-mail.

Reply-To: Enter the e-mail addresses to which the reply is sent.

Subject: Enter the subject line for the e-mail. The default value is "@ReportName was executed at @ExecutionTime."

Include Report: Choose whether to attach the report to the e-mail (assuming you have selected e-mail as the delivery method).

Render Format: Choose the render format for the report (see the "Exporting MOM Reports" section of this chapter for information on report export formats).

Include Link: Choose whether to attach a link to the cached report to the e-mail (assuming you have selected e-mail as the delivery method).

Priority: Select the priority setting for the e-mail.

Comment: Add comments if required (these comments will appear in the e-mail description).

The subscription processing options are as follows:

Select Schedule: Create a schedule for the report to run. Click the Select Schedule button to open a submenu to open the schedule selection dialog box.

The report parameter values will vary from report to report since all reports include different parameters. Enter values for the appropriate parameters as required.

Once you have entered values for all parameters, click OK and the subscription will be visible in both the Subscriptions tab in the report and as a SQL job (listed as a GUID) in SQL Enterprise Manager, as shown in Figure 7-13.

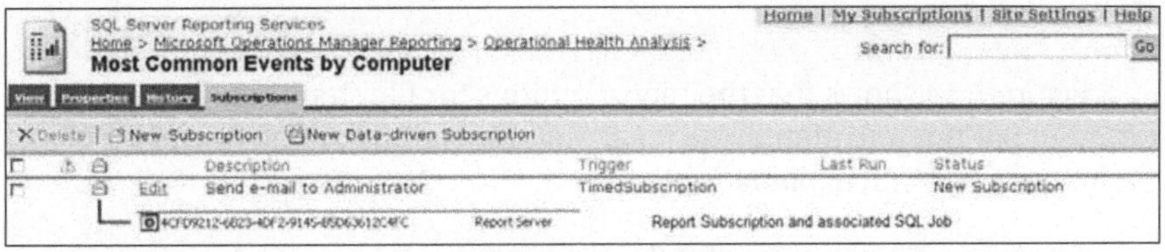

Figure 7-13. *The report subscription and associated SQL job*

Once a subscription has been created, the report will run at the scheduled time and e-mail the exported report file in the form of an attachment to the e-mail addresses specified in the report subscription properties.

If you select Report Server File Share from the Delivered by drop-down list in the report subscription properties window, the page will reload and display as shown in Figure 7-14.

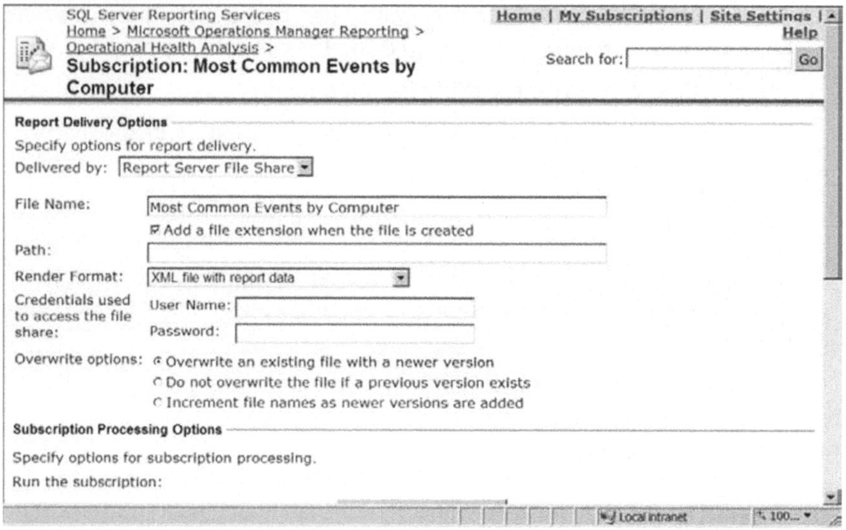

Figure 7-14. *The report subscription properties screen, with the Report Server File Share option selected*

Figure 7-14 shows that the report options for file share subscription have different parameters than those for e-mail subscription. Here is the list of parameters, with an explanation for each:

File Name: Enter a name for the file here.

Path: Use the parameter to specify the location of the file using a universal/uniform naming convention (UNC) path format (e.g., \\server1\share1).

Credentials used to access the file share: Enter the user account to be used to access the file share here, in the format domain\username.

Overwrite options: Specify whether to overwrite a file, leave the old file in place, or increment the files.

The parameters for subscription processing options and report parameter values for the file share subscription are the same as those for the e-mail subscription.

Summary

This chapter has covered the basics of MOM Reporting, including the generation of MOM reports and the configuration of report subscriptions to facilitate automated generation of reports.

In the next chapter, we will look more deeply at MOM Reporting, covering topics such as the creation of data-driven subscriptions and custom MOM reports.

CHAPTER 8

■ ■ ■

Advanced and Custom Reporting

MOM Reporting is an extremely powerful tool out of the box. However, to ensure that MOM provides the reports you need to suit your environment, the creation of custom reports may be necessary.

This chapter will cover the creation of reports in more detail and will also look at other more advanced aspects of MOM Reporting, such as data-driven subscriptions, which are subscriptions that allow the generation of multiple reports simultaneously.

Creation of Custom Reports

This section will look at the process for creating custom reports for MOM in SQL Server Reporting Services. We will create a custom CPU performance counter report as an example that can be used later in the chapter for the creation of a data-driven subscription. The differences between creating a performance report and an event report will also be looked at in this section.

In order to author reports in SQL Server Reporting Services, you must have Visual Studio .NET 2003 installed for SQL Server Reporting Services 2000, and Visual Studio 2005 installed for SQL Server Reporting Services 2005. I also strongly recommend that the MOM SDK be installed before you attempt to create a custom MOM report—this will facilitate the custom report creation through the SQL views that it creates. More information on the MOM SDK can be found in Chapter 11. The instructions in this chapter assume that the SDK has been installed.

For this section's example, we will use assume that SQL Server Reporting Services 2005 is being used, so we have installed Visual Studio 2005.

Note For all examples in this chapter, we will assume that SQL Server 2005 is being used. However, if you are using SQL Server 2000, then any reference to SQL Server Management Studio can be interpreted to mean SQL Server Enterprise Manager. Also be aware, however, that some of the menu options differ between SQL Server 2005 and SQL Server 2000, so some alterations to the instructions may be necessary.

In this chapter, you will also create a custom event report using Visual Studio 2005. Please be aware that this chapter is not a guide to using Visual Studio 2005. Experience with this product or a previous version is essential before attempting to create a custom MOM report.

Before creating a report with Visual Studio, it is necessary to install the business intelligence components. In order to do this, insert the SQL Server 2005 CD and install the workstation and client components. This will load the necessary objects into Visual Studio to allow reports to be created.

Open Visual Studio and Select New ➤ Project from the File menu. From the Business Intelligence Projects project type, select Report Server Project (located in the upper-right corner of the window). You can also use the wizard to create a report—however, for this chapter, you will create a report using an existing MOM report as a template. This ensures that your new reports are similar in appearance to the existing MOM reports that are included as part of a management pack. The project selection screen is shown in Figure 8-1.

Once the report project is opened, it is necessary for you to create a data source for the project to connect to the SystemCenterReporting database. This is necessary because the report gathers the required data from the database, and therefore requires a connection to the database during creation. The data source should be configured as shown in Figure 8-2.

You should set the data source credentials to "Windows," since SQL authentication is not supported for any of the MOM databases.

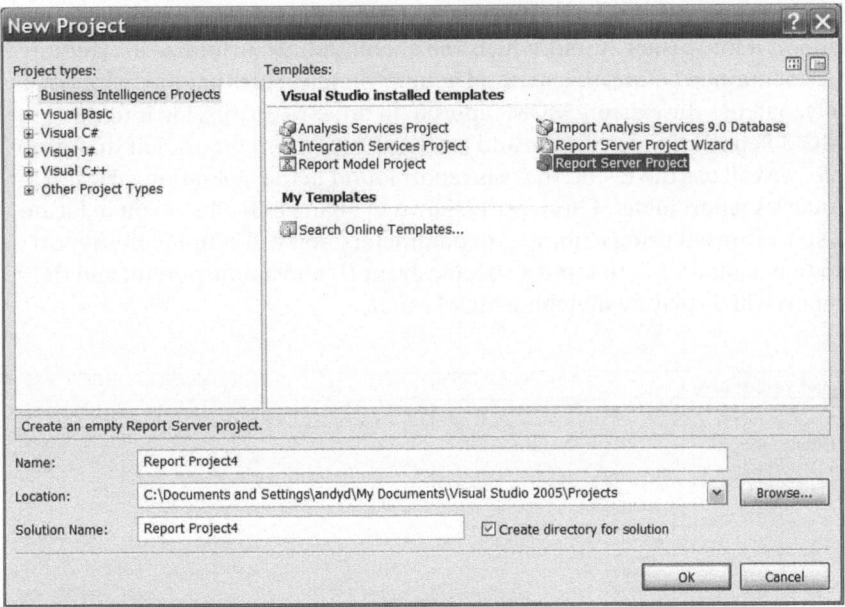

Figure 8-1. *Visual Studio 2005 project selection screen*

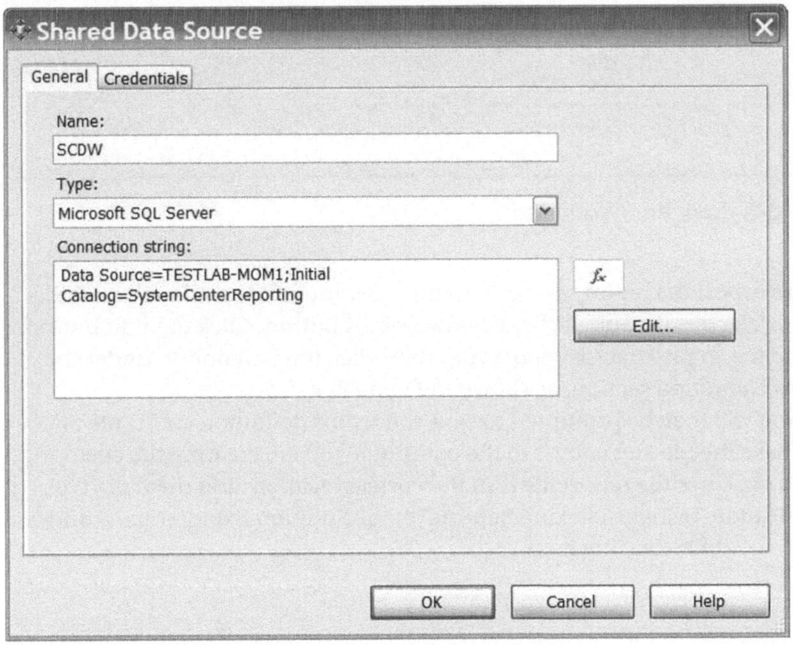

Figure 8-2. *Shared Data Source dialog*

Once the data source is created, copy an existing MOM event report and import it into Visual Studio, which will enable you to customize it as required (as mentioned before, this method allows you to ensure that the report visually matches the existing MOM reports). In order to do this, log into the MOM Reporting web console and locate a MOM event report. For this example, we will use the Event Analysis report found in the Operational Health Analysis report folder. This report (shown in Figure 8-3) allows you to locate a specific event using a number of parameters. You will simplify this report so that it allows you to input a specific event ID and a time period, and the report will display all matching MOM events.

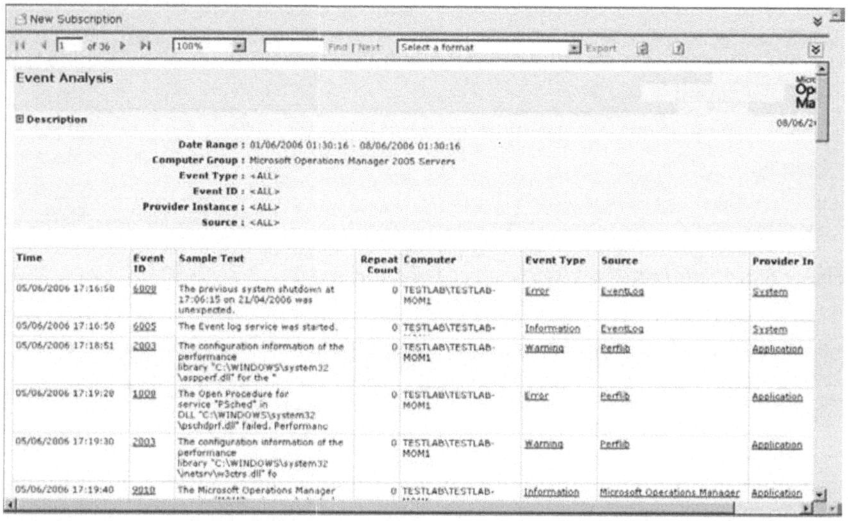

Figure 8-3. *Event Analysis report*

To export the report, navigate to the Operational Health Analysis folder in the web console, and click the Show Details button. Click the Edit button next to the Event Analysis report, and then click the Edit option under the Report Definition section, as shown in Figure 8-4.

You will then be prompted to save the report definition (.rdl) file to disk. Save the file and copy it to the computer you are creating the custom report on. Once the report file is in the correct location, add the report to Visual Studio by right-clicking Reports on the Solution Explorer pane and selecting Add ➤ Existing item.

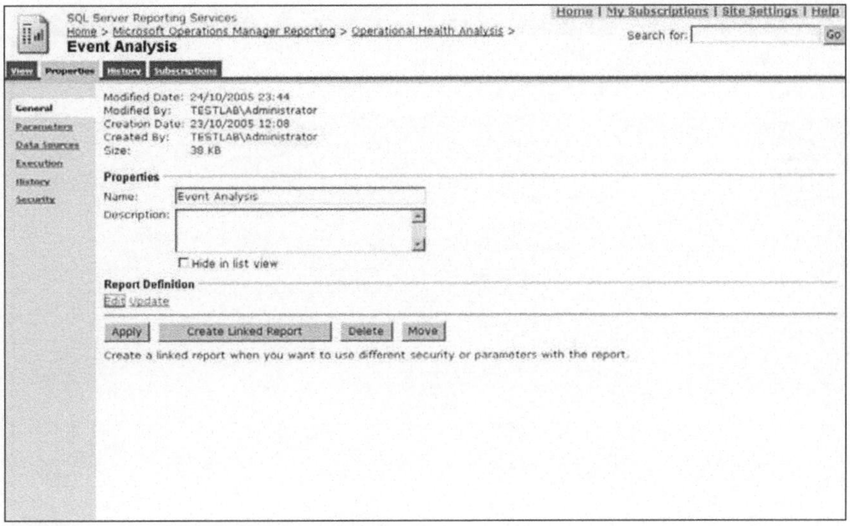

Figure 8-4. *Report definition screen*

Now that you have the template report, you will modify the report to remove all the input options except for the option to enter the event ID. First, you must remove the report parameters that are not required. Open the report and click in the report window.

■**Note** If you are prompted to convert the .rdl file, click Yes. This may happen if you are using Visual Studio 2005 to modify the reports.

You should now see a Report menu appear in the menu bar. Navigate to Report ➤ Report Parameters. The screen shown in Figure 8-5 will be displayed. This screen contains the report parameters that you need to modify.

You will be removing the parameters that are not required. You should remove the following parameters: CompGroup, EventType, PIName, Source, SortBy, and Direction.

Once you have removed the unwanted parameters, you need to modify the properties of the EventID parameter. Select the EventID parameter, click the Non-queried radio button in the Available values section, and click the Null radio button in the Default values section. Finally, click OK to save the changes.

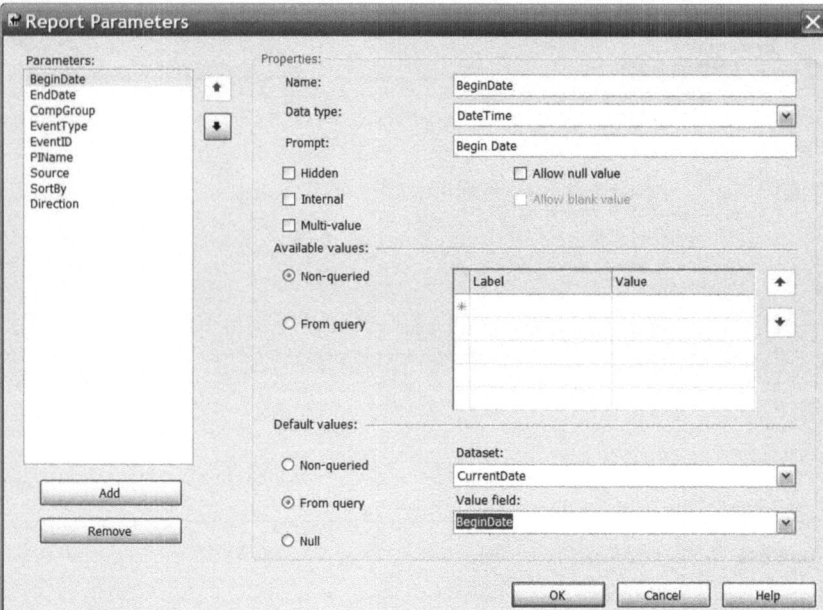

Figure 8-5. *Visual Studio 2005 Report Parameters dialog*

Next, you need to remove some of the unwanted items in the report itself. The items shown in Figure 8-6 should be removed and the report tidied up to fill in the gaps.

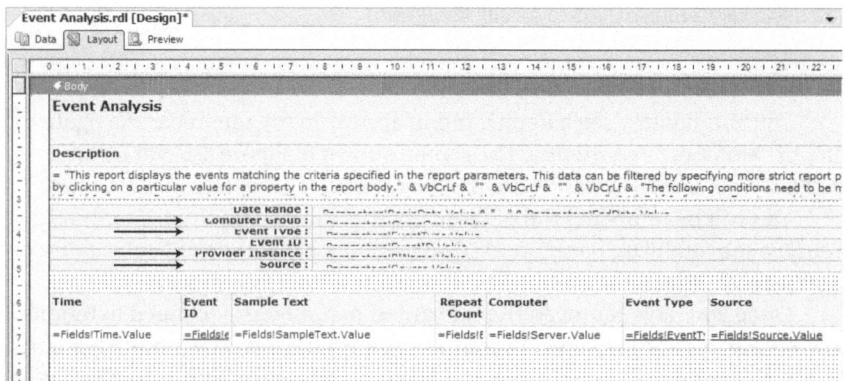

Figure 8-6. *Items to remove from the report*

Once you have removed the unwanted items and tidied the report layout as required, you need to modify the SQL query that gathers the data. Click the Data tab at the top of the report to display the data screen. Just as you removed the unwanted parameters, you now need to remove the unwanted datasets. Figure 8-7 shows a list of datasets from the drop-down list on the Data tab.

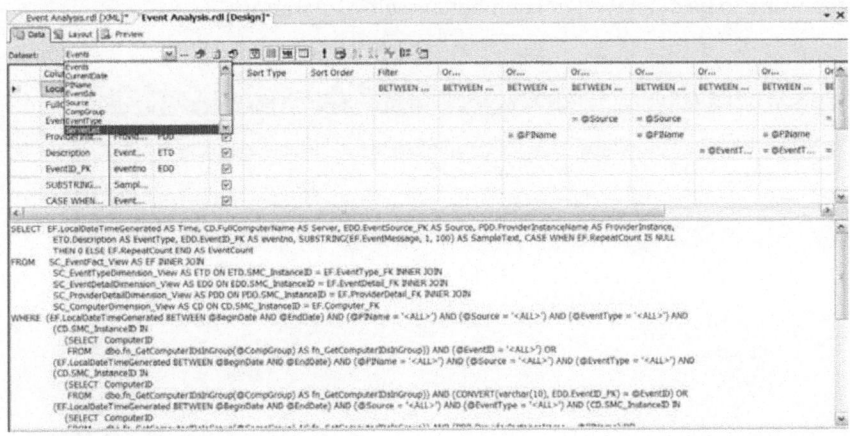

Figure 8-7. *Dataset drop-down list*

Remove the following datasets: Events, PIName, Source, CompGroup, EventType, and ServerList. Then change the query executed by the EventID dataset to this:

```
Select ComputerName, Message, NTEventID, Source,
TimeGenerated, RepeatCount
FROM SDKEventView
WHERE (TimeGenerated > @BeginDate)
AND (TimeGenerated < @EndDate)
AND NTEventID = @EventID
```

Finally, you need to change the main report to display only the information you require. Remove the following columns from the main table in the report: Event Type, Provider Instance, Source, and Repeat Count. Then change the Sample Text column name to Event Description. You now need to change the table properties to point to the correct dataset. In the Table Properties dialog box, change the dataset from Events to EventID.

The final thing you need to do before previewing the report is change the data fields in the table to display the correct data. To do this, open the properties dialog for each of the data fields—you can tell which fields are the data fields because they contain an expression, which means they start with an equals symbol (=). In the properties dialog for the data field (shown in Figure 8-8), change the data in the Value drop-down list to the data that should be displayed in the field. We will not cover each field in detail since the value to be displayed in each field is self-explanatory.

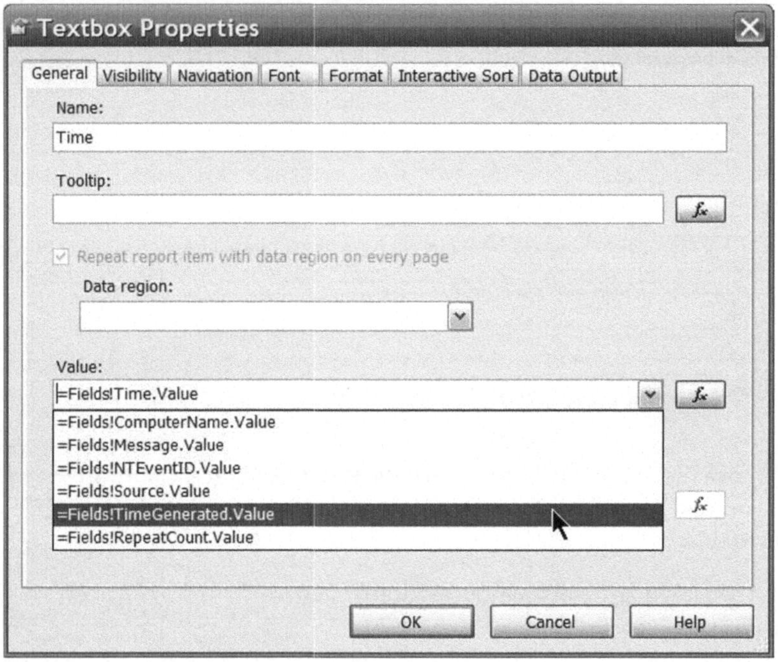

Figure 8-8. *Data field properties dialog*

Once you have done this, you need to change one final property in the EventID data field. In the properties dialog for the EventID data field, navigate to the Navigation tab and change Hyperlink Action to None.

The final thing you need to do . . . phew! . . . is change the sort order of the table. Open the Table Properties dialog and navigate to the Sorting tab. Configure the sort order to sort by ComputerName, and remove the second sort order (as shown in Figure 8-9).

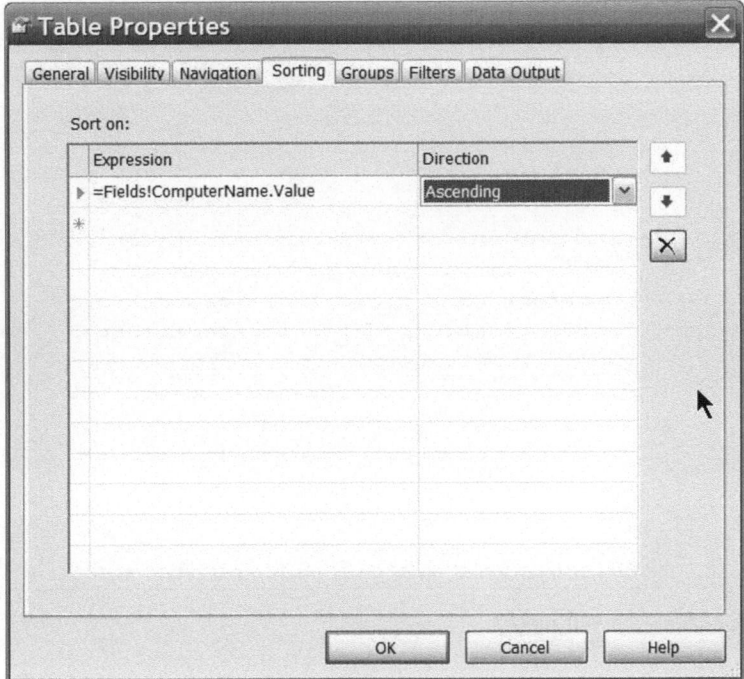

Figure 8-9. *Sorting tab in the Table Properties dialog*

Now that you have completed the reconfiguration of the report, click the Preview tab and enter a time period and an event ID. A report similar to the one shown in Figure 8-10 will be displayed. At this point, you can give the report a different name if you like by changing the name at the top of the report.

All you need to do now is to build the solution, which will create the .rdl file, and then import the file back into MOM Reporting using the MOM Reporting web console. Click Build ➤ Build Solution and, providing that the solution properties are correct, the solution will build and the report (.rdl) file will be created.

To import the report into MOM, copy the .rdl file to the reporting server and open the MOM Reporting web console. Navigate to the folder in which you wish to load the report, and click Upload Report. Browse to the report and click Upload. The report will now be visible and can be generated using the MOM Reporting web console.

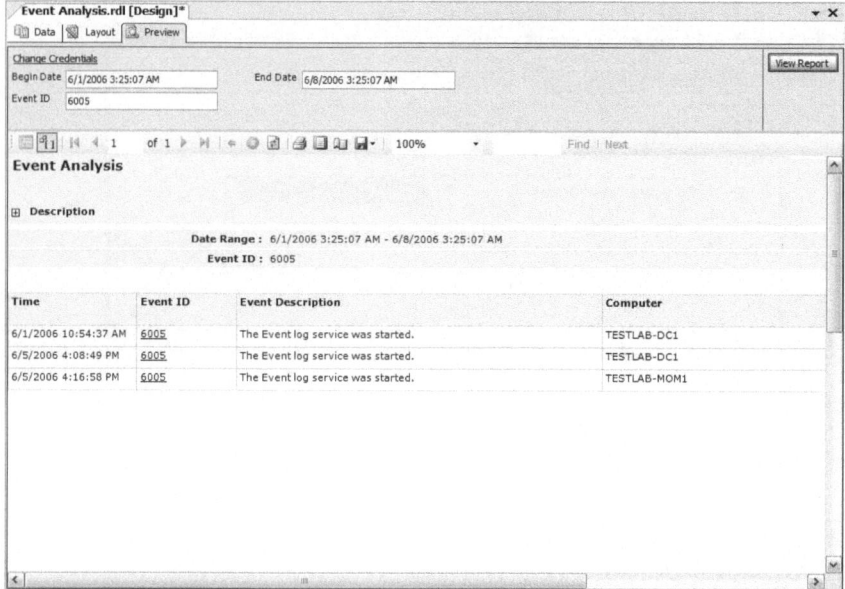

Figure 8-10. *Modified event report*

Data-Driven Subscriptions

Report subscriptions are used to automatically generate reports with a specified set of parameters. This feature is limited, however, since there may be a requirement to generate a report for a large number of computers. This would usually require the creation of a large number of report subscriptions, which would take considerable time and would be difficult to manage. In this case, data-driven subscriptions may be used to create a single report subscription that is able to execute multiple versions of the same report with different parameters. An example of this would be executing a CPU report for multiple machines.

Data-driven subscriptions work in a similar way to standard report subscriptions, except that the report parameters are not stored in the subscription, but are instead located within a small SQL Server database. Instead of the report parameters, the subscription contains connection information for the database that contains the parameters.

The SQL Server database consists of a separate table for each set of parameters (each report). The table contains a single column per parameter, with the column title being the name of the parameter.

Take, for example, the fact that you may want to generate a CPU report for a number of servers. You would not necessarily want to generate these reports one at a time, as this would be very time consuming. You would therefore create a data-driven subscription for CPU usage on a group of servers to combat this problem.

Note It is *very important* to note that, out of the box, the MOM reports do not support the creation of data-driven subscriptions, due to the fact that they carry out SQL queries within the reports to facilitate the use of drop-down lists in the reports. In order to customize a report for use with data-driven subscriptions, refer back to the Creation of Custom Reports section earlier in the chapter.

Assuming you have a custom report created that will allow you to generate a data-driven subscription, you must first look at the report and note the parameters that the report requires so that you can add them into the report subscription database. For this example, a custom CPU Report should be used. This can be created in a similar fashion to how the custom event report was created in this chapter.

Once you have identified the parameters required by the report, the report subscriptions database can be created. In order to create and populate the database, you must first manually create it using SQL Server Management Studio. Let's call it SQL_Report_Params. Once the database is created, you have two options: you can either create a table to hold the CPU report parameters or you can copy and paste the following SQL query and modify as required to reflect your environment. For this example, we will assume the table is called CPU_Report:

```
Use SQL_Report_Params
CREATE TABLE [dbo].[CPU_Report] (
    [Param1] [int] NOT NULL PRIMARY KEY ,
    [Param2] [int] ,
    [Param3] [nvarchar] (50) NOT NULL ,
    [Param4] [bit],
    [Param5] [nvarchar] (20) NOT NULL ,
) ON [PRIMARY]
GO
```

After the table has been created and fully populated, data-driven subscriptions can be created. The following INSERT statements are an example of what an INSERT statement might look like. Modify the test data in the columns to suit your environment.

```
INSERT INTO [dbo].[UserInfo] (SubscriptionID, EmployeeID,
LastName, FileType, Format)
VALUES ('1', '289', 'Valdez', '1', 'IMAGE')
INSERT INTO [dbo].[UserInfo] (SubscriptionID, EmployeeID,
LastName, FileType, Format)
VALUES ('2', '284', 'Alberts', '1', 'MHTML')
INSERT INTO [dbo].[UserInfo] (SubscriptionID, EmployeeID,
LastName, FileType, Format)
VALUES ('3', '275', 'Blythe', '1', 'PDF')
GO
```

Once the database is created and all of the parameters have been entered into the columns in the CPU_Report table, the data-driven subscription can be created.

Open the Report Server web page and navigate to the custom report created earlier. Click the Subscriptions tab and select New Data Driven Subscription from the top bar.

The first screen of the wizard, shown in Figure 8-11, allows you to specify a description for the report, as well as the method for the reports to be distributed: Report Server File Share, E-mail, or Null Delivery (not delivered). You also specify the data source to the reporting database from here. Here you should select "Specify for this subscription only."

Note You could also create a custom data source and select it from here.

Once you have specified a custom data source, the screen shown in Figure 8-12 will appear, on which you can configure the connection type, the connection string, and the Connect Using account settings. The connection type should be Microsoft SQL Server and the connection string should be Data Source=<SQL Server>; Initial Catalog=SQL_Report_Params. This will connect to the parameters database to obtain the report parameters. Under Connect Using, the "Credentials stored securely in the report server" radio button should be selected. An account with sufficient permissions to read from the SQL_Report_Params database should be specified in the format domain\username. You may also select the "Use as Windows credentials . . ." check box if the account is a domain user account and not a SQL Server user account.

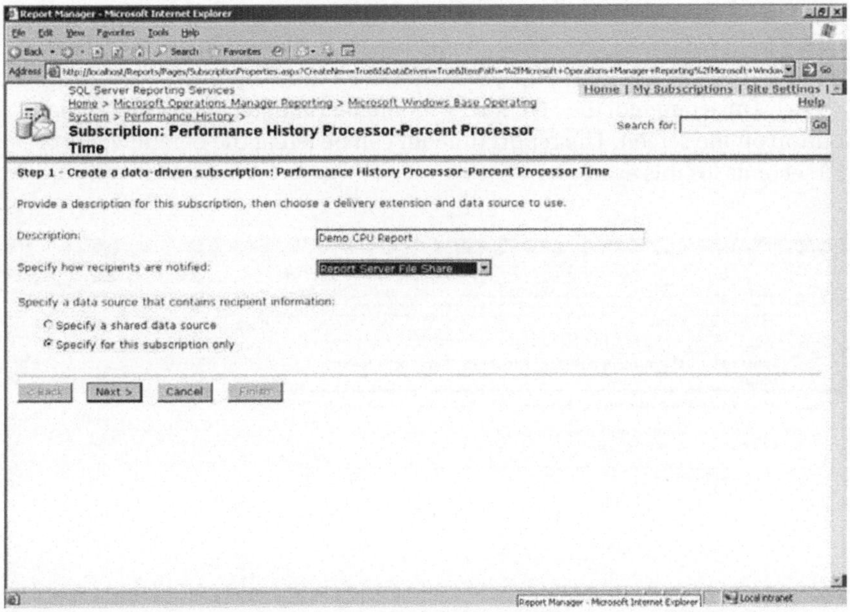

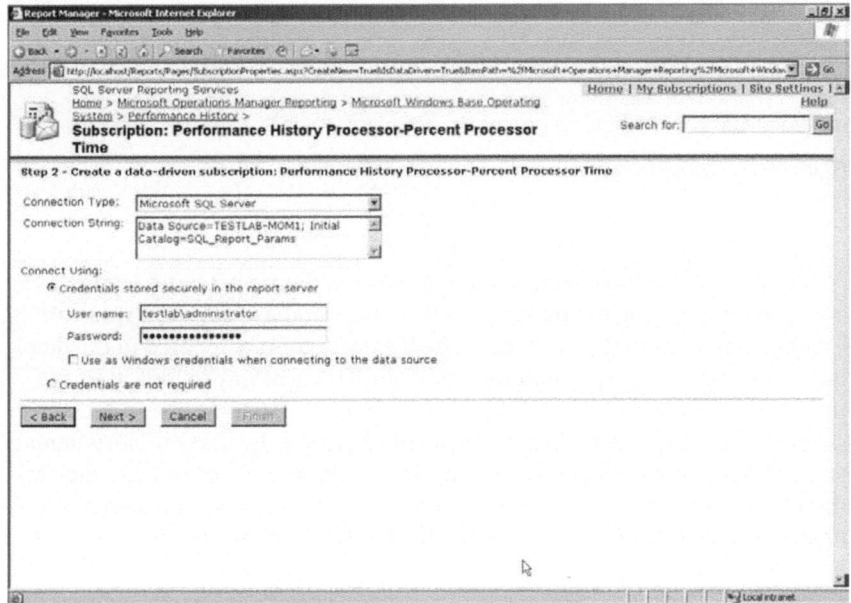

Figure 8-11. *Data-driven subscription wizard, screen 1*

Figure 8-12. *Data-driven subscription wizard, screen 2*

On the next wizard screen (shown in Figure 8-13), you specify the SQL query from which the report parameter data is retrieved. To retrieve the data for this example, the following query should be used: SELECT * FROM CPU_ Report. Once entered, the SQL query should be validated using the Validate button on the screen. The report timeout can be left at the default value of 30 seconds for this example.

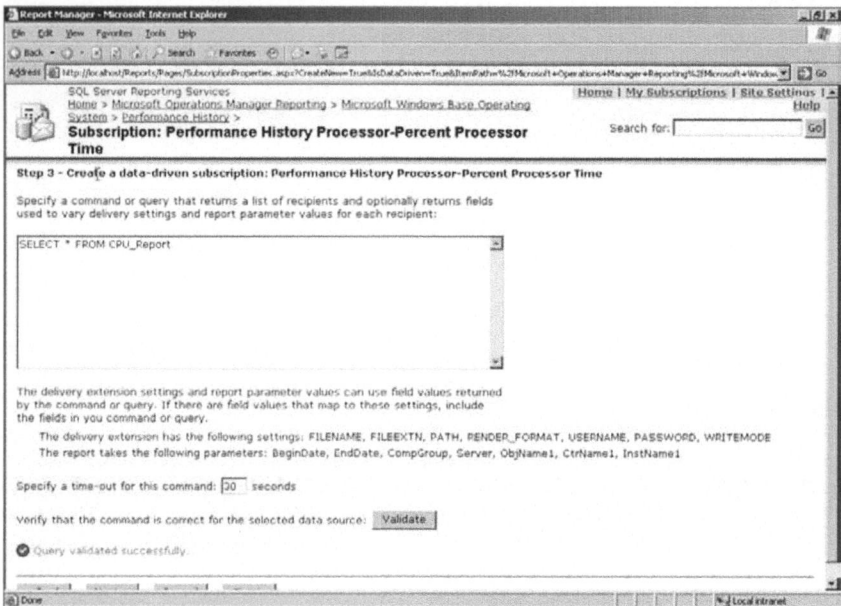

Figure 8-13. *Data-driven subscription wizard, screen 3*

After the query is validated, click Next.

The following two wizard screens (shown in Figure 8-14 and Figure 8-15) are used for mapping the parameters from the database back to the report. It is in these screens that you specify which parameters are located in the database and which should be entered manually. The best way to look at this is that any parameter that will change for each report (such as computer group) should be entered into and selected from the database table; whereas values such as the performance counter for a report will not change and can therefore be manually entered in this wizard screen. This simply reduces the need to duplicate information inside the database table in the report parameters database.

The screen shown in Figure 8-14 is used to specify the report generation settings (such as File name and Render Format). This defines how the report will actually be generated, and has no bearing on the data in the report.

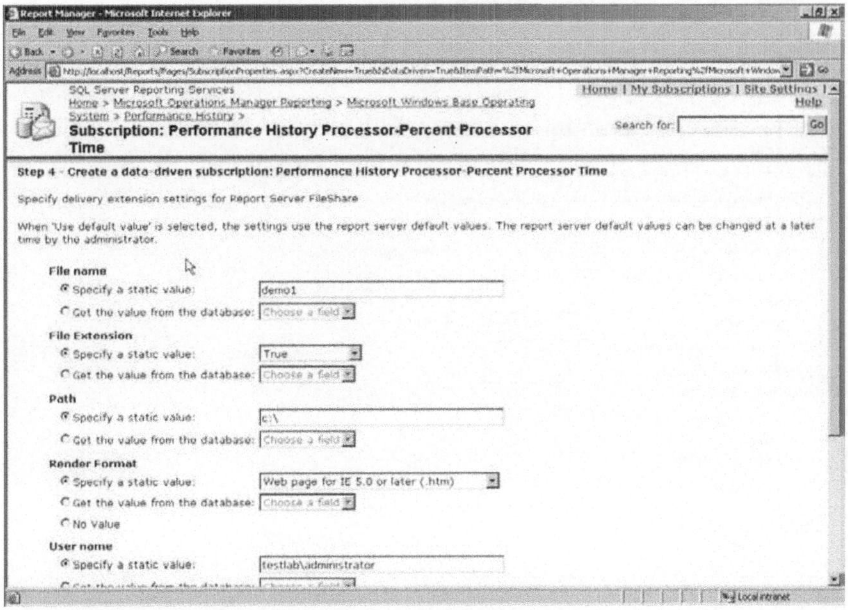

Figure 8-14. *Data-driven subscription wizard, screen 4*

The next of the two screens (shown in Figure 8-15) is where the actual parameters for the report are entered (if required). The parameters that will change per report should be read from the parameters database, whereas the static parameters should be entered manually to prevent duplication of data in the parameters database.

The next wizard screen is where the schedule for the report is specified. It is here that you define when the report should be run. The report can be run every time the data is updated on the report server (this will happen nightly after the DTS package has completed) or according to a schedule that you specify (recommended). If you select the option to specify a schedule and click Next, you will be presented with the screen shown in Figure 8-16, which allows you to specify the details for the schedule.

Finally, click Finish to create the data-driven subscription.

When the report executes according to the schedule, a number of reports will be created and named according to the option you specified in the report generation parameter options in the wizard. As you will see (if you have configured the subscription as defined in this example), each report gives the same performance counter for a different agent machine.

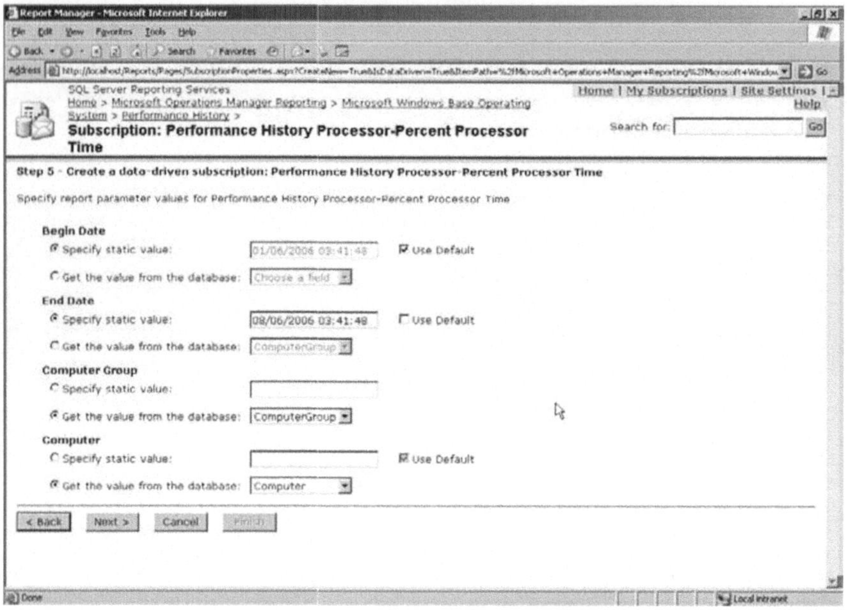

Figure 8-15. *Data-driven subscription wizard, screen 5*

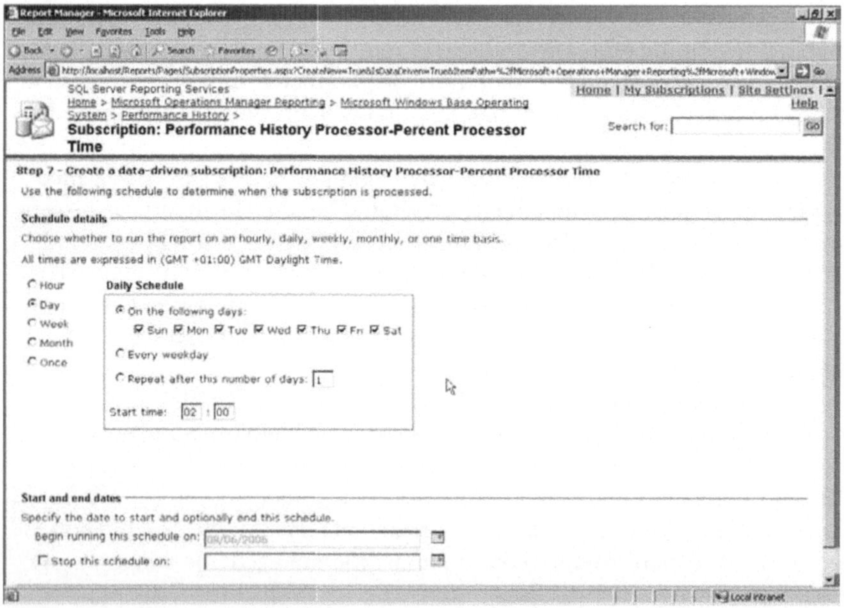

Figure 8-16. *Data-driven subscription wizard, screen 6*

Summary

In this chapter, we have looked at the method for creating custom reports to enable you to generate MOM reports that are appropriate to your environment. We have also looked at the basics for creating data-driven subscriptions to allow you to configure your report subscriptions to generate multiple reports under a single schedule.

In the next chapter, we will look at the MOM DTS package, which is used to transfer data from the operational (OnePoint) database to the MOM Reporting database (SystemCenterReporting). We will also show you how to troubleshoot issues with the DTS package in the next chapter.

CHAPTER 9

■■■

The DTS Package

In this chapter, we will look at the MOM DTS data transfer package, including what it does and its importance. We will also cover the configuration of the package and provide troubleshooting steps to follow in the case that it fails.

The OnePoint database should be optimized for writes, and the size and amount of data should be kept to a minimum to allow the database to function efficiently. For this reason, you need to utilize the SystemCenterReporting database.

The MOM Reporting DTS package is used by MOM to transfer data from the OnePoint (operational) database to the SystemCenterReporting (archive datawarehouse) database. The MOM DTS package consists of an executable that is run by a Windows scheduled task (found on the MOM Reporting Server) daily at 1:00 a.m. by default. The executable generates a SQL DTS package on the fly, which then ships data from OnePoint to SystemCenterReporting via the SQL server's TempDB database. The scheduled task is shown in Figure 9-1.

You need to ensure that the MOM DTS package is operating correctly in a working environment, since by archiving old data from the OnePoint database to the SystemCenterReporting database, the OnePoint database is kept small and streamlined, thus improving the performance of MOM.

The MOM DTS package dataflow is shown in Figure 9-2.

If the DTS package fails, you will see sluggish MOM performance and database issues with the OnePoint database. The OnePoint database has a maximum supported size of 30 GB—however, the database should never be allowed to exceed 18 GB, since at this point there will not be sufficient space to perform a SQL database reindex, which is very important to maintain the health of any SQL database.

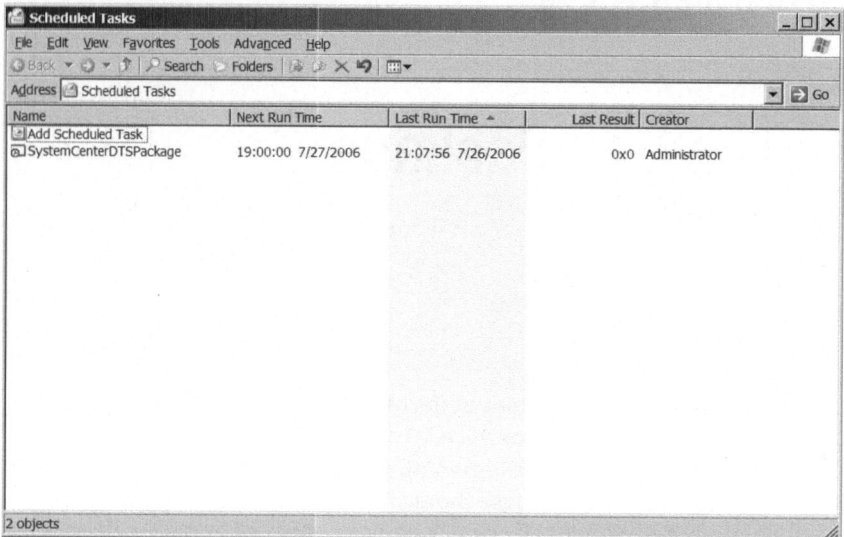

Figure 9-1. *The DTS package scheduled task*

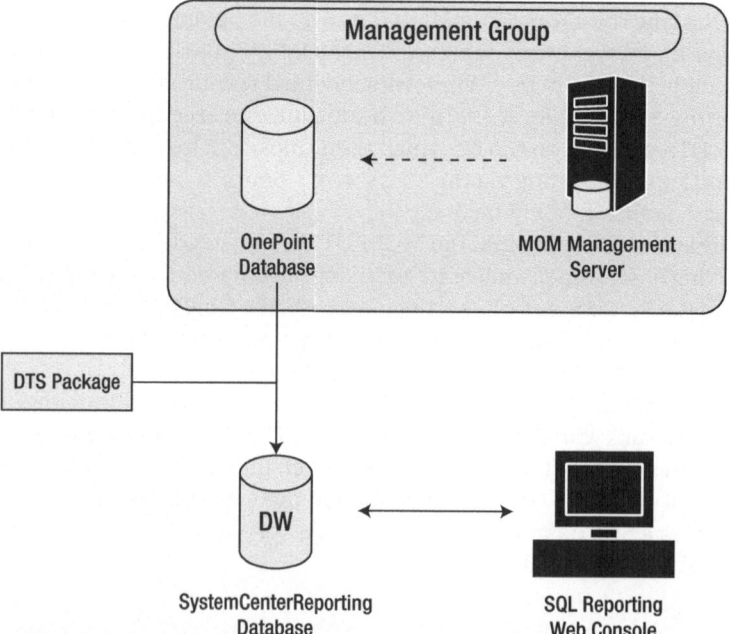

Figure 9-2. *DTS package dataflow*

Configuration of the DTS Package

Although the DTS package is run from a Windows scheduled task automatically, it may be necessary to run it manually from the command line on the MOM Reporting Server. This situation will usually arise when the DTS package has been failing and there is more than a single day's data to transfer from OnePoint to SystemCenterReporting.

In order to run the DTS package from the command line, you will need to browse to the location of the MOM.Datawarehousing.DTSPackageGenerator. exe file. You can find this file in the %Program Files%\Microsoft System Center Reporting\Reporting\ folder on the MOM Reporting Server.

At the command prompt, you can run the MOM.Datawarehousing. DTSPackageGenerator.exe file with the appropriate command-line parameters, which are listed in Table 9-1.

Table 9-1. *DTS Package Command-Line Parameters*

Parameter	Description
/silent	This switch is optional and runs the DTS package in silent (non-interactive) mode.
/srcserver	This is the server hosting the OnePoint database.
/srcdb	This is the name of the source database (OnePoint).
/dwserver	This is the server hosting the SystemCenterReporting database.
/dwdb	This is the name of the MOM datawarehouse database (SystemCenterReporting).
/product	This denotes the product for which you are transferring data; it should be set to "Microsoft Operations Manager."
/latency	This allows the transmission of small amounts of data for troubleshooting purposes. It is explained later in the section.
/chunk	This allows the transmission of small amounts of data for troubleshooting purposes. It is explained later in the section.

Note All parameters, with the exception of the /silent switch, are required for correct operation of the DTS package.

The final command should look like the command shown in Figure 9-3.

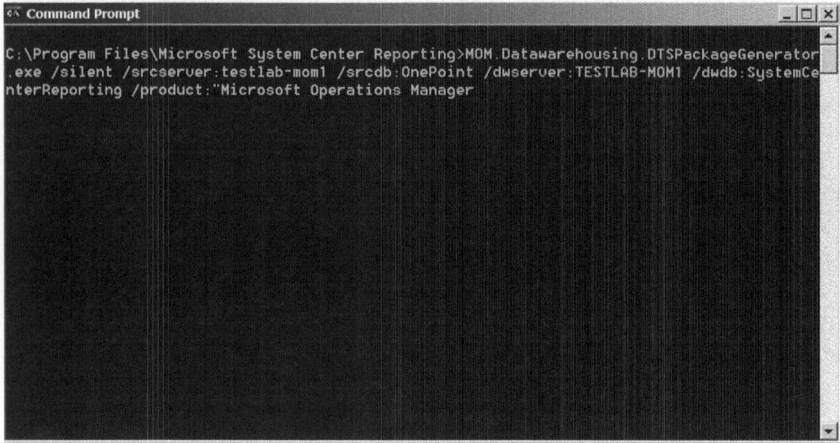

Figure 9-3. *The full MOM DTS package command*

There is one additional command-line parameter (two parameters in MOM SP1) that can be added to allow the transfer of sections of data from the OnePoint database to the SystemCenterReporting database. The /latency switch (and the /chunk switch in SP1) can be used to select sections of data to be transferred. The /latency switch is explained later in the chapter.

Monitoring the DTS Package

Because the correct operation of the DTS package is so essential to the proper operation of MOM, it is necessary to monitor the DTS package to ensure that it is consistently successful, and to identify any issues as soon after they occur as possible. In the following section, we will look at methods for monitoring the DTS package to ensure that it is working correctly.

The Microsoft Operations Manager Management Pack (installed by default) contains a rule to alert when the DTS package fails. The rule location is shown in Figure 9-4.

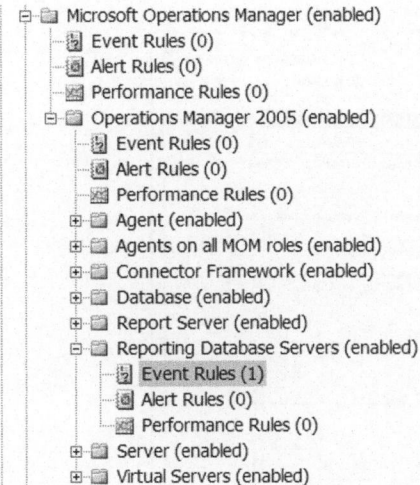

Figure 9-4. *The MOM DTS package failed rule location*

The rule is configured to look for a specific event in the event log of the
MOM Reporting Server. The rule details and criteria are shown in Figure 9-5.

The rule is configured to look for an event with a source of `MOM.`
`Datawarehousing.DTSPackageGenerator.exe` and an event ID of 1001, which
indicates a failure in the DTS package. This rule will generate an alert with
a severity of "Error" in the MOM Operator Console.

In addition to the built-in rule to detect DTS package failures, you need
to create at least one custom rule to generate an alert with a severity of
"Success" when the DTS package executes successfully.

To create this rule, refer to Chapter 5, which explains this rule in detail
and gives instructions on creating it.

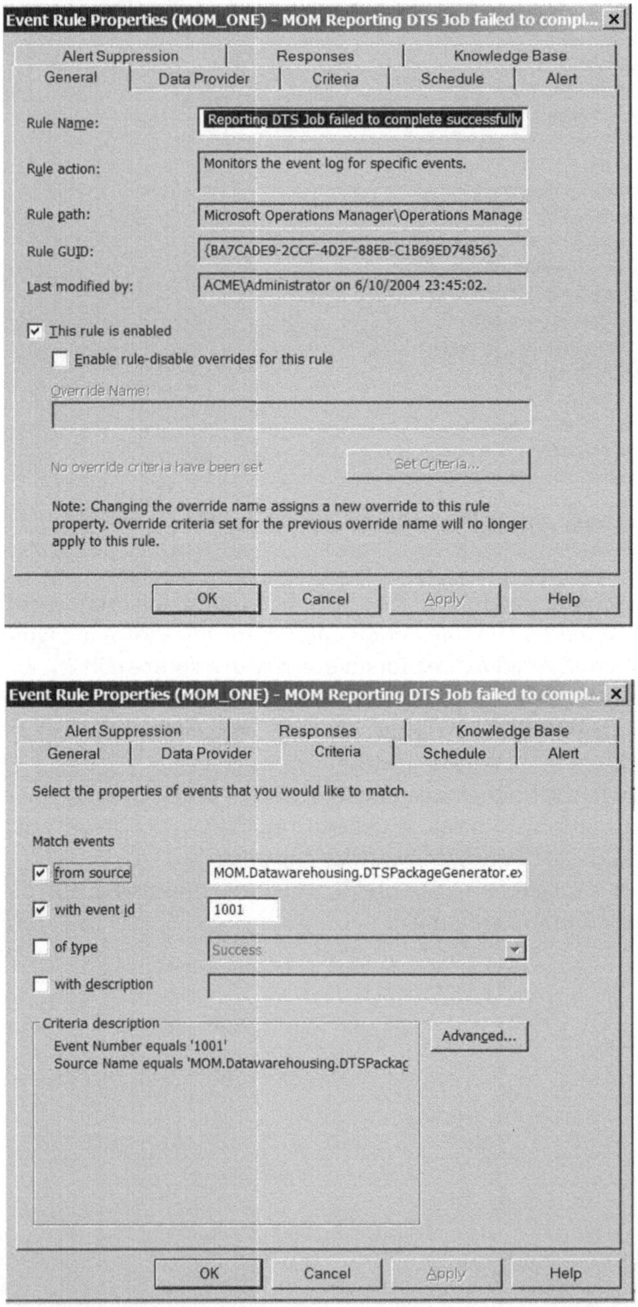

Figure 9-5. *MOM DTS failure rule details (top) and criteria (bottom)*

Troubleshooting Issues with the DTS Package

If your DTS package fails, it is important to address the issue immediately, as any delay could make the process of recovering from the problem more difficult. This is due to the fact that the DTS package runs more reliably when only transferring a small amount of data (a couple of GB maximum)—so, the more data you have to transfer, the more difficult the process becomes.

If you are unable to determine the last time that the DTS package successfully executed, you can run the following SQL query against the OnePoint database using SQL Query Analyzer or an equivalent tool:

```
SELECT * FROM GroomingSettings
```

The date in the TimeDTSLastRan column will indicate when the DTS package was last successfully executed.

Analyzing Event Log Entries

The first step to troubleshooting a DTS package failure is to analyze the event log entry that caused the failure alert to be generated. This can be looked at on the MOM Reporting Server itself or by inspecting the alert in the MOM Operator Console.

The event log entry has a very large description and is quite difficult to read. It is therefore important that you focus on the important information. This can usually be found at the end of the event log entry.

Common Causes of DTS Failure

Once the event log entry has been analyzed, troubleshooting can begin. Table 9-2 lists the common causes of DTS package failures and the basic steps to take to resolve them.

Table 9-2. *Common Failures of the DTS Package, and Resolution Steps*

Reason for Failure	Resolution Steps
The OnePoint/SystemCenterReporting and/or TempDB databases are out of space.	Increase the size of the affected database to compensate. It is worth noting that the TempDB database needs enough space to accommodate the entire DTS transfer (1.5 GB is usually sufficient as a starting point).

Continued

Table 9-2. *Continued*

Reason for Failure	Resolution Steps
The permissions on the scheduled task are incorrect or the user account has changed.	Change the account details on the scheduled task to an account with the appropriate permissions. The MOMDAS account usually has sufficient rights.
One or both of the SQL servers (the servers hosting OnePoint/ SystemCenterReporting) are unavailable.	Locate and resolve the cause of the server(s) being unavailable. This could be network related or an operating system failure.

As mentioned in Table 9-2, one of the common causes of DTS failure is insufficient space in one or more of the databases that are utilized during a MOM DTS transfer. The databases that are utilized during a DTS transfer include OnePoint, TempDB, and SystemCenterReporting. It is vitally important to ensure that the databases and log files have sufficient space to accommodate the data transfer prior to running the DTS package. I usually find that 1.5 GB of free space in TempDB is sufficient. It is expected that there will be considerably more free space already available in the OnePoint and SystemCenterReporting databases.

Note You may notice two additional databases on your MOM Reporting Server (ReportServer and ReportServerTempDB), depending on where SQL Server Reporting Services is installed. These databases are used to store reports and report subscriptions for SQL Server Reporting Services, and are not used during the MOM DTS transfer. For DTS troubleshooting, these databases can be ignored.

Usage of the /latency Switch

Once the issue has been identified and resolved, it may be necessary to transfer more than a single day of data (depending on how long the DTS package has been failing). If this is the case, the DTS package may need to be run manually to ensure that it runs correctly.

First, open a command prompt and browse to the `%Program Files%\ Microsoft System Center Reporting\Reporting\` folder. Copy the command line from the scheduled task (or from the "Configuration of the DTS Package" section earlier in this chapter) into the command prompt and replace the `/silent` switch with `/latency:x`, where x is the number of days since the DTS last ran successfully. For example, if the DTS package last ran successfully

4 days ago, then the switch would be /latency:4. After this has completed successfully, repeat with /latency:3, and then /latency:2, and so on, until you can run the DTS package normally without error.

Usage of the /chunksize and /maxchunks Switches (SP1 Only) and Their Relationships to the /latency Switch

The /chunksize switch is very similar to the /latency switch, and can be used in MOM SP1 instead of the /latency switch, as it offers an additional configuration option.

The /chunksize switch is configured with the chunk size in days. Data is processed in increments of the chunk size, thereby enabling transfer of a high volume of data with limited log space. Specifying 0 will not chunk the data. The /maxchunks switch is used to specify the maximum number of chunks to create when chunking is enabled.

Checking Data to Be Groomed

In order to help with identifying the amount of alert data to be transferred from OnePoint to SystemCenterReporting, you can query the OnePoint database to see how many alerts are awaiting transfer into the SystemCenterReporting database.

Run the following SQL query against the OnePoint database using SQL Query Analyzer or an equivalent tool:

```
SELECT COUNT(*) AS AlertsAwaitingGrooming
FROM dbo.Alert
WHERE (ResolutionState=255)
```

Grooming the SystemCenterReporting Database

The SystemCenterReporting database stores all archived MOM data, and therefore can grow to a large size (depending on the number of agents, number of rules, etc.). For that reason, database grooming is necessary.

The SystemCenterReporting database data is groomed according to age—it is currently not possible to groom it any other way. Therefore, it is important during the implementation of MOM to decide on the number of days of data you want to preserve. The default setting is 395 days, which may need to be changed to reflect your company's individual requirements.

If the default value of 395 days of data retention is not appropriate to your organization, it will be necessary to change the number of days of data that are retained in the SystemCenterReporting database.

Unfortunately, there is no GUI to make this change, and the change needs to be accomplished using a SQL query executed against the SystemCenterReporting database.

The following commands illustrate how to accomplish this.

To set the number of days for data retention within the SystemCenterReporting Database, run the following SQL script, where the @Groomdays variable is the number of days to retain data. In this example, the data is retained for 180 days.

```
--- Update the SystemCenterReporting data retention period
Declare @Groomdays int
--Retain data for 180 days
Select @Groomdays=180
exec p_updateGroomDays 'SC_SampledNumericDataFact_Table', @Groomdays
exec p_updateGroomDays 'SC_AlertFact_Table', @Groomdays
exec p_updateGroomDays 'SC_EventParameterFact_Table', @Groomdays
exec p_updateGroomDays 'SC_AlertToEventFact_Table', @Groomdays
exec p_updateGroomDays 'SC_EventFact_Table', @Groomdays
exec p_updateGroomDays 'SC_AlertHistoryFact_Table', @Groomdays
```

To check the current value for retention time, run the following SQL query:

```
select cs.cs_tablename 'Table Name', wcs.wcs_groomdays 'Groom Days'
from warehouseclassschema wcs
join classschemas cs on cs.cs_classID = wcs.wcs_classID
where cs.cs_tablename = 'SC_AlertFact_Table'
and wcs.wcs_mustbegroomed = 1
```

Replace the table name with the table you want to check.

Summary

In this chapter, we have looked at the importance of the MOM DTS package and how it relates to the rest of MOM. We have described how to configure the DTS package and also how to troubleshoot problems with it.

In the next chapter, we will look at the MOM Connector Framework, which allows MOM to connect to third-party management appliances and help desk systems, and also allows a MOM infrastructure to be created in a multitiered topology for enterprise scalability.

■ ■ ■

CHAPTER 10

Multitiered Management Groups

Many enterprises have servers in multiple geographical locations and require central monitoring of those servers. With MOM 2005, you can configure a multitiered management group that utilizes alert forwarding, which is a set of workflow processes designed to create a hierarchical systems management infrastructure.

Multitiered management groups can be used to achieve centralized monitoring. This type of monitoring is designed to forward only alerts, so it is very efficient, even for use by sites that do not have high bandwidth capacity. Alert forwarding enables management servers in one management group to send alerts to another management group, creating an efficient hierarchical alert management structure for large enterprise networks. This chapter will introduce you to the concepts and how to configure a multitiered management group.

This chapter covers the following:

- Design and installation of multitiered management groups
- Configuration of multitiered management groups
- Centralized reporting from multiple management groups

Multitiered Management Groups

Many organizations with servers in multiple geographical locations and with different support teams require a central view of their infrastructures. Multitiered management groups allow you to isolate monitoring activity according to logical business units or physical locations. Multitiered management groups can also be used if MOM is used to monitor an enterprise environment that is too large for a single management group. Multitiered management groups also maintain a centralized monitoring function.

Figure 10-1 shows the current infrastructure of a fictional company named ACME. With the current design, it is impossible to get a global view of the status of the ACME infrastructure, as each region has configured its own management group.

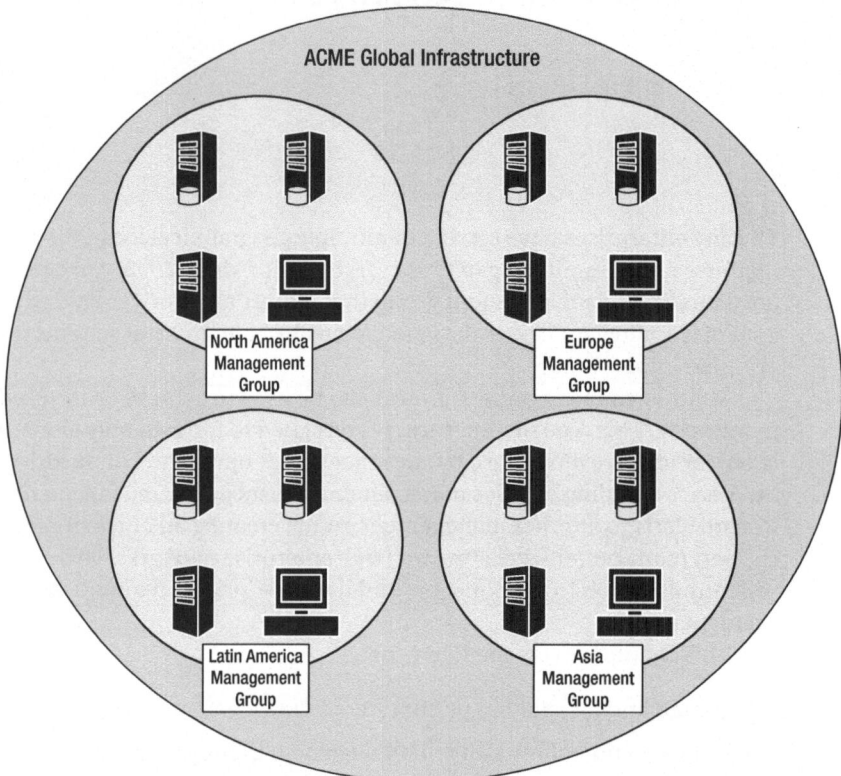

Figure 10-1. *The current ACME infrastructure*

If you work for ACME and want to create a view of its global infrastructure, then you should configure a multitiered management group. This will allow you to view the status of the global environment. Figure 10-2 shows a configuration example.

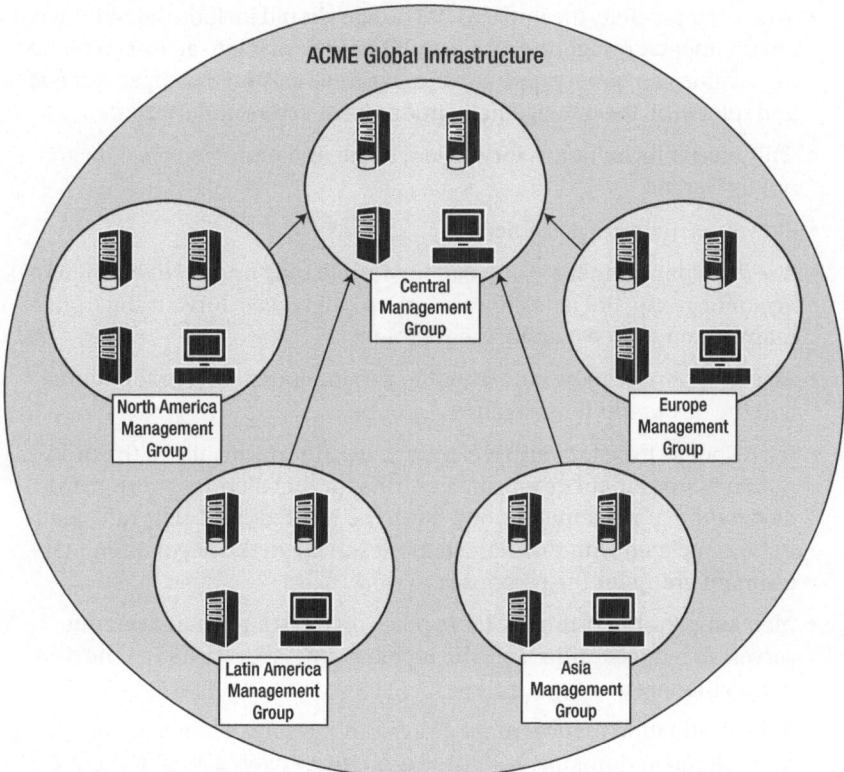

Figure 10-2. *An example multitiered configuration*

Design Considerations

Before you deploy a multitiered management group configuration, it is
important that you consider the following points:

- There is a management overhead associated with deploying a multitiered management group. You must ensure that any rules that are to
  be forwarded to another management group have the same rule GUID.
  This can be achieved by importing the same management pack into the
  source and destination management groups; any custom rules should
  also be imported. Keeping the source and destination rule bases in sync
  from that point forward can be difficult if your company does not have
  a change control process.

- Whenever possible, the initial MOM design should include the multitiered environment. Configuring a new multitiered design into an existing MOM installation can be very time consuming, as all existing management packs and rules in all the management groups have to be standardized.

- Only alert information is forwarded. Event and performance data are not forwarded.

- Only three tiers are possible.

- A source management group can forward to only one destination management group, but a destination group can receive forwarding from as many as ten source management groups.

- Alert responses can be configured to run independently in the source and the destination management groups.

- If a response for a forwarded alert is to be run specifically in the destination management group, an alert rule for that alert response in the destination management group has to be created. This alert rule needs to be associated with the management servers in the destination management group for the responses to work.

- Alert suppression primarily takes place on the source management server. To reduce traffic, only the repeat count is forwarded to the destination management group.

- If the destination management group and the source management group are in different domains, and there is no trust enabled, then a client certificate must be assigned for the MOM-to-MOM product connector service account, and the certificate is mapped to an account that is a member of the MOM Service Security group in the destination management group. The Microsoft Operations Manager 2005 Security Guide has all the steps you need to follow, documented at http://www.microsoft.com/downloads/details.aspx?FamilyID=812b3089-18fe-42ff-bc1e-d181ccfe5dcf&displaylang=en.

Once you have created your design, you have to ensure that it is documented and that this design document is updated with any changes that are made during the implementation and the implementation's operational life. Without this documentation, it becomes very difficult to spot unauthorized changes to the MOM infrastructure.

Installation Phases

There are a number of installation phases that you must follow to configure a multitiered management group. Figure 10-3 shows the phases if you are configuring the group as part of the install of a new MOM environment.

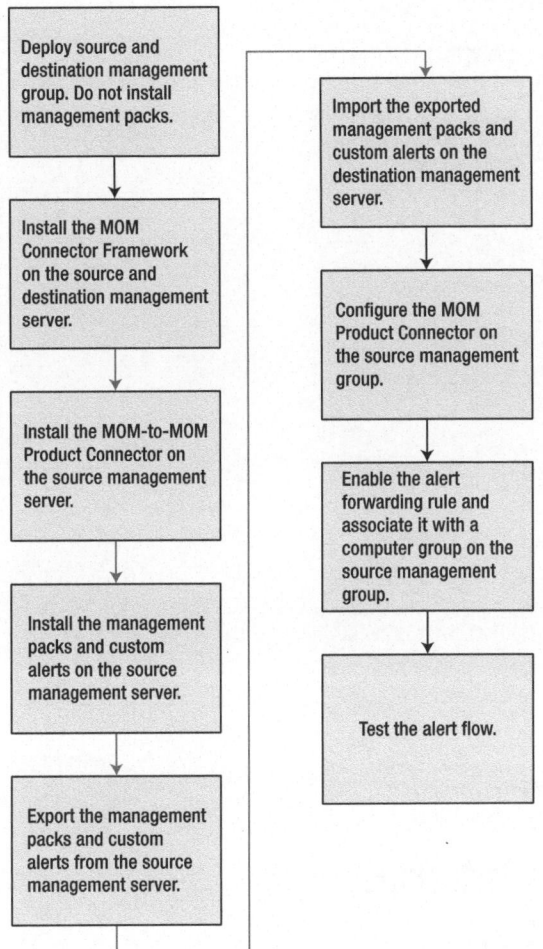

Figure 10-3. *A new MOM enviroment*

Figure 10-4 shows the phases you must follow if you are configuring the multitiered management group in an existing MOM environment.

When you implement a multitiered environment into an existing MOM installation, most of your time will be spent auditing the current installations to ensure that all installed management packs and custom rules are identified. The information that has been collected during the audit then has to be validated. Once the baseline configuration of management packs and rules has been identified, it has to be installed on the destination server.

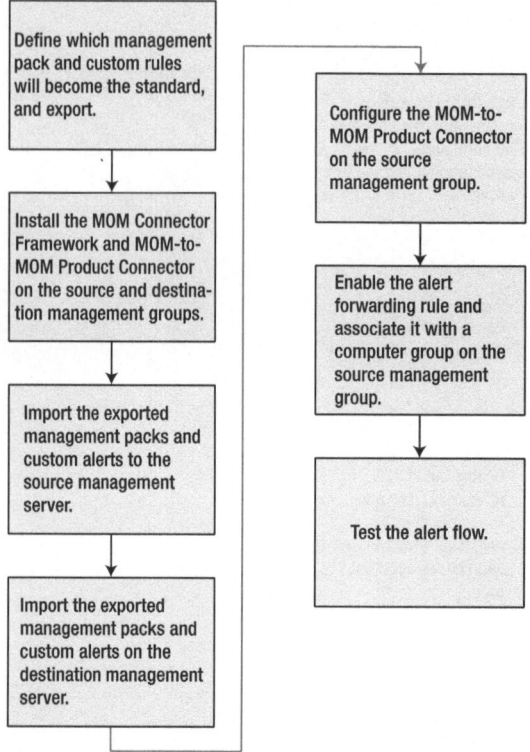

Figure 10-4. *An existing MOM enviroment*

Configuring a Multitiered Management Group

This section covers the steps to configure a multitiered management group. I recommend that you break the install down into a number of phases and thoroughly test each phase to ensure that the installation was successful. Breaking the install into phases will also make troubleshooting the install easier. The main phases are as follows:

1. Installing the MOM connector framework
2. Installing the MOM-to-MOM product connector
3. Configuring the management groups
4. Enabling alert forwarding

5. Testing the alert flow

6. Troubleshooting the MOM-to-MOM product connector

7. Configuring centralized reporting from multiple management groups

Phase 1: Installing the MOM Connector Framework

Here are the steps you need to install the MOM connector framework on the source and destination management servers:

1. Double-click setup.exe on the MOM 2005 CD.

2. Select Install Microsoft Operations Manager 2005.

3. Click Next.

4. Select Modify, and then click Next.

5. Select Microsoft Connector Framework, and choose the option to install, as shown in Figure 10-5.

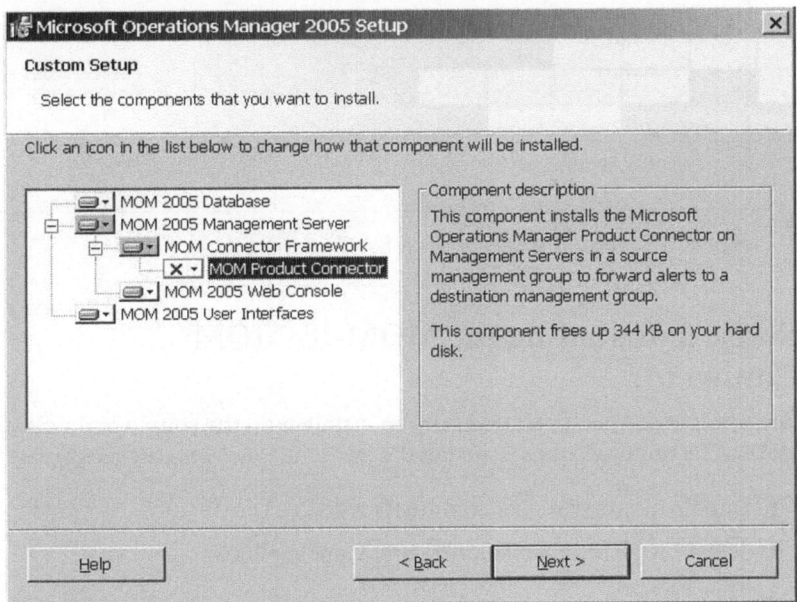

Figure 10-5. *The connector framework install*

6. Click Next.

7. Click Next on the prerequisites check screen.

8. Click Install.

9. Verify that the installation was successful by going to `http://ComputerName:1271/connectorserviceV2.asmx`. You should see a web page such as in Figure 10-6.

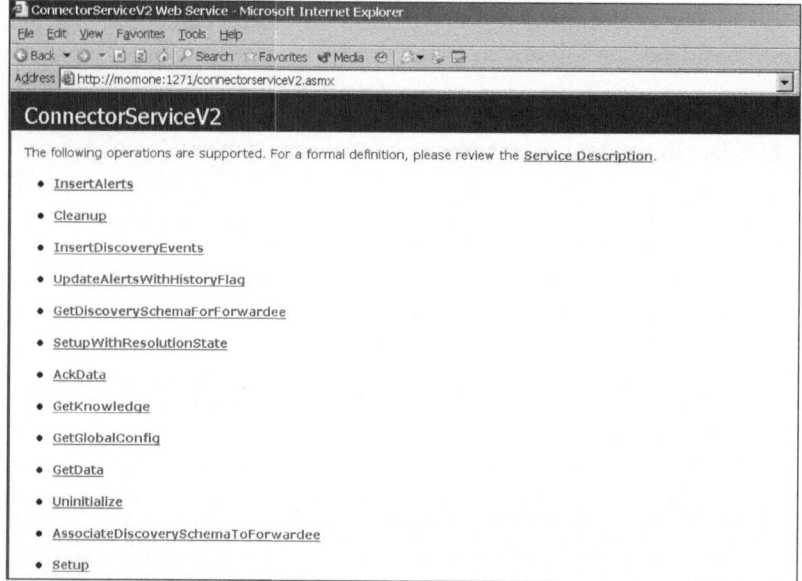

Figure 10-6. *Verfiying the connector serivce install*

Phase 2: Installing the MOM-to-MOM Connector

The product connector should only be installed on the source management server. The required steps to install the product connector are as follows:

1. Double-click `setup.exe` on the MOM 2005 CD.

2. Select Install Microsoft Operations Manager 2005.

3. Click Next.

4. Select Modify, and then click Next.

5. Select the product connector to be installed, and then click Next.

6. Click Next on the prerequisites checker screen.

7. On the Data Access Server Account screen, enter the DAS account of the source management group. Add the DAS account used in the source management group to the destination management group's MOM service group. This will allow the source management group to add alerts to the OnePoint database on the destination management group. Figure 10-7 shows the Data Access Server Account screen.

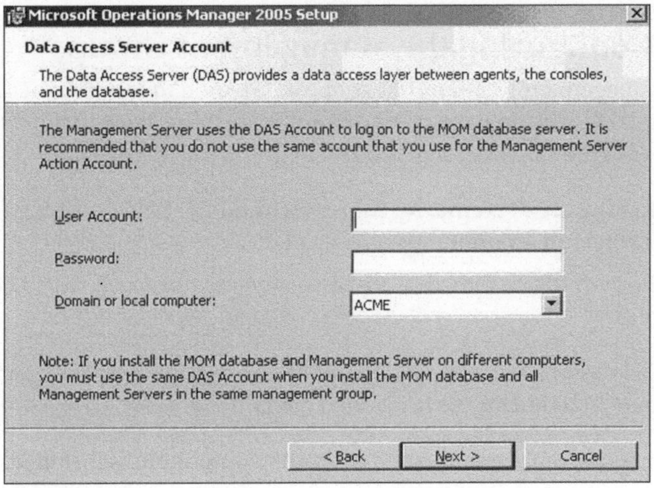

Figure 10-7. *The Data Access Server Account screen*

8. Click Next, and then click Finish.

If installing the MOM connector framework or MOM-to-MOM product connector on a Windows 2003 domain controller, then carry out the following steps:

1. Grant the IIS_WPG group read/execute permissions to the %WINNT%\Temp directory.

2. Grant the IIS_WPG group modify permissions to the `Temporary ASP.Net Files` directory.

3. Restart IIS.

If installing on a Windows 2000 domain controller, do the following:

1. Grant the IWAM_<computername> account read/execute permissions to the %WINNT%\Temp directory.

2. Grant the IWAM_<computername> account modify permissions to the `Temporary ASP.Net Files` directory.

3. Grant the IWAM_<computername> account the impersonate privilege (SeImpersonatePrivilege).

4. Restart IIS.

Once the connector framework and product connector are installed and verified, you need to configure the source and destination management groups to send and receive alerts.

Phase 3: Configuring the Management Groups

The source management group must now be configured to forward the selected alerts to the destination management group. The steps that must be followed to configure the source management group are as follows:

1. Ensure that the MOM connector framework and the MOM-to-MOM product connector components are installed.

2. Enable the alert forwarding rule and associate its rule group with a computer group.

The following steps must be carried out on the destination management group to prepare it to receive the forwarded alerts:

1. Ensure that the MOM connector framework component is installed.

2. Import management packs and any custom rule groups used in the source management groups.

Phase 4: Enabling Alert Forwarding

Here are the steps that you need to follow to configure alert forwarding from the source to the destination management group:

1. Enable the Microsoft Operations Manager\Operations Manager 2005\Connector Framework\Mark Alerts for forwarding to MOM Master management group rule. Figure 10-8 shows the location of the rule.

2. Identify the computer groups whose alerts you want to forward to the destination management group. As a minimum, the following computer groups should be associated:

   • Microsoft Operations Manager 2005 Agents

   • Microsoft Operations Manager 2005 Servers

   • Microsoft Operations Manager 2000 Agents, if applicable

3. Right-click "Mark Alerts for forwarding to MOM Master management group" and select Associate with Computer Group in the context menu, as shown in Figure 10-9.

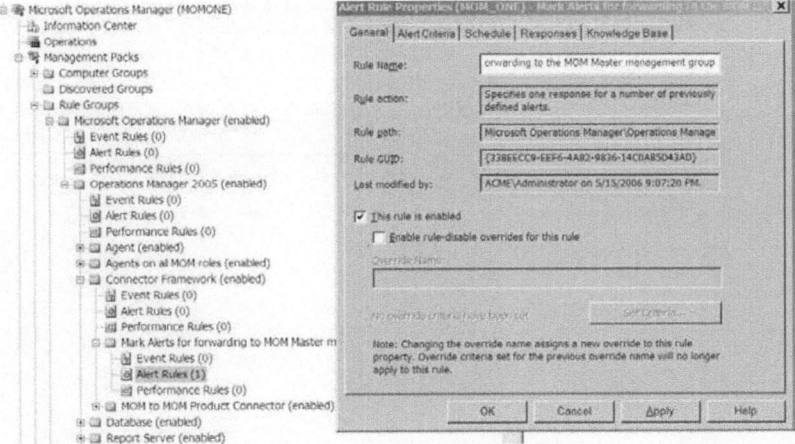

Figure 10-8. *Enabling the "mark alerts for forwarding" rule*

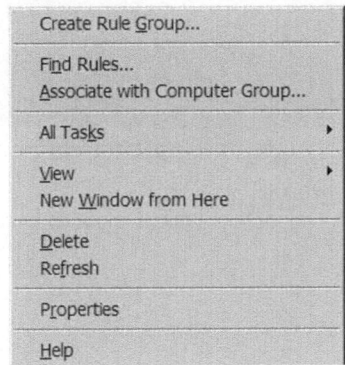

Figure 10-9. *Selecting Associate with Computer Group from the context menu*

4. Add the computer groups to which you wish to forward the alerts to the destination management group, and then click Apply. This is shown in Figure 10-10.

5. In the Administrator Console, expand Administration, right-click Product Connectors, and then click Create MOM-to-MOM Connection in the context menu, as shown in Figure 10-11.

6. Click Next on the Create MOM-to-MOM Connector Wizard.

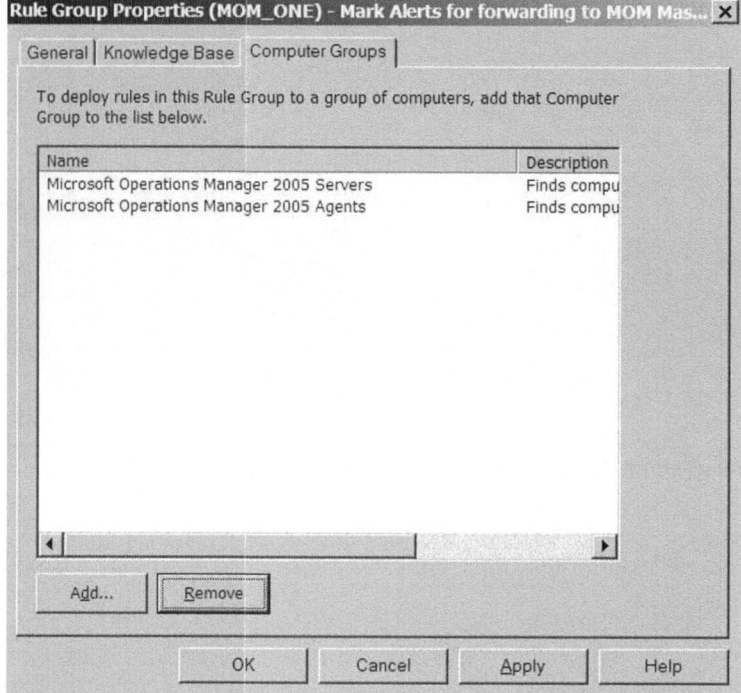

Figure 10-10. *The associated computer groups*

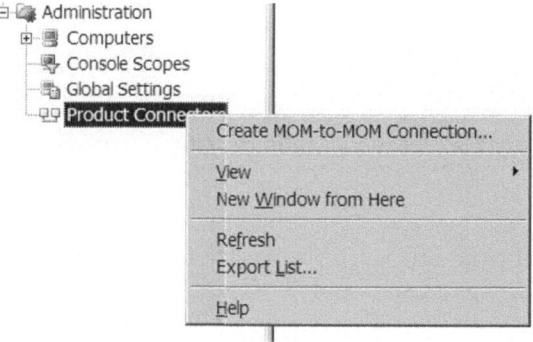

Figure 10-11. *Starting the Create MOM-to-MOM Connector Wizard*

7. On the Specify Connector properties page (shown in Figure 10-12), enter a connection name, a resolution state ID, and the polling interval, in seconds. For the connection name, I would recommended that you use the format *Management Group Name-Management Group Name* (e.g., MOM_UK-MOM_NA) so that you can quickly identify which management groups are connecting. Then click Next.

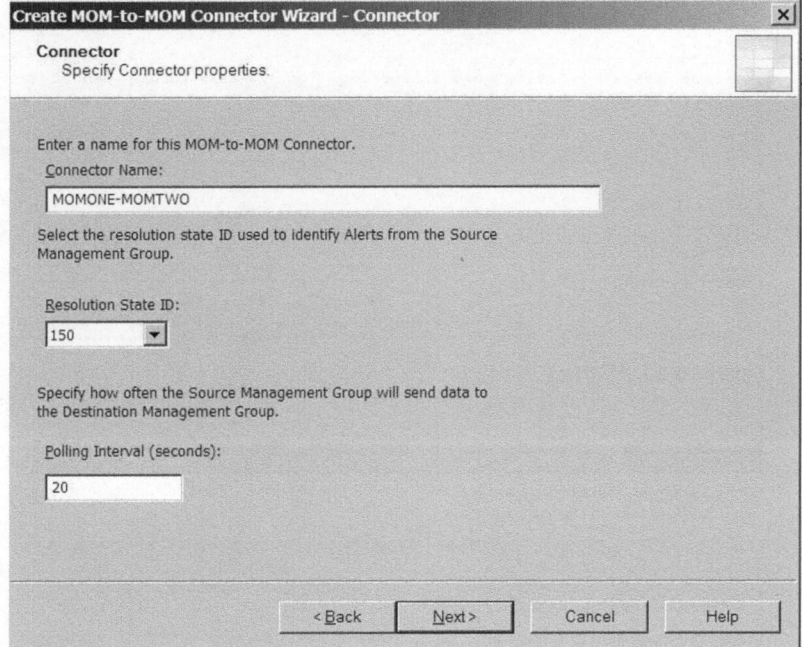

Figure 10-12. *MOM-to-MOM connector properties*

8. If you enter a resolution state ID other than 150, the "MOM Mark alerts for forwarding to MOM Master management group" script needs to be changed to match the new state ID. This is shown in Figure 10-13.

9. Add the target on the Add MOM Master Management Group screen (shown in Figure 10-14) for the connector. If you're using a different TCP port than 1271, or if you're using SSL encryption with connectors for the MOM connector framework, then you must use the Target MOM Web Service option using the following syntax: `http://ComputerName:1271/connectorserviceV2.asmx` (change the port number to match what your installation uses). If not, you can just specify a computer name. Then click Next.

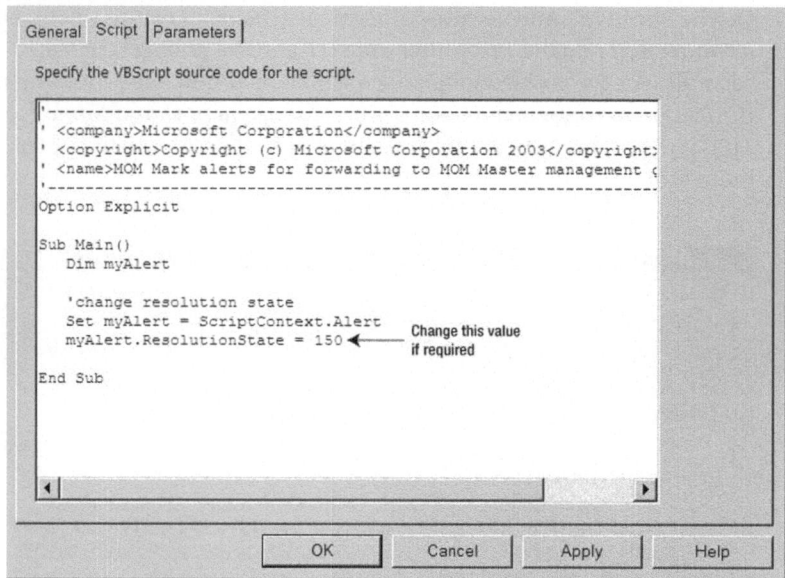

Figure 10-13. *Altering the script*

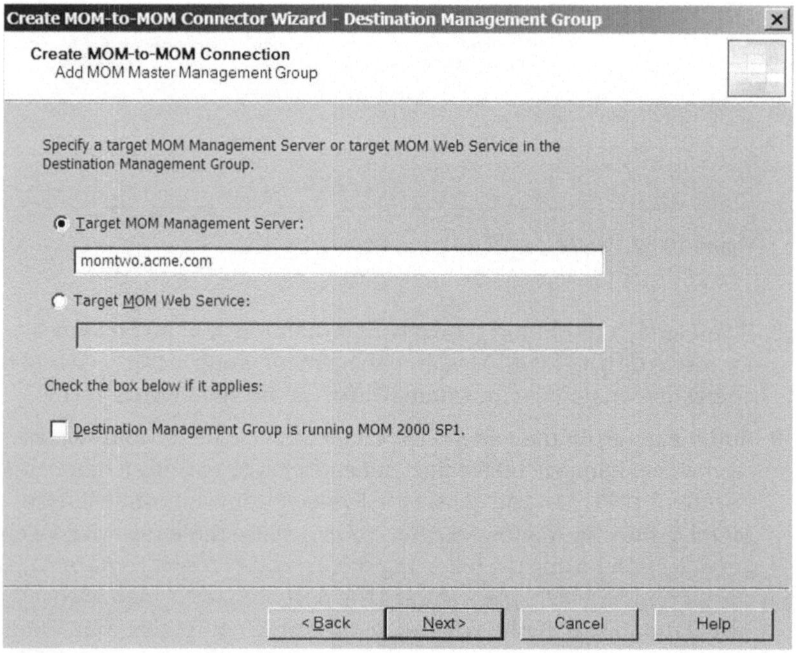

Figure 10-14. *Configuring the target management server*

10. On the Forwarding Properties page (shown in Figure 10-15), enter the settings that meet your requirements, and then click Next.

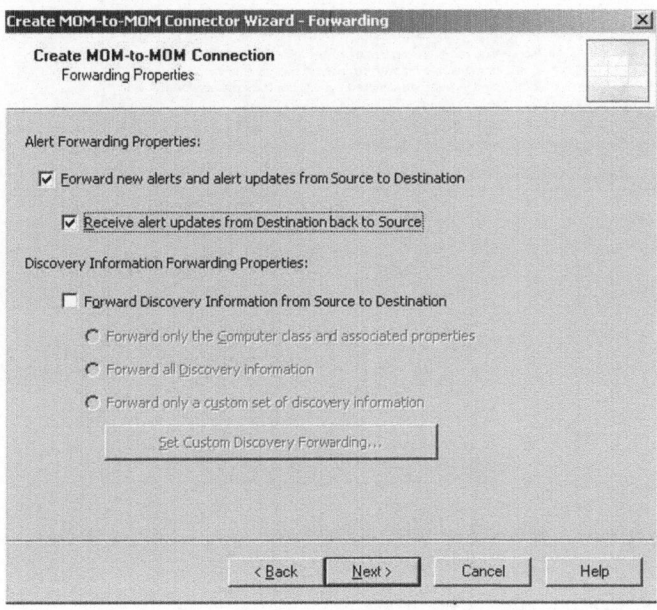

Figure 10-15. *Selecting the forwarding properties*

11. On the Failover Configuration page (shown in Figure 10-16), configure additional web services in the designated destination management group if you have more than one management server in the management group with the MOM connector framework installed. They can be used to provide resilience in the case of the primary server failing. Then click Next.

12. Check the confirmation screen and ensure that all settings are correct. Then click Next and Finish.

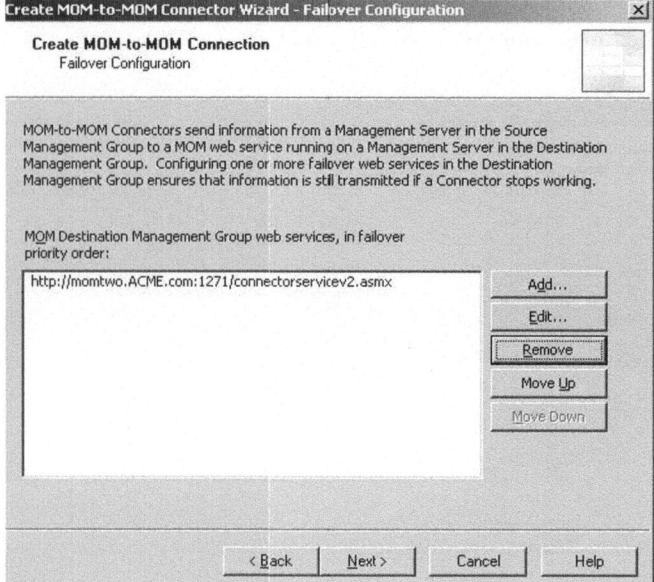

Figure 10-16. *Configuring resilience, if required*

Phase 5: Testing the Alert Flow

The next step is to manually verify that the alert information is being forwarded to the destination manager server. Use one of the following two options:

> *Option one*: Send an alert from the Operator Console by right-clicking the alert, and set the resolution name to the name you chose for the MOM connector. You should then see the alert in the destination management server's Operator Console. If you have configured the destination management group to send updates back to the source management group, you can resolve the alert. Click Set Alert Resolution State in the context menu, and you should see the alert in the source management group update its status to resolved. This is shown in Figure 10-17.

> *Option two*: You can use the Event Creator tool in the MOM 2005 Resource Kit to generate a number of test events to ensure that the alert forwarding is working as expected. This is shown in Figure 10-18.

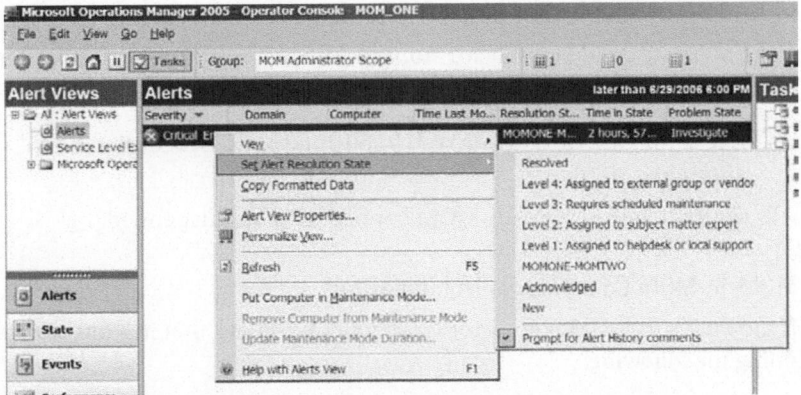

Figure 10-17. *Manually sending an alert via the Operator Console*

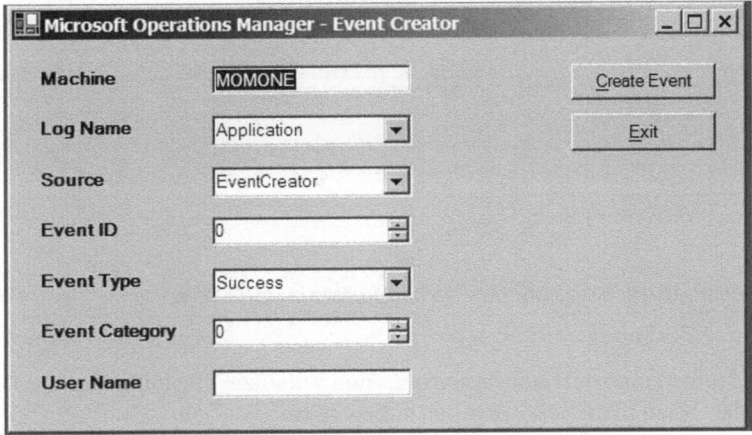

Figure 10-18. *The Event Creator tool*

Phase 6: Troubleshooting the MOM-to-MOM Connector

This section provides troubleshooting solutions for a couple of general issues that might occur when installing or using the MOM-to-MOM connector. Care should be taken when using the SQL commands contained in this section. As a precaution, I always recommended backing up the OnePoint database before making any changes via SQL.

MOM-to-MOM Connector Stops Forwarding Alerts

If the MOM-to-MOM connector stops forwarding alerts to the destination management group, you should do the following:

1. Check that the World Wide Web Publishing service is configured to Automatic Start.

2. Check that the MOM-to-MOM connector is not suspended.

MOM-to-MOM Connector Is Not Initialized

If the MOM-to-MOM connector is not working, check that it is initialized by doing the following:

1. Open the Administrator Console.

2. Go to Administration ➤ Product Connectors, and ensure that the connector is initialized (as shown in Figure 10-19).

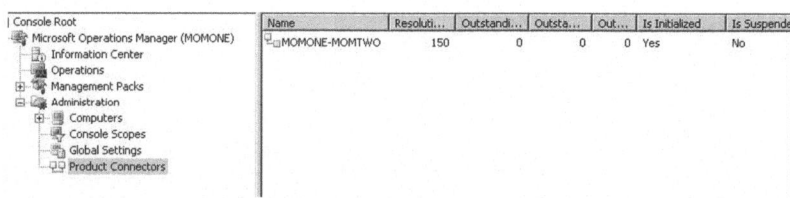

Figure 10-19. *Checking that the connector is initialized*

3. If the connector is not initialized, then initialize it by following the steps described in the following two subsections.

Initializing the MOM-to-MOM Connector on the Source Management Group

On the source management group, carry out the following steps to initialize the MOM-to-MOM connector:

1. Go to the OnePoint database and open SQL Query Analyzer.

2. Connect to the OnePoint database and run the following command:

```
use onepoint
select * from MMPC_Config
select * from MMPC_Forwardees
select * from MCF_Forwardees
```

The output will look something like Figure 10-20. If it the MOM-to-MOM connector is not initialized, the IsInitialized value will be set to 0.

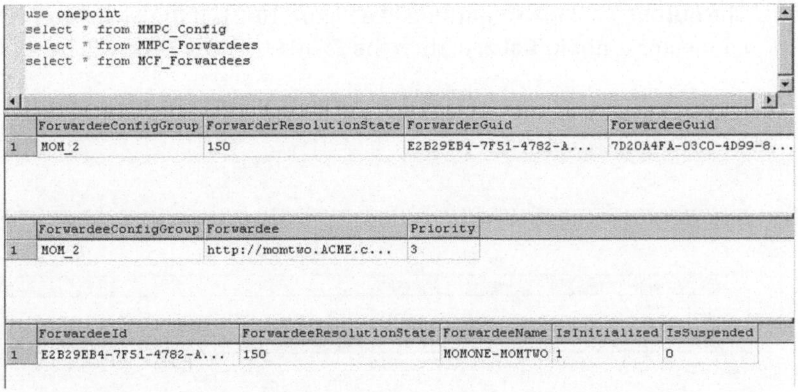

```
use onepoint
select * from MMPC_Config
select * from MMPC_Forwardees
select * from MCF_Forwardees
```

	ForwardeeConfigGroup	ForwarderResolutionState	ForwarderGuid	ForwardeeGuid
1	MOM_2	150	E2B29EB4-7F51-4782-A...	7D20A4FA-03C0-4D99-8...

	ForwardeeConfigGroup	Forwardee	Priority	
1	MOM_2	http://momtwo.ACME.c...	3	

	ForwardeeId	ForwardeeResolutionState	ForwardeeName	IsInitialized	IsSuspended
1	E2B29EB4-7F51-4782-A...	150	MOMONE-MOMTWO	1	0

Figure 10-20. *The source SQL output*

3. Copy the ForwardeeId value, and then run the following command:

```
exec mcf_doinitialize 'ForwardeeId value',7
```

For example, the following code will initialize the connector with the ID 'E2B29EB4-7F51-4782-A13D-FCE78C72B6A9':

```
use onepoint
exec mcf_doinitialize 'E2B29EB4-7F51-4782-A13D-FCE78C72B6A9',7
```

4. Then rerun the following command:

```
use onepoint
select * from MMPC_Config
select * from MMPC_Forwardees
select * from MCF_Forwardees
```

The value for IsInitialized should be 1.

Initializing the MOM-to-MOM Connector on the Destination Management Group

On the destination management group, carry out the following steps:

1. Go to the OnePoint database and open SQL Query Analyzer.

2. Connect to the OnePoint database and run the following command:

```
use onepoint
select * from MMPC_Config
select * from MMPC_Forwardees
select * from MCF_Forwardees
```

The output will look something like Figure 10-21. If the MOM-to-MOM connector is not initialized, then the `IsInitialized` value will be set to 0.

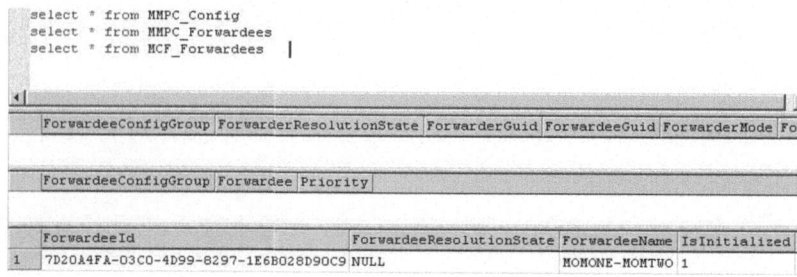

Figure 10-21. *SQL output from checking connector status*

3. Copy the `ForwardeeId` value, and then run the following command:

```
exec mcf_doinitialize 'ForwardeeId value',2
```

For example, the following code will initialize the connector with the ID '7D20A4FA-03C0-4D99-8297-1E6B028D90C9':

```
use onepoint
exec mcf_doinitialize '7D20A4FA-03C0-4D99-8297-1E6B028D90C9',2
```

4. Then rerun the following command:

```
use onepoint
select * from MMPC_Config
select * from MMPC_Forwardees
select * from MCF_Forwardees
```

The value for `IsInitialized` should now be 1.

Phase 7: Configuring Centralized Reporting from Multiple Management Groups

If your organization has deployed multiple management groups, there still may be a requirement to gather operational data into one central data warehouse so that trending and performance analysis can be carried out across the whole organization, rather than at the management group level. To aid this, MOM Reporting Server will take in multiple feeds from the different management groups. During the installation process, only one DTS job is created. To configure the reporting server to take feeds from the other management groups, you will have to manually configure the DTS jobs. Microsoft has released a Multiple Management Group Rollup Solution Accelerator, which is available at www.microsoft.com/technet/itsolutions/cits/mo/smc/ mmgp05.mspx. This URL also lists the steps you need to configure the DTS jobs. We primarily recommend that you use a batch file that contains all the different DTS jobs. Then configure a scheduled job to call the batch file. This will ensure that the DTS jobs will run in sequence and reduce the risk of a DTS job taking longer than expected to complete due to conflicts with another scheduled job. Before deploying this solution, you should take into account the network traffic that it will generate. If you have management groups on remote sites, then you should check the network to ensure that the DTS jobs that are required for centralized reporting do not impact the network performance, as large amounts of data can be transferred. You should also ensure that the DTS job finishes in an acceptable time period.

Summary

This chapter has shown how to install multitiered management groups, as well as the circumstances in which they should be used within your organization. The chapter has also covered design best practices for ensuring that multitiered management groups are used effectively.

Chapter 11 will discuss the tools that are available in the MOM 2005 Resource Kit.

CHAPTER 11

■ ■ ■

MOM Resource Kit and SDK

In this chapter, we will examine the tools provided in the MOM Resource Kit, and also look at the MOM Software Development Kit (SDK) and how it can be used to get the most from MOM. Finally, we will look at some of the third-party tools available to help you enhance MOM and extend it to better suit your environment.

MOM Resource Kit

The MOM Resource Kit is a collection of tools to enhance the MOM experience and assist in configuring and maintaining a MOM infrastructure. The MOM Resource Kit (which can be downloaded from www.microsoft.com/mom/downloads/2005/reskit/default.mspx) comprises a number of tools and scripts to enhance MOM and ease configuration and troubleshooting. You can install the MOM Resource Kit by means of an .msi file.

In addition to the tools included in the MOM Resource Kit, we recommend you use the SMSTrace tool, which makes not only the troubleshooting of MOM easier, but also the troubleshooting of any application that uses log files. The SMSTrace tool is included in the SMS Resource Kit, and allows you to do the following:

- Open and view a log file in real time without locking the file open. This means that the application writing to the log file can continue to do so while you are viewing the file.

- Filter the log file so that you see only log entries of interest (e.g., those pertaining to a specific problem that you are trying to solve).

- View errors and warnings in a log file in color-coded form, to assist in picking important lines out of a large file.

MOM SDK

The MOM SDK is written for developers who wish to write applications for MOM, and also for MOM administrators who may want to create scripts to write data into, pull data out of, or develop custom reports for MOM. In essence, the SDK allows you to extend and customize MOM to better fit your needs.

The MOM SDK contains documentation and code samples, as well as the code library for the MOM 2005 application. The SDK documentation includes information about creating MOM applications with the .NET Framework, creating custom reports, and connecting MOM to other management or help desk products. The documentation contains the full listing and detailed information about the following MOM code components:

- Runtime scripting objects
- MOM .NET Framework class libraries
- MOM WMI classes

The SDK also comes with a number of SQL views that are installed into the OnePoint and SystemCenterReporting databases to make extracting data directly from the MOM databases easier and faster. The following SQL views are included in the SDK, and are installed into both the OnePoint and SystemCenterReporting databases:

- SDKAlertsView
- SDKAlertsAndEventsView
- SDKComputerView
- SDKComputerGroupView
- SDKComputerToComputerGroupView
- SDKComputerAttributesView
- SDKEventView
- SDKEventParametersView
- SDKPerformanceView

The SDK also contains code samples of some of the tools created by developers at Microsoft, such as the MaintenanceModeUtility tool, which can be used to put agents in maintenance mode from the command line.

We recommend that you install the MOM SDK even if you do not plan to create any scripts or enhance MOM in any way, since if nothing else, it makes the data in the OnePoint and SystemCenterReporting databases more accessible.

Tools in the MOM Resource Kit

The following subsections describe the tools available to you from the MOM Resource Kit. Note that the MOM Resource Kit is subject to change, and the tools described in the following subsections may not be included at the time this book goes to press. There may also be additional tools included in the MOM Resource Kit that we do not describe.

Agent Helper

The MOM Agent Helper tool runs a set of responses to attempt to fix an agent that is no longer sending heartbeat packets to the MOM management server. It consists of two scripts that are run from within MOM:

- ReviveAgent
- ReviveDeadAgent

If an agent is not detected on the agent machine and the agent is defined as Agent-Managed in the MOM database, then the script will attempt to install an agent. If the agent is not functioning correctly, the Agent Helper will attempt to repair the agent.

This tool is useful if you experience problems with the MOM agent or you frequently rebuild servers, (e.g., in a development environment). In this case, as a server is rebuilt, the Agent Helper will run, detect that the machine should be defined as Agent-Managed, and attempt to install an agent (provided that the server name remains the same).

The Agent Helper consists of a management pack, which you should import by employing the same method as for importing other management packs.

Alert to RSS Utility

The Alert to RSS utility is an ASP.NET application that publishes MOM data as an RSS 2.0 syndication feed. The feed provides current information about the number of unresolved alerts on the management server, sorted by resolution state; and a summary of the number of agents managed by MOM. It can be extended to include more detailed information about the data in MOM. This is useful for keeping aware of issues using an RSS feed rather than the traditional SMTP e-mail method.

Business Activity Monitoring (BAM) Wizard

The BAM tool creates a management pack to monitor business processes using the BAM components of BizTalk Server. You can use the management pack to build key performance indicators (KPIs) and raise alerts when they exceed normal operating conditions.

Clean-up MOM

The Clean-up MOM tool is used to brute-force remove all aspects of a MOM deployment, including the following:

- MOM 2000 release to manufacturer (RTM)
- MOM 2000 SP1
- MOM 2005 beta builds (private beta, public beta, beta 3)
- MOM 2005 release candidate
- MOM 2000 and 2005 agent

This tool should be used as a last resort, as it forcefully removes MOM from a MOM server or agent. Its primary use is for removing MOM instances that have become corrupted or cannot be uninstalled by normal means. When you run it using the following command-line switch:

```
CleanupMOM.exe /z:All
```

All MOM components present on a machine will be forcefully removed, including all references in the Windows Installer registry location.

Computer Group Hierarchy Utility

The Computer Group Hierarchy utility can be used to export the computer group hierarchy from MOM so that it can be re-created on another MOM system. You may need to do this in a multitiered MOM configuration in which you have more than one management group with similar rule base configurations. (Multitiered configurations are explained in Chapter 10.) While it may not be necessary to duplicate standard computer group configurations, if you have nested computer groups or many custom computer groups, this tool will be useful. The following command-line parameters should be used when you run the tool:

```
CGHUtil.exe [option] [filename] [extendedOptions]
```

Let's take a look at an example:

```
CGHUtil.exe /dump CGroups.xml "Windows 2003 Servers" /WithComputers
```

This code will export all computer groups nested under the Windows 2003 Servers computer group; also, with the addition of the /WithComputers switch, all computers listed under the Included Computers tab will also be exported.

Configure Action Account

When you use a domain user account for the MOM Agent Action account in a low-privilege scenario, configuration of the local security settings for the account on all agents can take a long time. That is where the Configure Action Account tool comes into play. You can use this tool to set the default permissions for the MOM 2005 Management Pack (these are the same basic permissions for most of the other management packs).

The tool adds the Action account to the following local user groups:

- Users local group
- Performance Monitor Users local group

It also assigns the following permissions to the Agent Action account on the agent:

- The SeSecurityPrivilege user right
- The SeInteractiveLogonRight user right

Note When you run the tool, you must be logged in using an account that has local administrative rights on the agent machine.

To configure the permissions for the MOM Management Pack, you should run this tool using the following command line:

```
ConfigureActionAccount.exe /user:DOMAIN\User1 /mommp
```

To remove permissions, use the following command line:

```
ConfigureActionAccount.exe /user:DOMAIN\User1 /cleanup
```

Console Scope Utility

You use the Console Scope utility to synchronize Active Directory group members with MOM 2005 console scope members. This is useful when duplicating your Active Directory security model in MOM.

This tool should be executed on a MOM management server computer using the format of the following command line:

```
CSUtility.exe Action ScopeName GroupName
```

The parameters for the preceding command line are as follows:

- Action: The type of action to perform. Valid types include the following:
  - CreateScope: Creates the specified console scope.
  - DeleteScope: Deletes the specified console scope.
  - AddUser: Adds a user to the console scope.
  - RemoveUser: Removes a user from the console scope.
  - Synchonize: Synchronizes a console scope with the specified Active Directory group.
- ScopeName: The MOM scope name to use. If the scope does not exist, it is created. If you specify an empty string, the scope name is assumed to be the same as the Active Directory group name.
- GroupName: The Active Directory group name.

Following are examples of how you would create, add, remove, delete, and synchronize for the console scope:

```
CSUtility.exe CreateScope "Ops Group 1"
CSUtility.exe AddUser "Ops Group 1" MYDOMAIN\User1
CSUtility.exe RemoveUser "Ops Group 1" MYDOMAIN\User1
CSUtility.exe DeleteScope "Ops Group 1"
CSUtility.exe Synchronize "Ops Group 1" MYDOMAIN\ServerOperators1
```

Convert Management Packs to XML (MP2XML) and Management Pack Differencing Tools

These two separate tools are explored together, as they will usually be used as such. The convert tool (MP2XML) is used to convert an .akm (management pack) file to XML format to be used by the differencing tool.

In order to convert a management pack to an XML file, first export the management pack using the Import/Export Management Pack wizard from within the MOM Administrator Console. Once you have the .akm file, we recommend that you copy both the MP2XML.exe file and the .akm file to the same folder, somewhere on the local disk. Then simply run the tool using the following command line to execute the tool and convert the management pack into the XML format:

```
MP2XML.exe <AkmInputFile> <XmlOutputFile>
```

For example, the following creates the new file as XmlCustomRules.xml from CustomRules.akm:

```
MP2XML.exe CustomRules.akm XmlCustomRules.xml
```

You use the Management Pack Differencing tool to compare two management packs to determine any differences between the two. This is useful if you are trying to determine which (if any) changes have been made to a standard management pack. An example of this would be determining any rule changes that have been made to a MOM environment. You might need to do this if you have taken responsibility for the environment after it has been deployed and configured.

Note A standard text differencing tool such as WinDiff can also be used to compare management packs, but such tools are not provided as part of the Resource Kit. It is therefore recommended that you use the Management Pack Differencing tool, since it is included in the Resource Kit and is designed for use with MOM.

Once you have the two management packs that you want to compare in XML format, you should execute the MpDiff.exe file to use the GUI. (There is also a command-line version available, which we will cover later in this section.)

Once the utility loads, you will be presented with the screen shown in Figure 11-1.

Once you have loaded the utility, click the File menu and select Compare Management Packs. You will be prompted to enter the location of both XML files, one after the other. The results will then be displayed to reflect differences between the two management packs. An example of a set of results is shown in Figure 11-2.

You can also run the MpDiff tool using the following specified command-line parameters:

```
MpDiff.Console.exe
      /src:<Source MP xml file>
      /tgt:<Target MP xml file>
```

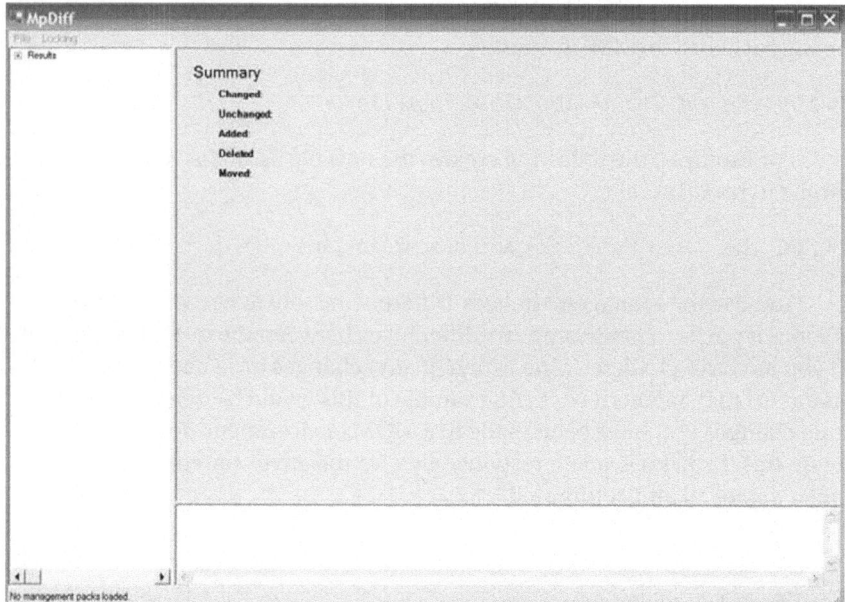

Figure 11-1. *The MpDiff utility*

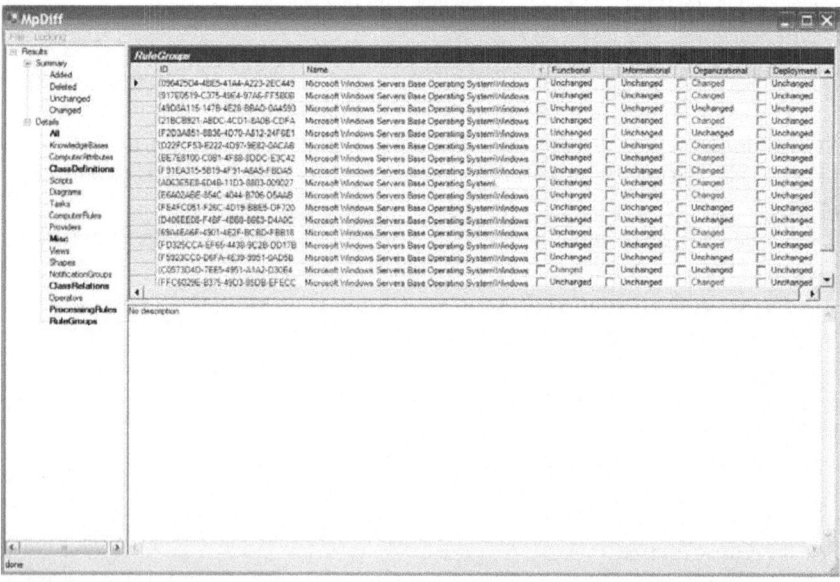

Figure 11-2. *MpDiff results*

The following optional switches may also be used:

- /lock: Applies a lock file against the diff result.
- /createLock:<filename.xml>: Creates a lock file from this diff result.
- /schema: Defines whether to validate against MOM XSD (default is on).
- /out: Outputs the XML diff result to a file (default file name is diffout.xml).
- /v: Sets the verbosity level. Items can be chained to one another. The available parameters are listed following, and should be used in the format: /v:cad:
    - u: Shows unchanged items
    - c: Shows changed items
    - a: Shows added items
    - d: Shows deleted items

Note Lock files allow you to keep track of changes in the management pack. If you want to be notified when an item in a management pack has changed, use a lock file.

DAS Role Update Utility

By default, MOM 2005 allows all members of the local administrator's group to access the Administrator and Operator Consoles in a manner equivalent to members of the MOM Administrators group. While not a security issue (as local administrators can always add themselves to the MOM Administrators group), this behavior may not be desirable for your environment.

The DAS Role Update utility (UpdateDASRoles) can reverse this default behavior and grant administrative access only to members of the MOM Administrators group if your environment requires this behavior.

It does this by locating the Microsoft Operations Manager Data Access Server (DAS) COM+ application, and removing the BUILTIN\Administrators group from the users list of this component. In order for this tool to function correctly, it should be run on all management servers in the MOM 2005 management group.

There are two command-line parameters that you can use when you are running this tool. To remove the BUILTIN\Administrators group from the

DAS COM+ application roles, run the tool with the following command-line parameter:

```
UpdateDASRoles.exe /update
```

To revert the changes made by the tool, run the following command:

```
UpdateDASRoles.exe /undo
```

■**Note** This tool does not prevent local administrators from adding themselves to the MOM Administrators group. Also, adding users to the MOM user groups will not grant them access until they log out and log in again.

Event Creator

The Event Creator tool is used to create events in the Windows event log for testing management packs. Event Creator allows you to choose event sources for the existing event logs that are currently registered.

After choosing an event source, you can simply choose an event ID, type, and category, and generate the event. Run the tool and input the required event details (as shown in Figure 11-3).

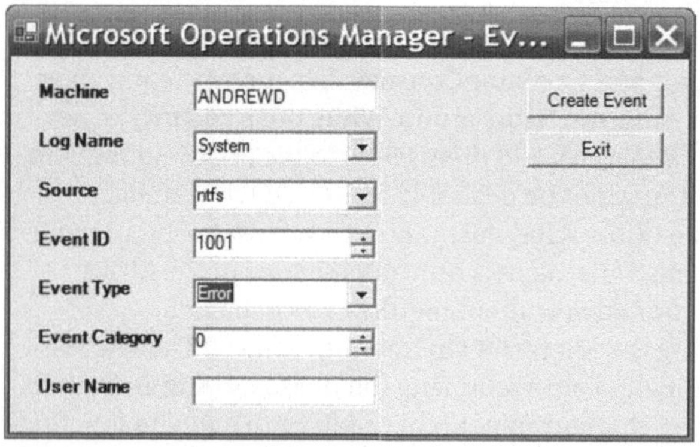

Figure 11-3. *The Event Creator tool*

Managed Code Response Utility

Use the Managed Code Response utility to assist in creating managed code responses in MOM. It allows you to gather the information to enter into the Managed Code Properties dialog for a rule.

Using .NET reflection, it is able to gather assembly names, fully qualified type names, method names, and method parameter types.

You should run the tool using the following command-line parameter:

```
MCRUtil.exe <AssemblyName>
```

The assembly name will output the full details for the assembly. For example

```
MCRUtil.exe AgentHelper.dll
```

will give the following output:

```
Assembly Name:
AgentHelper,
Version=5.0.2749.0,
Culture=neutral,
PublicKeyToken=9396306c2be7fcc4
```

There are also some additional command-line parameters that you can use; they can be found in the documentation accompanying the tool.

Management Group Utility

The Management Group utility can be used to output a list of management groups an agent reports to, and can also be used to detect and remove any computer groups that are corrupted. The following are some examples of how you can use the parameters. The first command line does not have a parameter:

`MGUtil.exe`: Outputs all management groups an agent is reporting to

`MGUtil.exe /c`: Outputs all corrupt management groups present on an agent

`MGUtil.exe /r`: Removes all corrupt management groups present on an agent

Management Pack Wizard

The Management Pack wizard is one of the best, most powerful tools in the MOM Resource Kit. It is a GUI-based tool that can be used to create a management pack. It can create rules to monitor Windows services, rules to monitor for events appearing in the event logs, and also rules to carry out performance monitoring and threshold alerting. The wizard also creates the state roles and components for management packs, allowing newly created management packs to take advantage of the capabilities of the MOM 2005 State view.

The wizard is simple to use. We will not cover the running of the wizard in detail since the documentation that accompanies the tool includes this information, along with screenshots to demonstrate the functionality of the tool. This tool is perfect both for MOM administrators who are unfamiliar or inexperienced with the concept of rule creation and MOM experts who need to create a management pack for a new application quickly, easily, and reliably.

MOM Information Utility

You can use the MOM Information utility (MOMInfo) to carry out the following tasks on an agent machine:

- Dumping the rules, responses, and VarSet values at the MOM agent into an XML file for analysis

- Clearing the queues on an agent

- Putting an agent into maintenance mode (when running the tool locally)

- Enabling script debugging on an agent

    You can use one or more of the following parameters with `MOMInfo.exe`:

    `/rules /out:<filename>.xml`: Outputs all the rules for all configuration groups to the specified XML file

    `/rules /out:<filename>.xml /config:<MG Name>`: Outputs only the rules for the specified management group (useful for agents that are multihomed)

    `/responses /out:<filename>.xml`: Outputs all currently running responses on the agent

/response /out:<filename>.xml /config:<MG Name>: Outputs all responses on the agent that are currently running against the specified management group

/clearqueue: Clears all MOM queues and restarts the agent

/clearqueue /config:<MG Name>: Clears queues for the specified management group and restarts the agent

/maintenancemode: Attempts to put the MOM agent into maintenance mode

---

Note If the agent cannot contact the MOM server, the agent will not appear to be in maintenance mode in the console.

/scriptdebugging: Enables the ActiveScriptDebugging registry key, which allows an administrator to attach a debugger or configure a JIT debugger to launch when a script fails or is hung

/errorhandling: Toggles the error handling in MOM

MOM Inventory

MOM Inventory is used to collect all information about a MOM infrastructure into a single .cab file. This can then be sent to Microsoft support to assist them in troubleshooting the issue. If you are familiar with reading MOM log files, you can use the tool to gather all the files into a single location.

MOM Remote Prerequisite Checker

The MOM Remote Prerequisite Checker is a version of the MOM Prerequisite Checker that can be run against a remote server. This is useful if you are not able to interactively log onto a server, but want to verify that it has the necessary prerequisites to allow an install of MOM. A screenshot of the utility is shown in Figure 11-4.

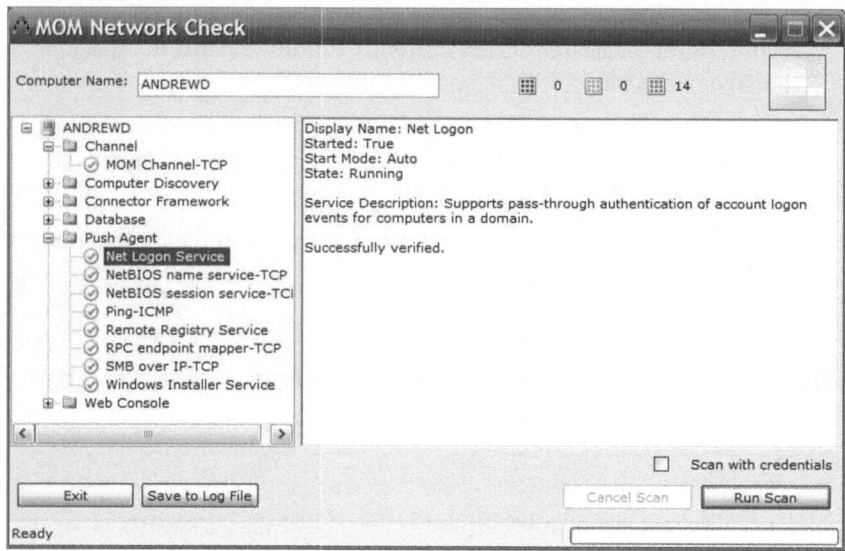

Figure 11-4. *The MOM Remote Prerequisite Checker*

MOM Trace Log Viewer

Using the MOM Trace Log Viewer, you can look at files with the .mc8 exten-sion. These files contain information about what MOM is doing in real time, and they cannot be easily viewed with any other tool. The tool includes filter-ing functionality to make reading large log files easier.

Operator Console Notifier

The MOM Operator Console Notifier is a very useful tool; it reduces the need for a user to continually monitor the MOM Operator Console. Provided that the tool is running, and you have a running Operator Console (which can be minimized) that is connected to a management server, the Operator Console Notifier will sit in the taskbar. When a new MOM alert is generated, the tool displays a slide-up bar and makes a sound, prompting you to look at the Operator Console and investigate the alert.

To install the tool, run the OpsConsoleNotifier.msi file. The resulting screen is shown in Figure 11-5.

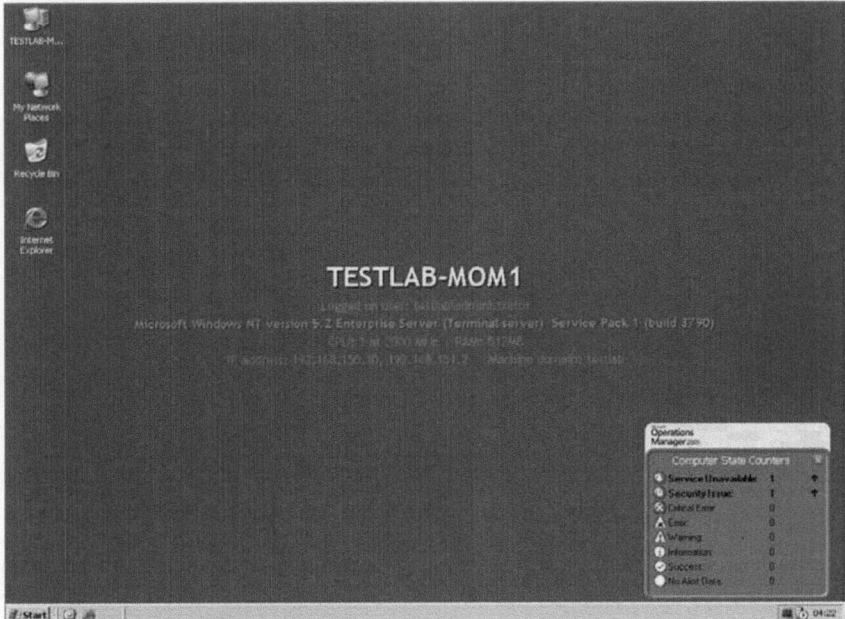

Figure 11-5. *The Operator Console Notifier tool*

Password Updater

The Password Updater tool is used to reset credentials for the following aspects of Windows:

- Windows services
- COM+ objects
- Scheduled tasks
- IIS virtual directories

From a MOM perspective, the Password Updater tool can be used to update the following items:

- The MOMDAS COM+ object on the MOM management servers
- The SystemCenterDTSPackageTask scheduled task on MOM Reporting Server
- The MOM connector Windows service on any management servers in the source management group

---

■**Note** This tool does not allow you to change the MOM Action account password. In order to do this, the SetActionAccount.exe utility should be used. This tool can be found in the MOM installation directory. Running the tool with the /? command-line switch will reveal the syntax that should be used to run the tool.

Following are some examples of parameters that you can use with the tool.

```
PasswordUpdater.exe /a DOMAIN\USER /p PASSWORD
```

This will search for all aspects on the current system that are running under the specified account, and update the passwords. You can add the /r switch to have the tool restart any services it changes.

```
PasswordUpdater.exe /a DOMAIN\USER /n DOMAIN\NEWUSER /p PASSWORD
```

This allows you to change the current account to a new account. Again, the /r switch can be used.

```
PasswordUpdater.exe /a DOMAIN\USER /p PASSWORD /f <filename>.txt
```

This will search through the specified file name (which has one server name per line), and will update all instances of the account on each remote system with the new credentials. Once again, the /r switch can be used.

Remove Blank Names

In MOM 2000 SP1, there was no enforcement to give MOM rules a name. In MOM 2005, rule naming is compulsory. Therefore, if you wish to import a MOM 2000 SP1 management pack that may have unnamed rules, you must first pass the .akm file through the Remove Blank Names tool. This tool will generate names for any rules that have blank names. The management pack can then be imported into MOM 2005.

Resultant Set of Rules (RSOR)

The RSOR tool allows a user to generate a plain text file showing the set of rules that would be deployed to an agent. This tool does not take into account rule overrides, however.

You can run the tool using the following command line:

```
RSOR.exe <MOMDBServer> <TargetAgent>
```

Rule and Computer Group Toggle Utility

The Rule and Computer Group Toggle utility is used to toggle the status of a rule group or computer group from enabled to disabled, and vice versa. Following are some examples of the parameters that you can use with this tool.

```
RuleUtil.exe /list:[All|Computer|Rule]
```

This set of parameters lists all computer or rule groups. Using the Computer or Rule switch allows you to filter by computer group or rule group.

```
RuleUtil.exe
   /enable | disable
   /compgroupname | compgroupid | rulegroupname | rulegroupid:<value>
```

This enables or disables a specified computer group or rule group. You can select the computer group or rule group to be affected using the name or the ID (GUID).

SharePoint Web Part

The MOM SharePoint Web Part allows you to add MOM information to an existing SharePoint site. For more information on configuring the web part, refer to the associated documentation included in the MOM Resource Kit.

Task Launcher

The Task Launcher tool allows you to run an existing MOM task from the command line. MOM tasks are located in the Operator Console. This tool allows these tasks to be run without using the Operator Console.

Note This tool only supports "runtime" tasks (i.e., tasks that run on the MOM server or agent). This tool does not support "console" tasks.

Run this tool using the following command-line parameters:

- TaskLauncher.exe /list: Lists all tasks in MOM
- TaskLauncher.exe /run /server:<TargetAgent> /taskpath:<TaskPath> | taskid:<TaskId>: Runs the specified task (using the task name or task ID) on the specified agent

Summary

In this chapter, we looked at the MOM Resource Kit and SDK, and how they can help you get the most out of MOM.

In the next chapter, we will show you how to carry out advanced troubleshooting of MOM in the event that you experience problems with your deployment.

CHAPTER 12

■ ■ ■

Troubleshooting

MOM is designed to provide important information about the nature and health of your infrastructure. It is essential that any problems with MOM are resolved as soon as possible—otherwise you may end up missing critical alerts from managed agents that represent a potential service outage to the business. This chapter will introduce you to the troubleshooting steps that will allow you to get your MOM infrastructure working again.

This chapter covers the following:

- MOM server and agent troubleshooting
- MOM agent installation troubleshooting

MOM Server and Agent Troubleshooting

To diagnose a fault within MOM, you need to know where to look to find information to troubleshoot the fault. The main places that you will check are the Operator Console alerts, the trace logs, and the event logs. It is also important to ascertain whether there have been any recent changes (e.g., configuration changes within MOM, service packs or hotfixes deployed, or network changes) that may be the cause of the fault.

Operator Console Alerts

When you install MOM 2005, by default the installation includes the MOM 2005 Management Pack. This management pack will monitor the health of the management server, the Operations and Reporting database server(s), and the agents. The Operator Console should be the first port of call when diagnosing faults, as the management pack monitors all the key components of the MOM infrastructure and provides suggestions on how to resolve the alerts. You must ensure that the alerts generated by the MOM 2005 Management Pack are responded to. It is not uncommon for the alerts to be missed, which over time can affect the operational effectiveness of the MOM infrastructure.

Trace Logs

Trace logs are used to debug the internal processes that MOM uses—by default, logging is not enabled. Trace logging can be configured to varying levels, as shown in Table 12-1.

Table 12-1. *MOM Trace Logging Levels*

Level Number	Level Name	Description
-1	Default	Logging is not enabled.
0	Error	Logs unexpected errors (e.g., catching an exception from a dependency, such as WinSock).
3	Warning	Logs expected errors, such as a user attempting an operation without sufficient privileges. Warnings do not affect MOM functionality; they do not indicate a problem with MOM so much as a problem with what a user is trying to do.
6	Info	Logs large amounts of data on MOM's operation (e.g., how long providers take to shut down).
9	Debug	Generates a combined log of error, warning, info, and debug data. Debug data would normally be used by Microsoft support.

Trace levels 6 and 9 will impact the performance of the MOM server, and should be switched off once the logs have been created. If the trace level is higher than 4, it will also generate alerts in the Operator Console, as in the following example:

```
The trace level is set too high.
The registry value "HKLM\Software\
Mission Critical Software\TraceLevel"
should be less than 4.
The current value is 9. Name: Trace level too high
Severity: Warning
Resolution State: New
Domain: XXXXXX
Computer: XXXXXXX
Time of First Event: 7/7/2006 6:00:01 AM
Time of Last Event: 7/7/2007 6:00:01 AM
Source: Microsoft Operations Manager
Rule (enabled):
Microsoft Operations Manager\Operations Manager 2005\
Agents on all MOM roles\MOM Logging Level Verification
```

The trace level can be set by altering the HKLM\Software\Mission Critical Software\TraceLevel registry key, as showing in Figure 12-1.

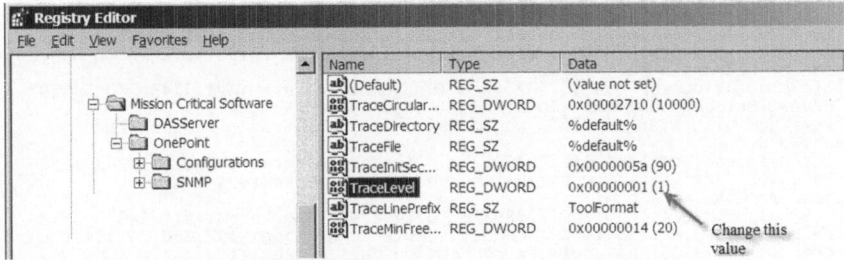

Figure 12-1. *Trace level registry entry*

Log files with the extension .mc8 can be found in two locations:

- %WinDir%\Temp\Microsoft Operations Manager\
- %UserProfile%\Local Settings\Temp\Microsoft Operations Manager\

MOM creates the following log files when trace logging is enabled:

- %WinDir%\Temp\Microsoft Operations Manager
  - MOMService*.mc8
  - MOMHost*.mc8
  - MOMAgentScriptHost-<ManagementGroupName>*.mc8
  - MOMAgentPerformanceHost-<ManagementGroupName>*.mc8
- MOM.UI.OpsConsoleExe*.log, located in %UserProfile%\Local Settings\Temp\Microsoft Operations Manager
- •DllHost.mc8 (DAS log), located in Documents and Settings\<Das account>\Local Settings\Temp\Microsoft Operations Manager or %systemroot%\Temp\Microsoft Operations Manager

The log files that MOM produces can be very difficult to read using Notepad or other text editors, so use the MOM Log Viewer utility to read the log files. Figure 12-2 shows the unformatted log file entry for an agent install failure because of an account failure.

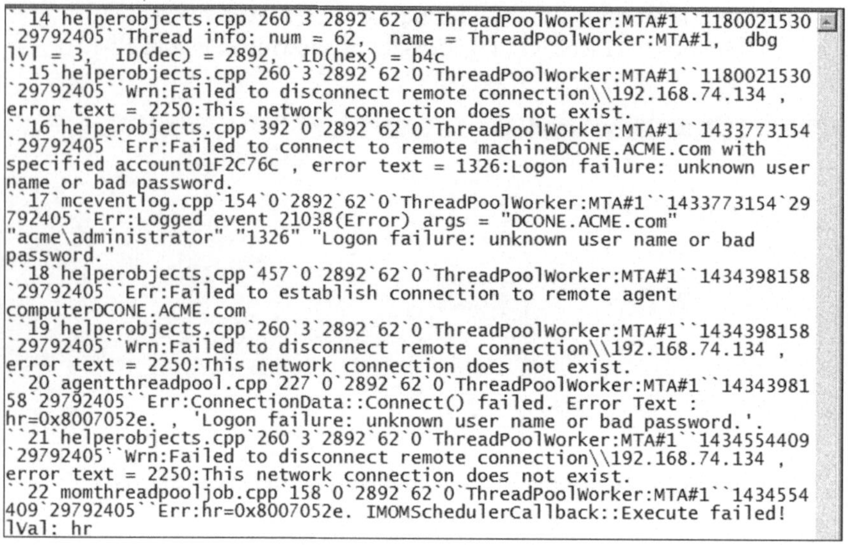

```
``14`helperobjects.cpp`260`3`2892`62`0`ThreadPoolWorker:MTA#1``1180021530
`29792405``Thread info: num = 62,  name = ThreadPoolWorker:MTA#1,  dbg
lvl = 3,  ID(dec) = 2892,  ID(hex) = b4c
``15`helperobjects.cpp`260`3`2892`62`0`ThreadPoolWorker:MTA#1``1180021530
`29792405``Wrn:Failed to disconnect remote connection\\192.168.74.134 ,
error text = 2250:This network connection does not exist.
``16`helperobjects.cpp`392`0`2892`62`0`ThreadPoolWorker:MTA#1``1433773154
`29792405``Err:Failed to connect to remote machineDCONE.ACME.com with
specified account01F2C76C , error text = 1326:Logon failure: unknown user
name or bad password.
``17`mceventlog.cpp`154`0`2892`62`0`ThreadPoolWorker:MTA#1``1433773154`29
792405``Err:Logged event 21038(Error) args = "DCONE.ACME.com"
"acme\administrator" "1326" "Logon failure: unknown user name or bad
password."
``18`helperobjects.cpp`457`0`2892`62`0`ThreadPoolWorker:MTA#1``1434398158
`29792405``Err:Failed to establish connection to remote agent
computerDCONE.ACME.com
``19`helperobjects.cpp`260`3`2892`62`0`ThreadPoolWorker:MTA#1``1434398158
`29792405``Wrn:Failed to disconnect remote connection\\192.168.74.134 ,
error text = 2250:This network connection does not exist.
``20`agentthreadpool.cpp`227`0`2892`62`0`ThreadPoolWorker:MTA#1``14343981
58`29792405``Err:ConnectionData::Connect() failed. Error Text :
hr=0x8007052e. , 'Logon failure: unknown user name or bad password.'.
``21`helperobjects.cpp`260`3`2892`62`0`ThreadPoolWorker:MTA#1``1434554409
`29792405``Wrn:Failed to disconnect remote connection\\192.168.74.134 ,
error text = 2250:This network connection does not exist.
``22`momthreadpooljob.cpp`158`0`2892`62`0`ThreadPoolWorker:MTA#1``1434554
409`29792405``Err:hr=0x8007052e. IMOMSchedulerCallback::Execute failed!
lVal: hr
```

Figure 12-2. *Log file viewed using Notepad*

Figure 12-3 shows the same log entry when viewed via MOM Log Viewer.

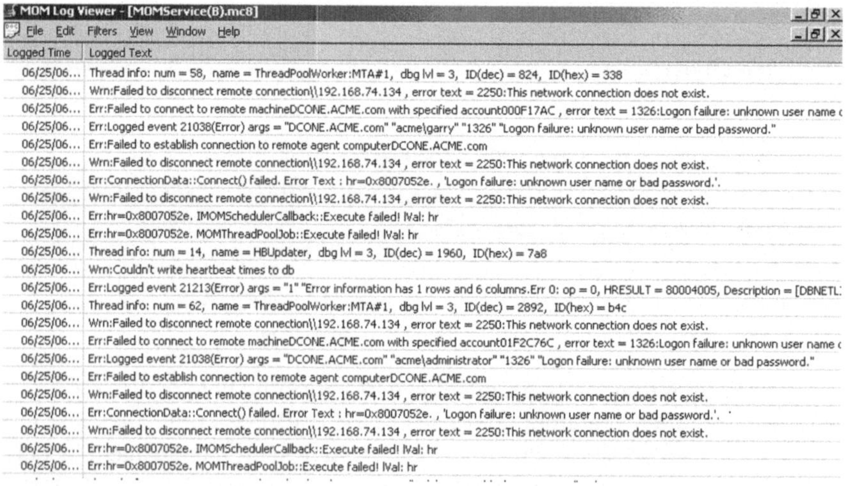

Logged Time	Logged Text
06/25/06...	Thread info: num = 58, name = ThreadPoolWorker:MTA#1, dbg lvl = 3, ID(dec) = 824, ID(hex) = 338
06/25/06...	Wrn:Failed to disconnect remote connection\\192.168.74.134 , error text = 2250:This network connection does not exist.
06/25/06...	Err:Failed to connect to remote machineDCONE.ACME.com with specified account000F17AC , error text = 1326:Logon failure: unknown user name c
06/25/06...	Err:Logged event 21038(Error) args = "DCONE.ACME.com" "acme\garry" "1326" "Logon failure: unknown user name or bad password."
06/25/06...	Err:Failed to establish connection to remote agent computerDCONE.ACME.com
06/25/06...	Wrn:Failed to disconnect remote connection\\192.168.74.134 , error text = 2250:This network connection does not exist.
06/25/06...	Err:ConnectionData::Connect() failed. Error Text : hr=0x8007052e. , 'Logon failure: unknown user name or bad password.'.
06/25/06...	Wrn:Failed to disconnect remote connection\\192.168.74.134 , error text = 2250:This network connection does not exist.
06/25/06...	Err:hr=0x8007052e. IMOMSchedulerCallback::Execute failed! lVal: hr
06/25/06...	Err:hr=0x8007052e. MOMThreadPoolJob::Execute failed! lVal: hr
06/25/06...	Thread info: num = 14, name = HBUpdater, dbg lvl = 3, ID(dec) = 1960, ID(hex) = 7a8
06/25/06...	Wrn:Couldn't write heartbeat times to db
06/25/06...	Err:Logged event 21213(Error) args = "1" "Error information has 1 rows and 6 columns.Err 0: op = 0, HRESULT = 80004005, Description = [DBNETL:
06/25/06...	Thread info: num = 62, name = ThreadPoolWorker:MTA#1, dbg lvl = 3, ID(dec) = 2892, ID(hex) = b4c
06/25/06...	Wrn:Failed to disconnect remote connection\\192.168.74.134 , error text = 2250:This network connection does not exist.
06/25/06...	Err:Failed to connect to remote machineDCONE.ACME.com with specified account01F2C76C , error text = 1326:Logon failure: unknown user name c
06/25/06...	Err:Logged event 21038(Error) args = "DCONE.ACME.com" "acme\administrator" "1326" "Logon failure: unknown user name or bad password."
06/25/06...	Err:Failed to establish connection to remote agent computerDCONE.ACME.com
06/25/06...	Wrn:Failed to disconnect remote connection\\192.168.74.134 , error text = 2250:This network connection does not exist.
06/25/06...	Err:ConnectionData::Connect() failed. Error Text : hr=0x8007052e. , 'Logon failure: unknown user name or bad password.'.
06/25/06...	Wrn:Failed to disconnect remote connection\\192.168.74.134 , error text = 2250:This network connection does not exist.
06/25/06...	Err:hr=0x8007052e. IMOMSchedulerCallback::Execute failed! lVal: hr
06/25/06...	Err:hr=0x8007052e. MOMThreadPoolJob::Execute failed! lVal: hr

Figure 12-3. *Log file viewed using MOM Log Viewer*

Figure 12-4 shows a line from the trace log showing that the wrong username or password was used when trying to install the agent.

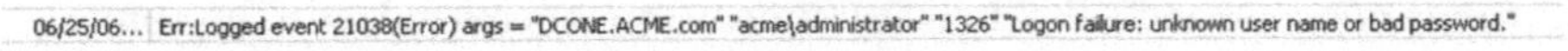

06/25/06... Err:Logged event 21038(Error) args = "DCONE.ACME.com" "acme\administrator" "1326" "Logon failure: unknown user name or bad password."

Figure 12-4. *Trace log entry*

Figure 12-4 also shows that MOM has logged an event in the event log
`Err:Logged event 21038(Error)`, and that the severity was *error*. The corresponding event in the event log is shown in Figure 12-5.

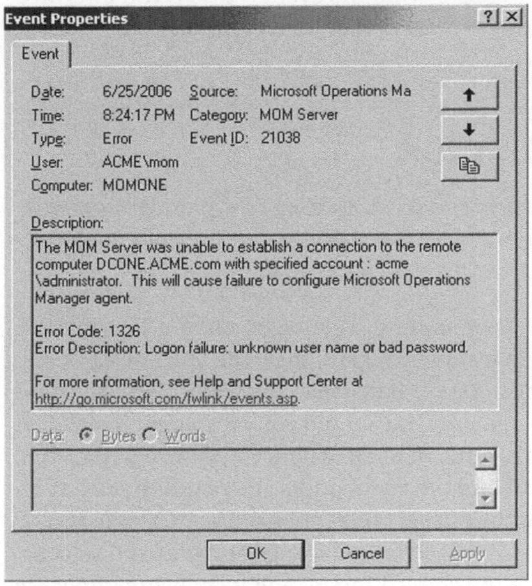

Figure 12-5. *Event log error*

When looking at errors in the event log, it is always worthwhile to look
for the errors in the log files and see what happened just before the event
was raised. This will often provide you with information that is useful when
you are troubleshooting.

Event Logs

The event logs on the MOM server or agent are helpful for both troubleshooting when things go wrong and monitoring performance and behavior.
An event log is a file that contains events, which are entries to the log that
notify the administrator of some occurrence relating to the operating system
or applications running on the system. An event includes information about

the type of occurrence, the date and time when it occurred, and the computer on which it happened. The main event logs that you will use are the application and system event logs.

When you're troubleshooting the management server, the event logs often provide you with the information you need to resolve an issue. However, you should ensure that you don't concentrate only on events generated by the MOM components, as the actual fault could be OS related. There is a community-based web site called `www.eventid.net` where you can search for additional information about obscure Windows events to help you interpret them. This web site also often shows what other administrators have done to resolve a particular event.

MOM Agent Installation

The MOM agent installation process is in most cases a very straightforward process. The main causes of failures are due to networks, firewalls, name resolution, and permissions.

Networks: If a slow network separates the management server and the client on which you plan to install the agent, then you will encounter timeouts if you try to carry out a push install of the agent from the management server. To overcome this, you should copy the agent install files to the agent, and then carry out a manual install. Once the agent install has completed, you should find the agent under the pending actions section of the Administrator Console on the management server. You should approve the agent install by right-clicking the agent and selecting Approve Agent Install from the context menu. Agents may not appear in the Pending Actions folder of the Administrator Console after you do a manual installation. If the agent already has a computer or discovery rule defined, or if the agent is listed in Unmanaged Computers prior to manual installation, it will not appear in the Pending Actions folder.

Firewalls: If a firewall separates the management server from the client on which the agent will be installed, a manual install of the agent will be required. You should ensure that the ports required by MOM are open (see Chapter 15 for more details). If the agent has a firewall installed (e.g., Windows 2003 SP1), then the required ports and exceptions need configuring on the agent. Microsoft Knowledge Base article 885726, located at `http://support.microsoft.com/kb/885726`, documents the steps that are required to install the agent on a firewall-enabled client.

Name Resolution: The agent and the management server need to be able to resolve each other's names via DNS or Windows Internet Naming Service (WINS). If there is no DNS or WINS infrastructure available, then LMHOSTS files can be used on the management server and agent. Microsoft Knowledge Base article 904866 (located at http://support. microsoft.com/default.aspx?scid=kb;EN-US;904866) provides an overview of the options available.

Permissions: To install the agent, you need administrative access to the system on which you intend to deploy the agent. This means that the Management Servers Action account needs to have administrative access (if used), or the account that you specify during the agent install process needs has administrative access.

To help find out what caused an agent install to fail, you can use the install logs and event logs to pinpoint the reason for the failure. The install logs for an agent install are located on the management server in the following location: %ProgramFiles%\Microsoft Operations Manager 2005\ AgentLogs. The two log files of interest are:

- %ComputerName%AgentInstall.log
- %ComputerName%AgentUninstall.log

MOM Log Viewer is the best tool to use to review these log files. Another tool that is worthy of mention is WiLogUtl.exe, which you can use to analyze the log files created when MSI packages are installed. WiLogUtl.exe can also be used to troubleshoot manual agent installs, and when installing any of the management server roles. WiLogUtl.exe can be downloaded from www. microsoft.com/downloads/details.aspx?FamilyId=A55B6B43-E24F-4EA3- A93E-40C0EC4F68E5&displaylang=en.

Resource Kit Tools

The Microsoft Operations Manager 2005 Resource Kit contains a number of downloadable tools that can help the troubleshooting process. The resource kit is a free download located at www.microsoft.com/mom/downloads/2005/ reskit/default.mspx. The tools that are used in troubleshooting are as follows:

- Clean-up MOM
- Management Group utility

- MOM Information utility
- Windows Server Cluster Detection utility
- MOM Inventory

Clean-Up MOM

The Clean-up MOM tool removes the MOM install on the server. It does not look at the role of the server in your MOM infrastructure, and if it is used on the management server, it will remove the MOM server if CleanupMOM.exe is not targeted against specific functions. By default, CleanupMOM.exe will remove all information on the server. However, when you use the /z parameter, you're able to target specific areas to remove. The other available parameters are as follows:

- :All: Removes all the MOM Windows Installer information
- :S: Removes all the MOM Server Windows Installer information
- :A: Removes Windows Installer information for MOM agent components
- :R: Removes Windows Installer information for MOM reporting components

Clean-up MOM is useful when you have been piloting MOM in your environment and need to clean up the pilot environment prior to deploying the production management group. When removing the agent function, you still need to remove the agent on the management server, as the management server will simply think that the agent is no longer heart-beating until you remove it.

MOM Information Utility

MOMInfo.exe allows you to export information on how the agent or management server is configured. The following list shows how the MOM Information utility can be used to troubleshoot agent issues:

- It can dump the rules, responses, and VarSet values at the MOM agent into an XML file for offline analysis.
- It can clear the queues on an agent.
- It can be run locally at the agent and put into maintenance mode.
- It can enable script debugging.

The following commands show the switches that are available for MOMInfo.exe:

- `MOMInfo.exe /rules /out:rules.xml`: Exports all the rules of all configured management groups in the `rules.xml` file. You can use `/config:ManagementGroup` to receive the information about one management group.

- `MOMInfo.exe /responses /out:responses.xml`: Dumps all running responses to a file called `responses.xml`. You can use `/config:ManagementGroup` to receive the information about one management group.

- `MOMInfo.exe /clearqueue`: Clears the queues on the agent; also restarts the agent service.

- `MOMInfo.exe /maintenancemode`: Puts the server into maintenance mode. The agent needs to be able to communicate with the management server to inform the management server that the agent is in maintenance mode.

- `MOMInfo.exe /scriptdebugging`: Enables script debugging on the agent.

- `MOMInfo.exe /errorhandling`: Turns on error handling to get information when MOM crashes.

Windows Server Cluster Detection Utility

`MOMClusterTool.exe` can be used to determine why a MOM agent is not detecting the virtual server on a Windows Server cluster. This tool performs the same checks as the MOM agent service, and provides a report of configuration problems that may prevent MOM from monitoring the virtual server. The Windows Server Cluster Detection utility can be run on one of the servers in the cluster group, or run remotely against the cluster.

MOM Inventory

`MOMInventory.exe` is used to collate all the information that Microsoft support will require to help you diagnose a support call that you have opened. The Mom Inventory tool will collect the following information:

- Windows Installer logs for MOM

- MOM trace logs

- MOM registry information

- MOM server configuration

- All event logs

It will also generate a list of all running processes. The information, once collected, is stored in a compressed CAB file that you can send to Microsoft for analysis.

Summary

The aim of this chapter has been to provide you with an understanding of the tools available in the Resource Kit that can be utilized to troubleshoot issues, and to introduce processes that you can follow to help resolve issues in the MOM infrastructure.

Chapter 13 will provide you with the information that you need to resolve issues with scripts that are utilized in your MOM installation.

CHAPTER 13

■ ■ ■

Troubleshooting Scripts

Scripts are an integral part of MOM. It is therefore important that you understand how to troubleshoot scripts that are used inside your MOM environment. This chapter will introduce the steps required to troubleshoot script failures; these steps can be used on existing scripts and custom-developed ones.

This chapter covers how you can use the following:

- Response Test
- Visual Studio

Response Test

Response Test is a command-line utility that is included in the MOM 2005 Resource Kit. It allows you to test the syntax of your MOM scripts from any machine on which the MOM agent is running, without having to make changes to your MOM infrastructure. It is very useful when testing custom scripts, as the only other solution is to use a MOM development environment and deploy rules that will call the script. Using the MOM development environment process can be very time consuming, as the events that will cause the rules to fire have to be simulated. The Response Test utility allows you to simulate the required events via an XML input file. The output from the Response Test utility is also sent to an XML file. The `ResponseTest.exe` file should be copied to the location where the MOM agent is installed, which by default is `C:\Program Files\Microsoft Operations Manager 2005`.

Using Response Test to Test a Script

Assume that you've developed the script shown in Listing 13-1 to check that DNS forwarding is working correctly on domain controllers. To test the script, `ResponseTest.exe` will be used.

Listing 13-1. *DNS Forwarder Check VBS Script*

```
Const Event_Type_Success = 0
Const Event_Type_Error = 1
Const Event_Type_Warning = 2
Const Event_Type_Information = 4
Const Eventid_Dnslookup_Failed = 41001
Const Eventid_Dnslookup_Success = 41002

Set Objshell = Createobject("Wscript.Shell")
Set Objwshscriptexec = Objshell.Exec("Nslookup Acme.Com")
Set Objstdout = Objwshscriptexec.Stdout

While Not Objstdout.Atendofstream
    'Loouparray(Intsize) = Objstdout.Readall
Strline = Objstdout.Readall
Wend

Srv="192.168.74.134"

If Instr(Strline,Srv)= 0 Then
  Createevent Eventid_Dnslookup_Failed,Event_Type_Information,Strline
Else
Createevent Eventid_Dnslookup_Success,Event_Type_Information,Strline
End If
Sub Createevent(Lngeventid, Lngeventtype, Strmessage)
  On Error Resume Next
  Dim Objnewevent
  ' Create A New Event
  Set Objnewevent = Scriptcontext.Createevent
  ' Set Event Properties
  Objnewevent.Message = Strmessage
  Objnewevent.Eventnumber = Lngeventid
  Objnewevent.Eventtype = Lngeventtype
  ' Submit The Event
  Scriptcontext.Submit Objnewevent
  Set Objnewevent = Nothing
End Sub
```

To check the code, use the following command line:

```
ResponseTest /script:c:\dns.vbs
```

The output will be sent to `ReponseTestOutput.xml`, which is located in `C:\Program Files\Microsoft Operations Manager 2005`. Use Internet Explorer to read the output file. Figure 13-1 shows the output from this test.

```xml
- <ResponseResults>
  - <Events>
    - <Event>
        <EventTimeGenerated>7/15/2006 10:20:19 PM</EventTimeGenerated>
        <EventID>41002</EventID>
        <EventSource>MOMXResponseTool Script</EventSource>
        <EventMessage>Server: dcone.acme.com Address: 192.168.74.134 Name: acme.com
          Addresses: 192.168.74.134, 192.168.71.128</EventMessage>
        <EventStrings />
        <EventLoggingComputer>MOMONE</EventLoggingComputer>
        <EventLoggingComputerDomain>ACME</EventLoggingComputerDomain>
        <EventSourceComputer>ACME</EventSourceComputer>
        <EventSourceComputerDomain>ACME</EventSourceComputerDomain>
        <EventType>4</EventType>
        <EventCategory>0</EventCategory>
        <EventMessageDLL />
      </Event>
  </Events>
</ResponseResults>
```

Figure 13-1. *ReponseTestOutput.xml output viewed in Internet Explorer*

As Figure 13-1 shows, the script in Listing 13-1 does not have any errors and has carried out the DNS Forwarder check and completed successfully. To show the output if there were a script error, the following lines of code have had the `Strline` parameter removed so that the incorrect number of parameters are passed to the `Createevent` procedure:

```
If Instr(Strline,Srv)= 0 Then
  Createevent Eventid_Dnslookup_Failed, Event_Type_Information
Else
  Createevent Eventid_Dnslookup_Success, Event_Type_Information
End If
```

The Response Test utility will now display errors in the command output. The command output can seem very complex, but the section you are interested in is located near the end. The output is shown in Listing 13-2; the sections in bold correspond to the error and the location in the script, which is shown as the line number.

Listing 13-2. *Output from the Command Line*

```
=== Status ===
HRESULT      = 0x80040202
Source       = Microsoft VBScript runtime error
Description  = Wrong number of arguments
or invalid property assignment: 'CreateEvent'
Resolution   =
Help File    =
Help Context = 0
Source File  =
Source Line  = 34
```

The output from Response Test can be very large if the script you are testing contains numerous errors. We therefore recommend that you either increase the DOS windows screen buffer size, or that you pipe the output into a text file (e.g., ResponseTest /script:c:\dns.vbs >output.txt). Having the output in a file makes it easier to search the output for errors.

Using Advanced Features of Response Test

Using Response Test to check that a script runs as expected is a very handy thing to do, but Response Test also allows you to go further by creating a testing scenario in a very controlled manner. For example, let's say you've created an alert in MOM that, when a service has more than 90 percent CPU usage, calls a script that will stop and start the service. To test this scenario using Response Test, you need to create the script to stop and start the service, and create an XML configuration file that will simulate the event being triggered. The script is shown in Listing 13-3; it is a simple VB script that stops and starts the service that is passed to it. The service name is received as the performance object instance that breached the threshold.

Listing 13-3. *The Script That Stops and Starts the Service*

```
Const Event_Type_Success = 0
Const Event_Type_Error = 1
Const Event_Type_Warning = 2
Const Event_Type_Information = 4
Const Eventid_Service_Restart = 41001

strComputer = "."
```

```
Set objPerfData = ScriptContext.PerfData
strSvc = objPerfData.InstanceName
strLine = strSvc &" Service Restarted"

Set objWMIService=GetObject("winmgmts:\\"
_& strComputer & "\root\cimv2")
Set colItems = objWMIService.ExecQuery("Select * _
from Win32_Service where name='strSvc'")

For Each objItem in colItems
   objItem.StopService
   objItem.StartService
Next

CreateEvent Eventid_Service_Restart, Event_Type_Error, strLine

Sub CreateEvent(lngEventID, lngEventType, strMessage)
  On Error Resume Next

  Dim objNewEvent

  ' Create a new event
  Set objNewEvent = ScriptContext.CreateEvent
  ' Set event properties
  objNewEvent.Message = strMessage
  objNewEvent.EventNumber = lngEventID
  objNewEvent.EventType = lngEventType
  ' Submit the event
  ScriptContext.Submit objNewEvent
  Set objNewEvent = Nothing
End Sub
```

You now need to create the XML configuration file. This XML file contains the performance counter, performance instance, and performance value. Listing 13-4 shows the configuration settings to use in testing the script from Listing 13-3. Notepad can be used to create the file, and it should be saved as an XML file—for example, config.xml.

Listing 13-4. *XML Configuration File*

```
<ConfigData>
    <PerfData>
        <PerfObject>Process</PerfObject>
        <PerfCounter>% Processor Time</PerfCounter>
        <PerfInstance>spoolsv</PerfInstance>
        <PerfTime>06/06/2006 5:34:11 PM</PerfTime>
        <PerfValue>90.</PerfValue>
        <PerfComputer>MOMONE</PerfComputer>
        <PerfDomain>ACME</PerfDomain>
    </PerfData>
</ConfigData>
```

To test the script, run the following command-line `ResponseTest.exe` file:

```
/script:c:\service.vbs /config:c:\config.xml
```

If there are no errors in the script, the output will be sent to `ReponseTestOutput.xml`, and will be similar to Figure 13-1; if there are errors in the script, then those will be visible in the command output. It is possible to configure the configuration file to simulate scenarios not based on performance events. The configuration file can be configured to simulate events, alerts, and performance data. The configuration options for simulating an event are as follows:

```
<Event>
    <EventTimeGenerated> - The time of the event
    <EventID> - The event id
    <EventSource> - The event source
    <EventMessage> - The event message
        <EventStrings>
            <String Num='1'>Testing Event Strings</String>
        </EventStrings>
    <EventLoggingComputer> - The Computer that logged the event
    <EventLoggingComputerDomain> - The domain of the computer
    <EventSourceComputer> - The Computer the event came from
    <EventSourceComputerDomain> - The domain of the source computer
    <EventType> - Integer representing the event type
    <EventCategory> - Integer representing the event category
    <EventMessageDLL> - The message dll of the event
</Event>
```

Substituting the values, the following example will create an event with an ID of 4199 that will be raised by the computer MOMONE:

```
</Event>

<EventTimeGenerated>06/06/2006 7:40:55 AM</EventTimeGenerated>
    <EventID>4199</EventID>
    <EventSource>MOMXResponseTool Script</EventSource>
    <EventMessage>Testing Events</EventMessage>
    <EventStrings>
        <String Num='1'>String Value One</String>
    </EventStrings>
    <EventLoggingComputer>MOMONE</EventLoggingComputer>
    <EventLoggingComputerDomain>MOMONE</EventLoggingComputerDomain>
    <EventSourceComputer>MOMTWO</EventSourceComputer>
    <EventSourceComputerDomain>ACME</EventSourceComputerDomain>
    <EventType>1</EventType>
    <EventCategory>0</EventCategory>
    <EventMessageDLL></EventMessageDLL>
</Event>
```

The configuration options for simulating an alert are as follows:

```
</Alert>
    <AlertID> - The GUID of the alert (registry format)
    <AlertRuleID> - The GUID of the alert rule (registry format)
    <AlertName> - The alert name
    <AlertOwner> - The alert owner
    <AlertDescription> - The alert description
    <AlertLevel> - Integer representing the alert level
    <AlertResolutionState> - Integer representing the alert state
    <AlertTime> - The time of the alert
    <AlertSource> - The alert source
    <AlertComputer> - The alert source computer
    <AlertDomain> - The domain of the source computer
    <AlertSummary> - Summary of the alert history
    <AlertCustomField1 />
    <AlertCustomField2 />
    <AlertCustomField3 />
    <AlertCustomField4 />
    <AlertCustomField5 />
    <AlertServerRole> - The alert server role
    <AlertServerRoleInstance> - The alert server role instance
```

```
    <AlertSubGroupRole> - The alert sub group role
    <AlertSubGroupRoleInstance> - The alert sub group role instance
    <AlertProblemState> - Integer representing the problem state
</Alert>
```

Substituting the values, the following example will create an alert called Test Alert from Response Test, raised by the computer MOMONE.

```
<Alert>
    <AlertID>{00000000-0000-0000-0000-000000000000}</AlertID>
    <AlertRuleID>{00000000-0000-0000-0000-000000000000}</AlertRuleID>
    <AlertName>Test Alert from ResponseTest</AlertName>
    <AlertOwner>GarryM</AlertOwner>
    <AlertDescription>Test Alert from ResponseTest</AlertDescription>
    <AlertLevel>50</AlertLevel>
    <AlertResolutionState>B</AlertResolutionState>
    <AlertTime>02:00:00 AM</AlertTime>
    <AlertSource>AlertSource</AlertSource>
    <AlertComputer>MOMONE</AlertComputer>
    <AlertDomain>ACME</AlertDomain>
    <AlertSummary>Alert by Script ResponseTool</AlertSummary>
    <AlertCustomField1>Update Field 1</AlertCustomField1>
    <AlertCustomField2>Update Field 2</AlertCustomField2>
        <AlertCustomField3>Update Field 3</AlertCustomField3>
        <AlertCustomField4>Update Field 4</AlertCustomField4>
        <AlertCustomField5>Update Field 5</AlertCustomField5>
  <AlertServerRole></AlertServerRole>
  <AlertServerRoleInstance></AlertServerRoleInstance>
  <AlertSubGroupRole></AlertSubGroupRole>
  <AlertSubGroupRoleInstance></AlertSubGroupRoleInstance>
  <AlertProblemState>0</AlertProblemState>
</Alert>
```

In the examples shown so far in this chapter, the Response Test script has always been separate from the XML configuration file. It is possible to include the script inside the XML configuration file, but this is not recommended. Having a separate script file allows you to transfer the script easily into your MOM environment without worrying about accidentally changing any contents of your script when you remove the Response Test configuration information.

Note Response Test runs under the context of the account that ran it. When you test out scripts, it is important to remember that the MOMHost process runs the scripts under the credentials of the MOM action account; so the results could be different when implemented into your live MOM environment.

Visual Studio

Visual Studio is an advanced integrated development environment (IDE) by Microsoft. It lets programmers create programs, web sites, web applications, and web services. It can be used by MOM administrators to help debug scripts in the MOM environment. To debug a script, you either need to have Visual Studio installed locally, or have remote debugging tools installed on the server. It is therefore the safest option to—whenever possible—debug in a development environment so that you do not have to install any extra components onto a production system. If this is not possible, then the safest option is to just install the remote debugging tools, as this does not require a reboot.

Installing Remote Debugging Tools

The remote debugging tools are located on Visual Studio's install media. To install the remote debugging tools, you need to carry out the following steps:

1. Go to the location of the Visual Studio media.

2. Double-click Setup.exe.

3. The Visual Studio .NET setup screen will appear. Double-click the Remote Components Setup link (located near the bottom of the screen), as shown in Figure 13-2.

4. This will open the Remote Components Setup page. Scroll to the Full Remote Debugging support area, and then click Install Full.

Once the install has completed, you can use Visual Studio to remotely attach to processes on the remote system.

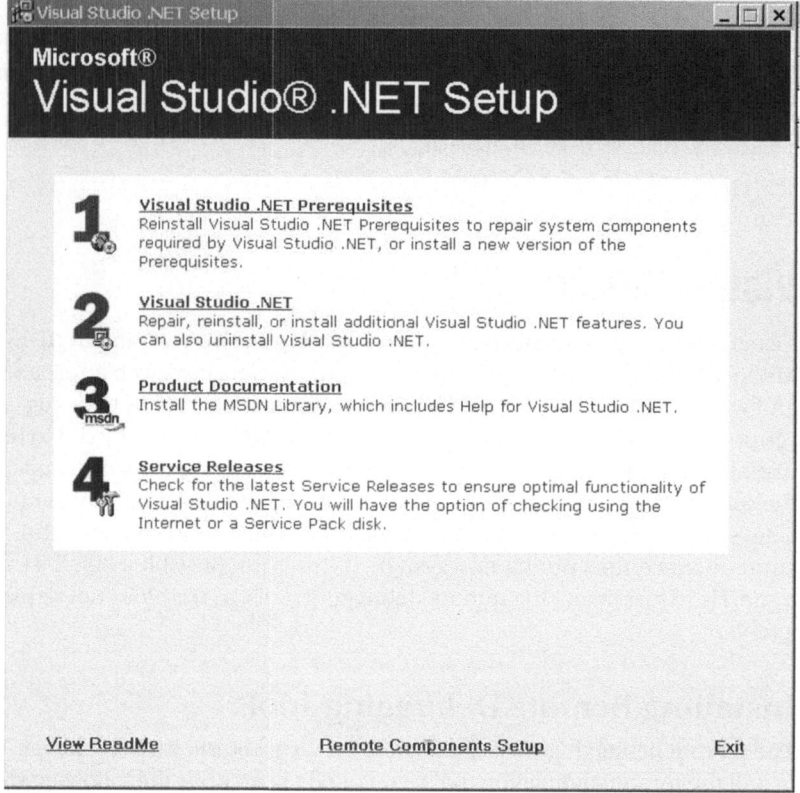

Figure 13-2. *The .NET Setup Screen*

Debugging a Script

A typical MOM agent will at times run multiple scripts; so when you try to debug a script, it is important to restrict the debugger to the script that you want to troubleshoot. To achieve this, go to the following section in the registry:

HKEY_LOCAL_MACHINE\SOFTWARE\Mission Critical Software\OnePoint\

and configure the following registry key values:

DebugEnabledScripts: Enter the name of the script(s) you wish to debug. This can be either one script, multiple scripts separated by commas, or all scripts that run on the agent, which is specified by a *.

EnableActiveDebugging: Enter the value 1 to enable active debugging. Once debugging has finished, the value should be set to 0.

Figure 13-3 show an example of the agent being configured to allow debugging of the DNS check script.

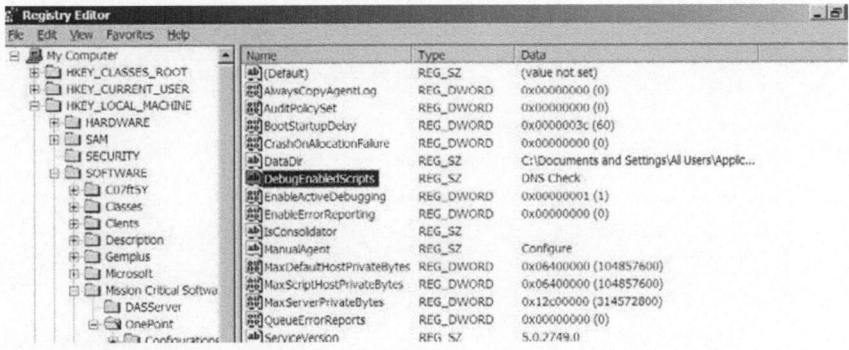

Figure 13-3. *Registry entries*

The next step is to attach the debugger to the MOMHost process on the agent that you installed the remote debugging tools on. To attach Visual Studio to the MOMHost process, follow these steps:

1. On the system with the full Visual Studio install, start Visual Studio and select Processes from the Debug menu, as shown in Figure 13-4.

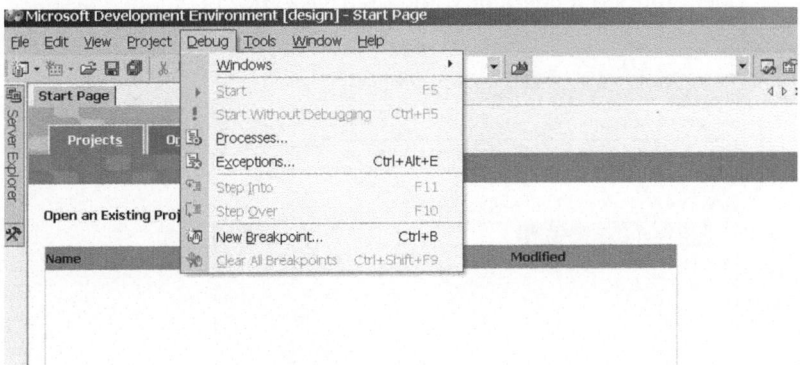

Figure 13-4. *Selecting Processes from the Debug menu*

2. The Processes dialog will now appear. In the Name field, enter the name of the agent that you installed the remote debugging tools on, and click Refresh. In Figure 13-5, the remote debugging tools have been installed on an agent called MOMONE.

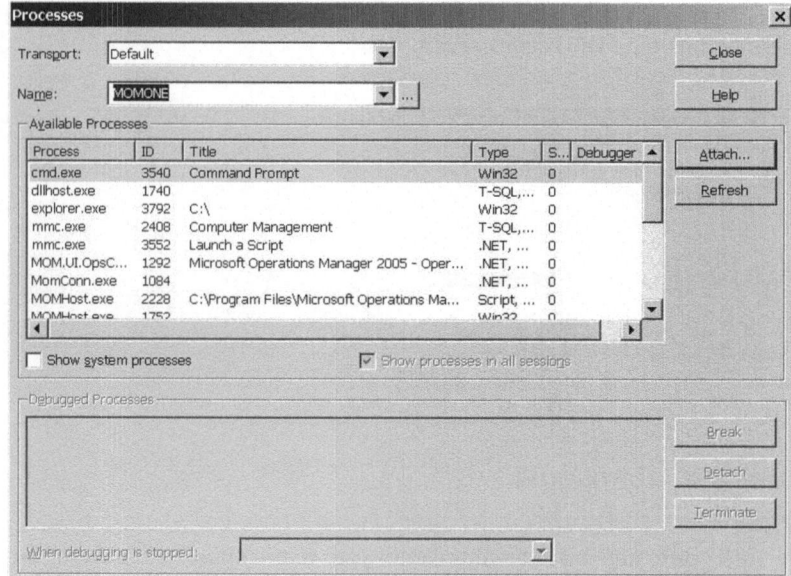

Figure 13-5. *Selecting the agent*

3. Select the MOMHost.exe process by clicking it, and then clicking Attach.
   The Attach to Process dialog will then appear, as shown in Figure 13-6.
   Check the Script check box, and then click OK.

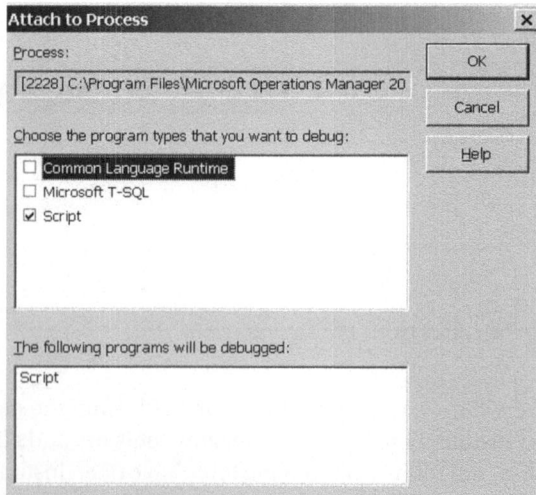

Figure 13-6. *Selecting Script*

4. The Processes dialog will now reappear, as shown in Figure 13-7. In the bottom pane, highlight the `MOMHost.exe` process, click Break, and then click Close. This will take you back to the Visual Studio start page.

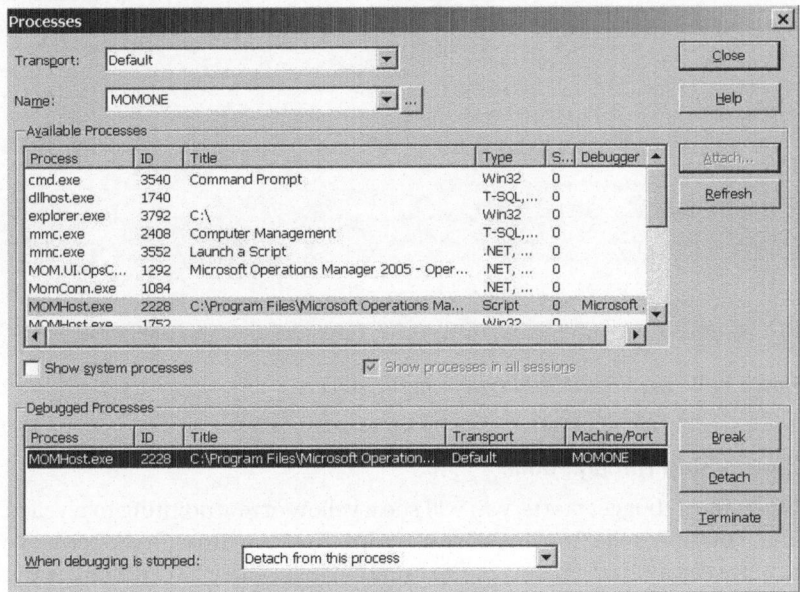

Figure 13-7. *Configuring the break options*

Visual Studio is now configured to start the debugging tool when the DNS check script is run. When the agent calls the script, the Visual Studio screen will change to the debugging screen, as shown in Figure 13-8.

This screen may take a while to appear, as it is only started when the agent starts the script you specified. From the debugging screen, you can now step through the code and inspect the values of the variables that configured in the script.

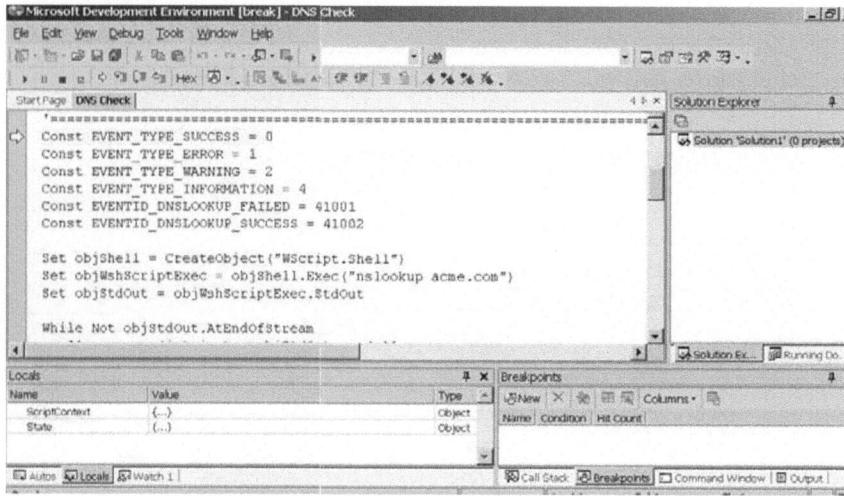

Figure 13-8. *The Visual Studio debugging screen*

How to Step Through Code

When the debugger starts, you will see a yellow arrow pointing to a yellow line. This line is the first line of your script. To move through the script, you can use the toolbar of icons or the function keys. Table 13-1 describes the functions of the toolbar and the function keys.

Table 13-1. *Debugging Toolbar Icons and Function Keys*

Menu Icon	Description	Function Key
⤵	Executes the current line, and then stops at the next line.	F11
⤷	Steps into the code line by line. If the next line calls a function or subroutine, the procedure will be completed before returning to the main code body.	F10
▶	Starts execution of the code from the current line, until the end or a breakpoint is reached.	F5
■	Stops the execution of the code and ends the debug session.	Shift+F5

How to Inspect the Values of the Variables

A variable is a placeholder that refers to a computer memory location where you can store program information that may change during the time your script is running. Variables are often used in conditional checks. For example, in the DNS script, a variable is used to hold the expected IP address of the web server. This is then compared to the input from the NSLOOKUP command. When troubleshooting scripts, it is often useful to inspect the value of these variables as the script is running. This can be achieved by stepping through the code and inspecting the variables in the Locals window. This window will be populated with the variables as they are used throughout the script. Figure 13-9 shows the variables that are used in the DNS check script.

Locals		
Name	Value	Type
ScriptContext	{...}	Object
State	{...}	Object
EVENT_TYPE_SUCCESS	0	Integer
EVENT_TYPE_ERROR	1	Integer
EVENT_TYPE_WARNING	2	Integer
EVENT_TYPE_INFORMATION	4	Integer
EVENTID_DNSLOOKUP_FAILED	41001	Long
EVENTID_DNSLOOKUP_SUCCESS	41002	Long
⊞ objShell	{...}	Object
⊞ objWshScriptExec	{...}	Object
⊞ objStdOut	{...}	Object
strLine	"Server: dcone.acme.com□□Address: 192.168.74.	String
srv	"192.168.74.134"	String

Figure 13-9. *The Locals window*

Summary

This chapter has covered how to troubleshoot and test scripts that you use (or intend to use) in your MOM environment. Chapter 14 will cover the steps to take to ensure that your MOM environment is secure, and also how to deploy and manage agents that are separated by a firewall.

CHAPTER 14

■ ■ ■

Security

Securing your MOM environment and also running MOM agents behind a firewall can seem like a challenging task. However, MOM supports agents separated by a firewall out of the box, and it can also be configured to run in a low-privilege scenario, so most security restraints can be managed. This chapter aims to cover the main areas relating to managing security for your MOM infrastructure, and gives recommendations on how to remain secure and avoid creating a complex environment to manage.

This chapter covers the following:

- Service accounts
- Configuration of agent computers to run in low privilege
- Security groups
- Configuration options
- Agents behind firewalls

MOM Service

In MOM 2005, you can run the MOM service under the context of either Local System on Windows 2000 and Windows 2003, or Network Service on Windows 2003. The MOM service is not responsible for agent management or database communication. The MOM service is responsible for communications between the agent and the management server, and for running the agent on the client. It is important to note that the MOM service will not start unless it is running as either Local System or Network Service.

Caution Run the MOM service under the Network Service context. Do not change the context under which the account runs, as this can result in communication failures in your MOM environment.

Service Accounts

MOM 2005 has a requirement on a number of service accounts. Before deploying MOM, you need to ensure that you have all the required accounts configured and the correct permissions granted to the accounts. These accounts need to be carefully managed after installing MOM to ensure that the MOM infrastructure continues to work correctly.

MOM Installation Account

When you install MOM 2005, you must use an account that has administrator access on all servers on which you are installing MOM components. During the installation process, a number of SQL jobs are created. The account that was used to install MOM 2005 will become the owner of these jobs.

Note The installation account must have administrator access on the management server, database server, and report server (if used).

DAS Service Account

In MOM 2005, you can run the DAS service under the context of a standard domain user account. During the installation, the DAS account will be granted the required SQL privileges on the OnePoint database. The DAS Service account is used for database access and the MOM-to-MOM product connector.

If the MOM connector framework is installed, then the DAS Service account must be a member of the SCDW DTS security groups on the MOM Reporting Server and the MOM Database Server.

If the MOM installation has been upgraded from MOM 2000, the access rights that were granted under MOM 2000 remain. The account will have extra permissions that are no longer required in MOM 2005.

Tip Run the MOM service under the context of a standard domain user account.

Management Server Action Account

Under Windows 2003, you can run the Management Server Action account under either an administrator or user account context. Under Windows 2000, the Action account must have local administrator access. If the management server is carrying out any agentless monitoring, then the Management Server Action account must have a local administrator on the remote machine.

The Action account on the management server is used to gather data from the management server, and to run response on the management server. This allows the separation of the MOM service context from the response context on managed computers, including the agent on the management server. You can also use the Action account on the management server to run computer discovery, as well as install, uninstall, and update settings on agents on remote computers, if the Management Server Action account has administrative access.

Recommendation   Run the Management Server Action account as domain user. When the account is run under user context, any uninstall or update settings on agents will require you to provide an account that has the required administrative rights. If you run the Management Server Action account with an administrator account, then you should carry out the following steps, as the account will have administrator access on all managed servers:

- Configure a complex password.
- Audit and monitor account usage.
- Restrict account details.

Agent Action Account

Under Windows 2003, you can run the Agent Action account under Local System context. For any Windows 2000 systems, you must run the Agent Action account with local administrator access.

If system context access is higher than your security policy permits, then you can use a domain or local account that has the following minimum access on the managed agent:

- Member:
    - Local Users group
    - Local Performance Monitor Users group
- Privileges:
    - Access to Windows event logs
    - Manage auditing and security logs
    - Log on locally

Running with a domain account or a local account can add a significant management overhead. The account information also needs to be secured, as this account will have access to all your managed systems.

You should check the management pack guide, as some management packs may require the Agent Action account to have different access rights on the managed agent.

The Agent Action account runs any defined responses to events, and is also used by any tasks that may be run via the Operator Console.

Recommendation Check the management pack access requirements that will be deployed to the agent. If the agent is Windows 2003, and no additional access rights are required by the management pack, run the Agent Action account under Local System context. If the managed agent is Windows 2000, then run with local administrator's rights. The context under which the Action account is running can be checked and changed with the `SetActionAccount` utility, which you can locate on the agent, in the `%Program Files%\Microsoft Operations Manager 2005` directory. The syntax is as follows:

```
SetActionAccount.exe <configname> <options>
-query
```

(Returns the current Action Account settings)

```
-set domain username
```

(Sets the Action account to the given account. Use the machine name for local accounts.)

You must restart the MOM service if the account is changed.

Reporting Accounts

The Report User Access account is used by SQL Server Reporting Services to connect to the SCDW.

The DTS Transfer account is a domain account that the scheduled DTS job will use to transfer data from the MOM database to the SCDW.

Recommendation Use the DAS account for the DTS Transfer account and create a new domain user account for the Report User Access account.

Security Groups

During the installation, the groups shown in Table 14-1 are created. In an upgrade to MOM 2005, the MOM 2000 SP1 groups are renamed. During the upgrade, the memberships are retained from MOM 2000 SP1. Table 14-1 provides a summary of the MOM security groups and their use within MOM.

Recommendation Using your company's naming standards, create separate domain local or universal groups that can be added to the MOM Administrators, MOM Users, MOM Authors, and SCDW Reader groups. This will reduce the management overhead of managing access to the MOM infrastructure. You should also carry out regular checks on the group memberships to ensure that there is no unauthorized access to the management infrastructure. You can also create an alert in MOM if there are any changes to the group membership.

Table 14-1 *Summary of MOM Security Groups*

Group	Use	Location	Default Membership	Comments
MOM Service	Internal functions within the MOM infrastructure.	Management server	None	The DAS account is automatically added to this group when the MOM-to-MOM product connector is installed. The MOM-to-MOM Product Connector (MMPC) account is added during setup to the MOM Service group; it should not be removed from this group. No other accounts should be added to this group.
MOM Administrators	Members can perform any task in MOM 2005 in either the Administrator or Operator Console, apart from the reporting functions.	Management server	None	Members of the built-in administrators group on the management server also have administrative rights in MOM; therefore membership of this group should be restricted. To access the reporting functions, the user must also be a member of SCDW Reader group.

Group	Use	Location	Default Membership	Comments
MOM Authors	Members can import, export, create, and modify management packs in the MOM Administrator Console. Members can perform any task in the Operator Console. Members cannot modify the computers managed by MOM.	Management server	None	
MOM Users	Members can perform any action in the Operator Console (if console scopes are used, the users are restricted to the assigned scope, but they will have full access within that scope), apart from run-time tasks. Members have no access to the Administrator Console other than to launch the Operator Console.	Management server	DAS account	
SCDW DTS	Members can perform data archiving functions from the MOM 2005 Database Server to the MOM 2005 Reporting Database.	Database server	None	
SCDW Reader	Members can view reports via SQL Server Reporting Services on the MOM Reporting Server.	Database server	None	

Configuring Agent Computers to Run in Low Privilege

This section will provide the agent security levels that can run the main management pack with a low privilege account (e.g., not in Local System context). The core requirements that low privilege accounts require for Windows 2003 Servers are as follows:

- They must be members of the following groups:
  - Local Users
  - Local Performance Monitor Users
- They must have the following privileges:
  - Access Windows event logs
  - Manage auditing and security logs
  - Log on locally

On Windows 2000, the Action account has to be a member of the local Administrators group.

Windows Server Base Operating System Management Pack

You cannot run the following management pack tasks using a low privilege account. These tasks require that the Action account have the following administrator rights on the agent computer:

- Share Configuration Query
- NBTStat Adapter Query
- NBTStat Cache Query
- NetStat Display Total Active TCP Connections
- Network Statistics Server Service Query
- Session Query

Cluster Management Pack

The MOM Agent Action account requires full control of the cluster. This can be carried out by opening the Cluster Administrator console and connecting to the cluster. Click the server name, go to File ➤ Properties, and on the Security tab, add the account. Allow full control permissions to the account.

Exchange Management Pack

You must configure the Agent Action account on Exchange Server to run as Local System. This management pack will not run under low privileges.

Active Directory Management Pack

The Agent Action account requires the additional access rights shown in Table 14-2.

Table 14-2. *Agent Action Account Access Rights*

Object	Access Rights	Comments
MomLatencyMonitors container	Full access	Create the MomLatencyMonitors container as a child container of the root of each domain and application directory partition that is going to be monitored. If an application directory partition crosses domains, provide the appropriate access to the Action account in each domain. If the configuration partition is going to be monitored, create the MomLatencyMonitors container as a child object of the configuration partition. The MomLatencyMonitors container needs to be created on only one domain controller, as the object will replicate to the other domains in the forest.
HKLM\System\Current ControlSet\Service\ NTDS\Parameters	Read access	This must be applied to all monitored domain controllers.
Directories containing NTDS.dit and Active Directory log files	Read access	This must be applied to all monitored domain controllers.

Configuration Options

There are a number of settings that can be configured to enhance the security of your MOM implementation. How you use these settings depends on the monitored environment, as some management packs require these settings to be disabled or enabled.

Mutual Authentication

Using mutual authentication, the management server and agent authenticate each other with the Kerberos V5 protocol before transmitting data. Mutual authentication helps prevent man-in-the-middle attacks and reduce the possibility of rogue management servers or agents performing actions on other managed systems.

Mutual authentication is a global management group setting and cannot be overridden at the agent level. Mutual authentication is disabled by default when upgrading from MOM 2000 SP1. When enabled, MOM SP1 agents cannot connect to the management server. The Block MOM 2000 and MOM 2000 SP1 setting is automatically enabled. The management server and agents must be in an Active Directory domain.

Recommendation Whenever possible, ensure that mutual authentication is enabled. If you are upgrading from MOM 2000 SP1 or managing legacy systems in NT domains, you need to ensure that mutual authentication is enabled once the migration has been completed. If you are monitoring systems in separate Active Directory forests, you will have to disable mutual authentication, as a trust must be available between the management server and the agent.

Custom Server-Side Responses

Server-side responses are run on the management server in response to data collected from a managed computer. There is a potential security risk in that spoofed data sent to the management server could trigger a server-side response.

The option to enable or disable server-side responses affects only custom server-side responses. Server-side responses are disabled by default for new and upgraded installations of MOM 2005.

You should check the management pack documentation to see if this setting must be enabled.

The following types of responses are affected by this setting if it is enabled:

- Script responses configured to be launched on the management server
- Notification responses when a command is specified
- Command/batch file responses configured to be executed from the management server
- Managed-code responses

The following responses are not affected by this setting, and will always be executed:

- Any responses to be executed locally on the managed computer
- Notification responses that use e-mail or page notifications
- Update state variable responses
- SNMP trap responses

Recommendation   Leave this setting disabled unless a management pack requires this setting to be enabled.

Agent Proxying

In MOM 2000, alerts may be generated by a managed server on behalf of another server. In this situation, the reporting server is called a proxy. This is required to monitor servers, virtual servers, or clusters that cannot host a MOM agent. MOM 2005 disables agent proxying by default. This feature, when enabled, could be used to spoof data on behalf of another server to generate malicious action. The setting can be managed globally or on individual agent level.

To find the global setting, go to Administration ➤ Global Settings ➤ Agents, and click the Security tab (see Figure 14-1).

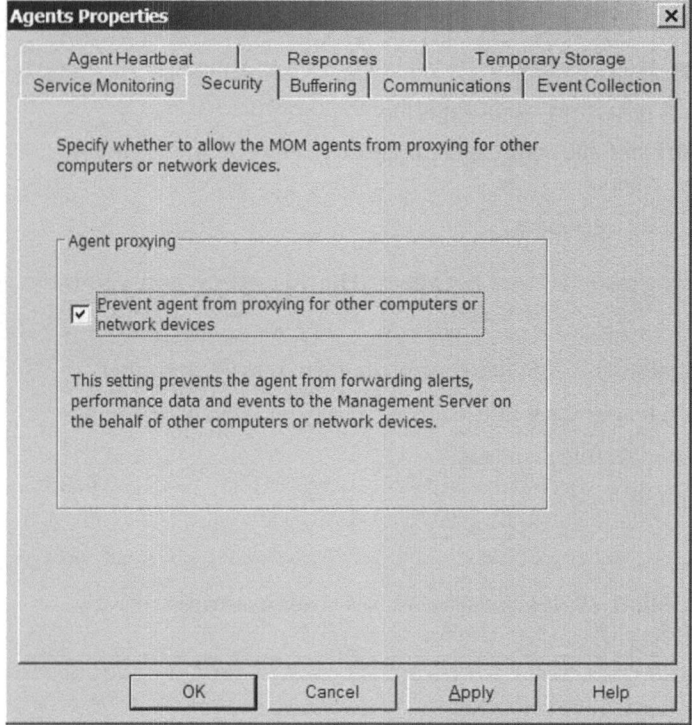

Figure 14-1. *Global agent proxying configuration*

To find the individual agent setting, go to Administration ➤ Computers ➤ Agent-Managed Computers, double-click the agent, and then select the Security tab (see Figure 14-2). You need to uncheck the Use global settings box if you wish to change the settings for this agent.

The management pack documentation should be checked to see if agent proxying is required for the management pack to function correctly.

■**Recommendation** Managing individual agent proxy settings can be difficult for large-scale deployments if the majority of agents need to proxy for other computers. In this situation, as long as the security implications are understood and accepted, it may be easier to set the proxy setting at the global level.

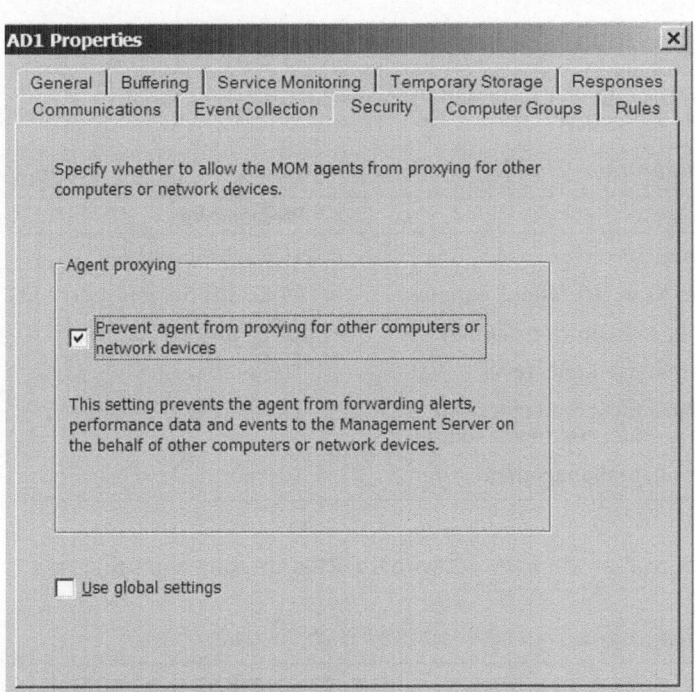

Figure 14-2. *Agent proxying configuration on an individual agent*

Encryption

The agent always initiates the communication between the MOM agent and the management server. The agent-server communication channel uses the TCP/IP protocol, and communications are secure, authenticated, and encrypted. In a trusted Active Directory environment, communications are also signed.

Firewalls

The configurations that will work with firewalls are shown in Table 14-3.

Table 14-3. *Configurations That Will Work with Firewalls*

Configuration	Protocol/Port
Agent to management server	TCP/UDP port 1270
Management server to Operations database	OLEDB Tunneling, port 1433
Reporting console to Reporting database	HTTP port 80
Web console to management server	TCP port 1272
MOM-to-MOM product connector destination to MOM-to-MOM product connector source	TCP port 1271
Management group to management group	TCP port 1271

The configurations that will *not* work with firewalls are shown in Table 14-4.

Table 14-4. *Configurations That Will Not Work with Firewalls*

Configuration	Protocol/Port
Management server to agentless monitoring	RPC port (TCP 135) and DCOM port range
Administrator Console to management server	RPC port (TCP 135) and DCOM port range
Operator Console to management server	RPC port (TCP 135) and DCOM port range
Operations database to Reporting database	DTS port (TCP 1433)

Agent Limitations

While MOM will function adequately behind a firewall, there are a number of limitations that you need to be aware of. The main limitations are as follows:

- The Reject New Manual Agent Installations check box on the MOM management server must be cleared.

- Local administrator rights on the server that the agent is going to be installed on are required.

- The Mutual Authentication Required check box on the MOM management server must be cleared.

- The agent control level must be set to None to ensure the following:
  - The MOM management server will not attempt to uninstall the agent.
  - The MOM management server will not set the agent state to Pending Uninstallation.
- The MOM Administrator Console cannot be used to update agent settings for these computers.
- The MOM Administrator Console cannot be used to upgrade or uninstall the agents for these computers.
- The MOM agents will not be configured to upgrade automatically if the MOM management server is upgraded.
- The MOM Administrator Console cannot be used to remotely install MOM product updates for the agents.

Note There is an issue with running the Active Directory management pack on agents in the DMZ or in untrusted domains. When agents are manually installed, computer discovery is not run. This means that the FQDN field in the computer table is not populated. A number of Active Directory management pack scripts require the FQDN information for parameters in the script. Please read Chapter 6 for the steps you need to take to resolve this issue.

Summary

In this chapter, we looked at managing MOM security. We also looked at how to manage agents behind firewalls, and provided tips on how to reduce the overhead of managing the security of your MOM environment. In Appendix A, we will show you how to upgrade your MOM infrastructure to SP1, and also how to upgrade a SQL Server 2000 installation to SQL Server 2005.

■ ■ ■

Upgrading MOM

Once MOM has been deployed in an environment, it may be necessary to upgrade from time to time. In this appendix, we will look at the process for upgrading MOM in the most common scenarios we have come across. We will cover the installation of MOM 2005 SP1 onto an existing MOM 2005 installation, and the procedure for upgrading SQL Server from 2000 to 2005 in an existing MOM infrastructure.

Upgrading MOM 2005 to SP1

If you have installed MOM 2005 from the installation media, it is likely that you are running a non-SP1 version of MOM. In order to confirm this, open the Administrator Console and click Help ➤ About. Check the version number, and use Table A-1 to verify the version of MOM you are running.

Table A-1. *MOM Version Numbers*

MOM Version	Version Number
MOM 2005 base	5.0.2749.0
MOM 2005 SP1	5.0.2911.0

Deciding Whether You Need an Upgrade

If you are running the MOM 2005 base version, you will benefit from upgrading to SP1. MOM 2005 SP1 provides the following enhancements:

- Support for more OSs and databases, including Windows Server 2003 SP1, SQL Server 2000 SP4, and SQL Server 2005

- Support for x64 platforms, allowing MOM 2005 to monitor and run on the most current high-performance hardware

- Alerting based on MOM licence usage, allowing you to keep track of your MOM licenses

MOM 2005 SP1 also offers a number of security and code enhancements over the base version of MOM 2005. The following are just some of the updates that are provided in SP1:

- Support for disjointed namespaces when using mutual authentication

- Support for NETBIOS names that contain dots (e.g., SERVER1.HQ)

- Much improved heartbeat mechanism, which is used to detect when agents are down

- Improved MOM connector framework

Planning for an SP1 Upgrade

Before you deploy MOM 2005 SP1, you need to carry out some planning to ensure that the upgrade is successful. First, you need to look at your MOM infrastructure and audit all instances of the MOM software installed. This includes all MOM database servers, management servers, and instances of MOM consoles installed across your environment.

Once you have a list of all instances of MOM software in your environment, you can begin to plan the procedure for upgrading to SP1.

Deploying MOM 2005 SP1

In order to ensure a successful upgrade to SP1, we recommend that you update the individual components in the order shown in the following list:

1. OnePoint database

2. Management servers

3. MOM consoles

4. Management packs

5. Agents

Once you have run the MOM SP1 executable on the OnePoint database server, all the management servers, and the machines that have MOM consoles installed, any non-SP1 management packs should be updated.

■Note While updating the management packs to SP1 is not strictly necessary, it is recommended that you do so to ensure that you have the latest rules and fixes to the management packs, and also to ensure that the management packs take advantage of the added functionality in MOM 2005 SP1.

After you have updated the main MOM components, you then need to update the MOM agents. This should be done from the MOM Administrator Console when possible (i.e., when the agents' control mode is set to Full). Once the MOM database and management servers have been updated, you will notice that the agent-managed machines will appear in the Pending Actions screen in the Administrator Console. Their status in the Pending Actions column will be Agent upgrade, as shown in Figure A-1.

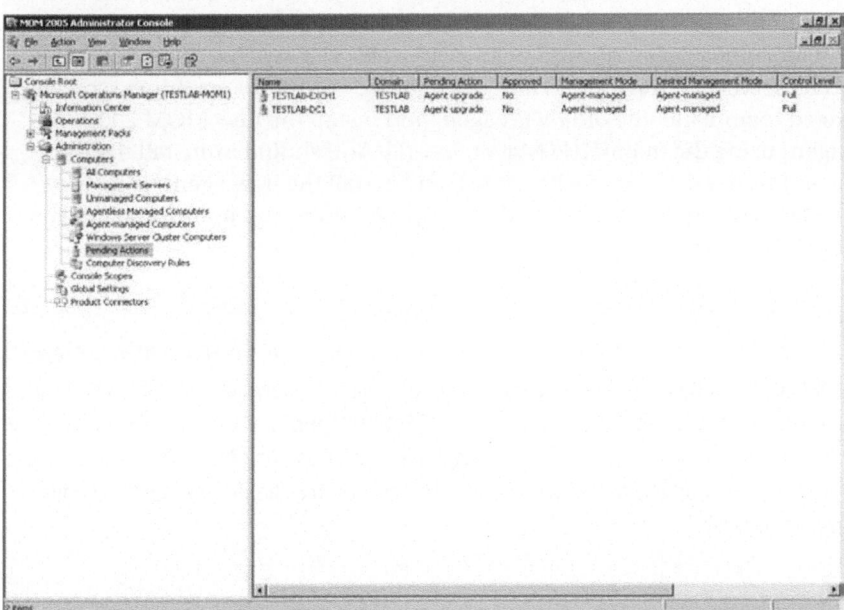

Figure A-1. *The Pending Actions screen, showing MOM agents awaiting upgrade*

From here, you can right-click the agents and select Upgrade Agent Now, and the agents will be updated automatically.

Please be aware that there is a prerequisite to running the SP1 version of the MOM 2005 agent. Windows Installer 3.1 version 2 is required on the agent machines prior to the installation of the MOM SP1 agent. While the

MOM agent update does not usually require a reboot of the machine, the update to Windows Installer 3.1 *does* require a reboot, and you should therefore plan this update and schedule the server downtime for the affected agents as necessary.

■**Note** You may find that some agent updates fail. This will most likely be due to the fact that Windows Installer 3.1 version 2 is not installed on the agent. Ensure that this update is installed prior to attempting to update agents. This update can be downloaded from the Microsoft Windows Update site (`http://windowsupdate.microsoft.com`).

The aforementioned procedure will allow you to update the MOM agents on the machines that are fully managed by MOM (those with a control level of Full). However, in your environment, you may have some machines that have had their MOM agents manually installed. This will include machines deployed behind firewalls, ISA servers, and Windows 2003 servers with Windows Firewall enabled. For these machines, you will need to uninstall the old MOM agent and install the new MOM 2005 SP1 agent using the updated `MOMAgent.msi` file. You should uninstall the old agent from Add/Remove Programs, and install the new agent using the MOM 2005 Agent Setup wizard, supplying the settings appropriate to your environment.

■**Note** The updated `MOMAgent.msi` file is not supplied with the MOM 2005 SP1 executable. You can obtain this file directly from Microsoft, or download the SP1-integrated copy of MOM 2005. In the SP1 copy of MOM, the `MOMAgent.msi` file can be found in the `i386` folder on the disk or `.iso` file. If you have MOM Reporting installed, it will be necessary to upgrade this to SP1 also. To accomplish this, run the SP1 executable on the reporting server.

Upgrading MOM Database Servers from SQL Server 2000 to SQL Server 2005

With the release of SQL Server 2005, you may upgrade your MOM database servers to take advantage of the new features and improved performance and security in the latest version of SQL Server. Before you consider an upgrade to SQL Server 2005, make sure you are running MOM 2005 SP1, since the non-SP1 version of MOM does not support SQL Server 2005.

Once you have decided to upgrade to SQL Server 2005 and you have prepared MOM by upgrading it to SP1, you should follow the procedure documented here to upgrade with the least amount of impact on the MOM environment. First, I recommend backing up both of the MOM databases (OnePoint and SystemCenterReporting) in addition to the system databases, and also the SQL Server Reporting Services databases (ReportServer and ReportServerTempDB). Once you have a backup of these databases, you can proceed with an upgrade of SQL Server.

Before starting the upgrade, be sure to put the MOM database and MOM management servers into maintenance mode in the MOM Operator Console. You need to put all MOM servers into maintenance mode, as the databases will be taken offline, which will generate alerts; and the management servers will be unable to connect to the database, which will also generate alerts.

It does not matter which database server you decide to upgrade first, and if you have both databases hosted on the same server, this decision will be easy! To upgrade SQL Server to 2005, run the SQL Server 2005 installation package (setup.exe from the SQL Server 2005 CD). First, the setup program will install the prerequisite components, and then the main setup wizard will launch and upgrade SQL Server.

Note You will also need to upgrade SQL Server Reporting Services using the same method you used to upgrade SQL Server.

We will not explain the upgrade process in detail in this book for two reasons: first, the upgrade may vary across environments; and second, we do not specialize in SQL Server and therefore are not in the best position to offer advice on the SQL Server 2005 upgrade process.

Once SQL Server has been successfully upgraded to 2005, the first thing you should verify is that the MOM databases are mounted and available for immediate use. To do this, launch SQL Server Management Studio and expand Databases. Check the status of the OnePoint and SystemCenterReporting databases, and also the ReportServer and ReportServerTempDB databases. This is shown in Figure A-2.

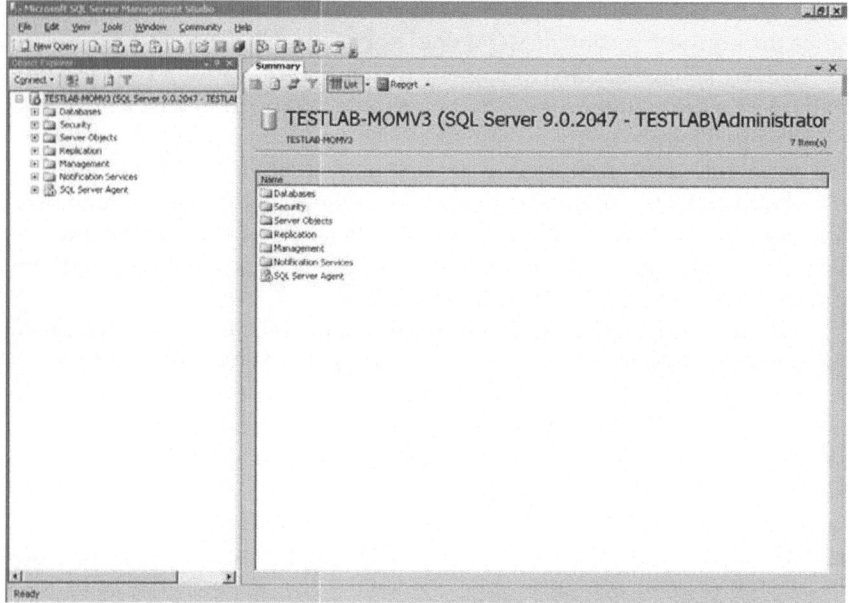

Figure A-2. *SQL Server 2005 Management Studio*

Once you have verified that the databases are online, check that the MOM Operator and Administrator Consoles load correctly.

Finally, you must be aware that there are three hotfixes to apply to the various MOM servers that fix issues related to SQL Server 2005. The hotfixes are detailed in Table A-2.

Table A-2. *MOM Post–SQL Server 2005 Hotfixes*

Knowledge Base Article Number	Web Location	Applies to
913801	http://support.microsoft.com/kb/913801	Management servers
913812	http://support.microsoft.com/kb/913812	Management servers
915785	http://support.microsoft.com/kb/915785	SystemCenter Reporting database

Note While the download locations are correct at the time of this book going to press, be aware that they may change in the future.

Install the hotfixes onto the servers listed in Table A-2 by running each `.msi` package from each respective location shown in the table.

The last thing you should be aware of is an issue that may produce an error when importing MOM reports into SQL Server 2005 Reporting Services. You may get an import error and the report import will fail. Microsoft has confirmed this to be an issue with a number of management packs, and has updated the packs accordingly. You can find more information at `http://support.microsoft.com/kb/919598`. You can download and import the reports of the updated copies of the affected management packs to resolve this issue.

Index